The Pro-Incumbency Century

The Pro-Incumbency Century

Yashwant Deshmukh
Sutanu Guru

PRABHAT PRAKASHAN

Published by
PRABHAT PRAKASHAN PVT. LTD.
4/19 Asaf Ali Road,
New Delhi-110 002 (INDIA)
e-mail: prabhatbooks@gmail.com

ISBN 978-93-95386-28-9
THE PRO-INCUMBENCY CENTURY
by Shri Yashwant Deshmukh • Shri Sutanu Guru

Edition
First, 2023

Paperback Price
₹ 500.00 (Rupees Five Hundred only)

Printed at
R-Tech Offset Printers, Delhi

PREFACE

There are a few subjects on which every articulate Indian has a view. One of these is politics. (The silent voter also has a view, not necessarily articulated.) Therefore, whenever there are elections, there will be discussions and debate, even betting, sometimes a bit more formalized through the Satta Bazar. There are opinion polls, exit polls and post-mortems about why exit polls went wrong. Indeed, there are surveys even if no elections are in the offing. This great deal of interest in politics, at least on the part of the voluble voter, is desirable in a democracy and barring a deviation in mid-1970s, India has always been that, in sharp contrast with the immediate neighbours. Democracy has three layers, but most interest is devoted to elections to Parliament and State assemblies, not to elections to local bodies, though a considerable amount of social empowerment has occurred because of this. Psephology is an art. It is not an exact science. Findings, eventually proved right or wrong, are functions of sample size, sample design, questions asked and veracity of responses, not to speak of possible subjectivity in tweaking responses. CVoter has been in this business for almost twenty years and its surveys transcend elections. CVoter has been wrong. But more often than not, it has also been right. This book is by Yashwant Deshmukh and Sutanu Guru, both associated with the CVoter Research Foundation.

This book isn't about any forthcoming elections. It is about what determines electoral behaviour. Is bad governance punished and is good governance rewarded? What do we mean by governance? Is voting behaviour at all explained by governance variables, moving beyond caste and religion? Are voters prescient enough to recognize long-term costs of populism? Is there anti-incumbency, or can a specific template convert it to pro-incumbency? These aren't easy questions to answer. Is an absolute improvement in an indicator important, or is it the increment? Is presumed anti-incumbency against the PM/CM, the political party, or the incumbent MP/MLA? How different is voting behaviour for Parliament different from that for State assemblies? Researchers have sought to answer these questions, without any conclusive answer. Ex ante expectations have gone wrong. Hence, there has been ex post rationalization. This is not quite a book that is based on academic research. It is best described as a popular book, based on case studies. Given the contentious nature of political discourse and strong views many people have, propositions stated will be countered and debated. That should be the intention, to trigger a discussion. There are insights, some not that obvious. It's a welcome addition to the corpus, on a subject few people quite understand.

1 May, 2023 **—Bibek Debroy**

ACKNOWLEDGEMENT

It might sound cliched and done to death; yet it needs to be repeated. Books, particularly those related to painting a canvas of contemporary political, social, and economic landscapes is more about collaboration than bouts of frenzied and inspired writing by any author. Even the most successful and best-selling fiction writers rarely fail to acknowledge the help of a team of editors who simultaneously nurse and temper the individual brilliance of the writer to create a coherent masterpiece. When it comes to nonfiction, the role of non authors is even more critical and decisive. Take this book for instance. Each chapter is based on analysis of both historical and contemporary data that would have taken the authors years to just compile; forget analysing the data points in a meaningful manner. Insights on political, economic, and social transformations might appear on surface to be the result of wisdom acquired by the authors. In reality, they reflect hours and hours of brainstorming, fiery debates, arguments, ideological and identity-based polemics, and often just good-natured banter about election results. Let us also not forget the importance of seemingly cruel but powerfully insightful jokes on political leaders that the authors would prefer not to repeat here!

Any structure or work that can survive the vagaries of time and new data sets depends on the strength of the foundation. We owe big to honourable Achyutanand Mishraji who is not only Chairperson of CVoter Foundation but also remains the moral compass in most turbulent times of our lives. The authors salute Gaura, who has been encouraging, prodding, provoking and often scolding the lead author for more than two decades to distil his experience of studying elections into a paper or a book that readers interested in contemporary India can enjoy reading and debating.

Shailendra has not just been a colleague and friend for decades, but also a constant source of comfort, advice and plain simple common sense. He is the power engine of CVoter, works as backup of that power engine, and remains the only back up of that backup as well. There would be no CVoter research without the leadership of the three amazing women: Gaura, Shaleja and Aakanksha; who actually run CVoter. From spending endless hours in Questionnaire design to training the researchers to managing the CATI operations and meeting the deadlines; these ladies are no-nonsense tough taskmasters. They work with hands on cut-the-crap agenda, their pretty smiles notwithstanding.

And then there would certainly be no CVoter data without Mannanji. He has been our data and archives encyclopaedia when it comes to harnessing, studying, analysing, and interpreting data for more than two decades. Neelabh and Haider have always ensured that our IT logistical backbone and programming stays sturdy. Rahul Sharma is the unsung warrior who enjoys envious success in making possible what looks seemingly impossible. The qualitative inputs of Ajitji, Khalid, Manish, Sushil and Sanjay are critical. Ajit Shukla and Khalid Akhtar are always there to harness their vast experience and offer invaluable insights and suggestions. Manu Sharma always comes up with different take with his world view on local issues and local view on global issues. On a lighter note, we are contemplating pay-per-view live webcasting our interactions with Qualitative team during elections for making extra bucks, but we are not sure if they would come under action or comedy genre.

The CATI team members Raja, Amit, Sundar and Vitul who hardly say no to any extra responsibility whatsoever. Yash is our permanent man Friday for God knows how many years. Anu ensures we get our due salaries, no matter how late they are running. Satyendraji is the silent and truthful face managing our office. Santosh is the 24x7 lifeguard as he only moves us physically. And last but not the least, our dear Mukesh for making all these names work effectively with his unending supply of Caffeine and Mohit for repairing every short circuit in office at the right time. Armies used to march on their stomachs. Today, they march on the coat tails of computers and data crunching software and algorithms. Without them, there would be no book.

And yes, thank you Priyamvada for the lovely cover design. We owe you and promise that we will repay by designing the cover of your book the day you decide to publish.

WHY PRO-INCUMBENCY HAS BECOME THE NORM IN INDIAN ELECTIONS

CONTENTS

1
INTRODUCTORY

As usual, at about 5 am, he was up and awake fiddling with both his Rudraksha Malas and his I-pad. This monk, Yogi Adityanath, the sitting chief minister of Uttar Pradesh, was not selling a Ferrari. The reddish glow of the sun began turning golden brown and then red, as dawn gave way to morning and then the cacophony of delirious and dejected voices boomed across tens of millions of TV sets, tablets and mobiles on March 10, 2022. By noon, it was clear that the monk who was born in a lower middle-class family in neighbouring Uttarakhand and become the Head Priest of the powerful Gorakhpur Sect at the ripe young age of 25, was creating history by winning a second successive term.

This was history. For the first time ever since India became an independent sovereign republic, a sitting chief minister in Uttar Pradesh had led his party to a second successive victory. The scale of his repeat performance awed even his fierce critics of whom there are legion. This was the man who faced global flak for dead bodies floating down rivers during the second wave of the Covid-19 pandemic. This was the leader of a state where unemployment and inflation were playing havoc with households whose livelihoods had already been battered by the pandemic. This was the man who confronted a young, resurgent rival in the form of Akhilesh Yadav who threatened to make history by crafting an alliance of backward caste and Muslim voters. This was the man who was reviled for his 'Muslim baiting' rhetoric and the alleged actions of his administration of targeting and persecuting minorities. This was the man under whose nose highly publicised rapes became symbols of failed law and order.

This was a monk who faced the implacable hostility of farmers in Western Uttar Pradesh. This was the leader accused of shielding a party colleague's son accused of running over his SUV over protesting farmers in Lakhimpur Kheri and killing three of them in Lakhimpur Kheri. And yet he won a thumping victory. Journalist Rajdeep Sardesai who had hinted at a BJP victory in a February, 2022 column sent out a Tweet: "No result exemplifies gaps between political narratives and electoral outcomes quite like Lakhimpur Kheri. The BJP won all eight seats in a district despite horrific farmers killings/violence here. Voter behaviour is often disconnected to constitutional morality"[1]

The bespectacled boy next door who is now considered and rated as one of the most successful start-up founders is as different from Yogi Adityanath as chalk and cheese. We are talking about Arvind Kejriwal, undisputed boss of the Aam Aadmi Party who also visited a Hanuman Temple on March 10. The visit, metaphorically speaking, was a thanksgiving one. He too had created history in Punjab by winning an unprecedented mandate to rule. It was almost a repeat performance of his back-to-back sweeping victories in Delhi where AAP had won 67 out of 70 seats in 2015 and 63 out of 70 in 2020. In Punjab, his party not only made its debut as the putative ruler, but also smashed the traditional powerhouses by winning 92 out of 117 seats. No one was spared in Kejriwal and his aide chief minister Bhagwant Mann's victory march across the state. Those who lost their own assembly seats were the 94 year-old five time chief minister Prakash Singh Badal (much more about him in the book), his son Sukhbir Singh Badal, the irrepressible Navjot Singh Sidhu, Congress chief minister Charanjit Singh Channi in two seats, former chief minister Captain Amarinder Singh and a host of others. Delivering a speech in the afternoon, Kejriwal made his national ambitions clear. In 2017, Narendra Modi had talked about a 'New India' after sweeping Uttar Pradesh. In 2022, the 'Jhadu' man offered his own version of another 'New India' after sweeping Punjab.

Commentators were quick to draw comparisons as well as speculations. One of them, Sagarika Ghosh wrote in a column in NDTV the day election results were announced: "Along with

Kejriwal, Yogi Adityanath is the other big headline of this election. Yogi is the saffron-clad Hindu prelate identified with hard, religious majoritarianism who has an unprecedented second-term win under his belt and can justifiably be called the BJP's No. 2 leader. Kejriwal has expanded his footprint and done what no other leader has been able to—create a political start-up and win two states in a relatively short period, focused on a non-identity politics model of health and education. Kejriwal is not a dynast, he has a middle class connect, he does not bear the baggage of any kind of 'Muslim appeasement' and appeals to a younger demographic tired of politics as usual. So will the two new political disruptors Arvind Kejriwal and Yogi Adityanath be potential national rivals, if not in 2024 then perhaps in 2029? Both will still be relatively young, 61 and 57, respectively. An IIT-educated engineer versus a saffron-clad monk: can Indian politics get a more unlikely yet fascinating contest?"[2]

In the hype and hysteria over the results, only a few more discerning commentators noticed the elephant in the room: How in God's name had the BJP managed to tide over visible and much discussed 'anti-incumbency' sentiments? And not just in Uttar Pradesh where the Modi-Yogi combination was always a potent force, but also in Uttarakhand where it had changed three chief ministers in six months? Uttarakhand had till then never re-elected an incumbent since it was formed in 2000. And how in God's name did it manage to win 20 seats out of 40 in Goa after ten uninterrupted years of 'unpopular' rule and retain power? The obvious conclusion missed by most was that pro-incumbency has replaced anti-incumbency theme as far as Indian voters are concerned.

Pro-Incumbency is the Real Thing

This book is all about pointing out the simple **FACT** that pro-incumbency verdicts by voters is the most significant and most neglected phenomenon of 21st century Indian politics. While analysing Indian politics in the contemporary era, pundits have analysed many trends that appear clearly visible. The first is the decline of the Congress. The second is the rise of the BJP. The third is the remarkable durability and resilience of regional parties. The fourth is the constant efforts by the subalterns to grab their share of political and economic power. The fifth is the virtual exclusion of Muslims in many regions of India from power-sharing platforms and opportunities. But most ignore the elephant in the room: pro-incumbency verdicts that seem to defy logic and history. Except Rajasthan, Karnataka, Jharkhand (and Kerala till 2021) and the very small states Himachal Pradesh and Uttarakhand, pro-incumbency verdicts seem to have become the norm in elections, unless the ruling party commits hara-kiri. This is too fascinating a phenomenon to ignore.

Let's look at the whole thing from the perspective of cricket and understand why and how the polity of a country goes through structural changes every few decades. Till Kapil Dev came along, the Indian bowling attack was virtually monopolised by spinners. So when it came to analysis and more by pundits, there was the usual lament over the absence of a 'quality' and 'effective' pace bowling attack. This was akin to the lament that politics and elections in India were completely monopolised by the Congress and there was a terrible dearth of a 'quality' and 'effective' opposition. The arrival of Kapil Dev was preceded and accompanied by the Indian cricket team finally winning some matches against powerful opponents. As the Indian cricket team added variety and zing to its bowling attack, so did opposition parties in Indian politics. The virtual monopoly of the Congress was broken in politics and opposition parties started winning a few elections here and there; just as the Indian cricket team started winning a few matches here and there.

Then came the '1977' moment for the Indian cricket team. Rated as minnows who would offer tone resistance if at all since Kapil Dev was the captain. The team scripted history in 1983 when it humbled the mighty and seemingly invincible West Indies led by Clive Lloyd to win the World Cup in One Day Cricket, a trophy monopolised till then by West Indies. In many ways, this was like the underdog Janata Party, a hurriedly cobbled up conglomeration of disparate political parties with differing ideologies, that humbled the seemingly invincible Indira Gandhi and the Congress.

The Indian cricket exam has faced many setbacks since then, but victories have become more common.

In the 21st century, the Indian cricket team entered a new and assertive era led by Saurav Ganguly and then M.S. Dhoni and even became the number one team in the world in rankings. Meanwhile, the Congress that once enjoyed a monopoly over power in India started resembling the West Indies team that had started living off past glory rather than current performances. The invincible had become also-rans; just as the Congress has become in contemporary times.

In a nostalgic piece for the portal *The Scroll* in 2020, Vinay Mahanarangan quoted an ageing fan Pankaj Mithel: "The celebrations when Indian won were grand. It was an unbelievable high. I can watch that final again and again and again. Just like it was in 2011, everyone was on the streets back then as well. There were hundreds of people all around. My friends and I set off on our two-wheelers and enjoyed the moment with strangers in different parts of the city. When the team arrived from England in Mumbai, my friend and I were there at the airport, along with hundreds of people, to receive the players. There was chaos. Everyone wanted a glimpse of the champions. We even rode on our two-wheeler behind the team bus. The victory gave our generation hope...the hope that we as Indians can be winners. It made us believers. That triumph was for our generation, the ones who grew up in the late 50s and early 60s.[3] Opposition parties after 1983 too started believing they could win, as they started doing in the early 1980s and gave birth to the 'anti-incumbency' phenomenon.

But perhaps the most significant change in the Indian cricket team is one that was largely ignored by the media, except the prescient commentators that had seen it coming more than a decade ago: the relentless rise of a world-class fast bowling attack. Then, if someone had suggested that it is fast bowling that would become India's most potent and dominant narrative, experts would have laughed. Not anymore. Something similar has happened with pro-incumbency verdicts. India had become so used over time to 'anti-incumbency' that the polar opposite was difficult to comprehend; forget about attempts to analyse it. Exactly in the same manner, fans had become so used to spinners winning matches for India that it was difficult to comprehend a fast bowling attack doing the same. But over time, the fast bowling attack, like pro-incumbency verdicts, has given such a preponderance of data on its ability to win matches that it is now considered more lethal and a bigger match winner than spin bowling. That doesn't mean spin bowling, like anti-incumbency, has disappeared (remember the Punjab assembly elections of 2022?). It is still a potent weapon in the Indian arsenal. But like fast bowling, only the naïve and the ideologically blinkered would ignore the growing frequency and importance of pro-incumbency verdicts.

The 2022 Verdicts

By the time it was noon on March 10, 2022, the celebrations and recriminations were well and truly underway in Panaji, Imphal, Dehradun, Chandigarh, Lucknow, and even Delhi. The TV channels and digital platforms were inundated with instant analysis and hasty post-mortems that quickly arrived at a few correct conclusions. The first was that Narendra Modi continued to be the most popular, charismatic and powerful leader of India. Some veterans compared his dominance over Indian polity with that of Indira Gandhi in the halcyon days of the Congress party. The second was that the halcyon days of Congress now appeared destined to remain a fading memory as it continued on the path of self-destruction and political suicide. Many commentators who are not terribly fond of the BJP marvelled at the inability of the Congress to defeat the BJP in Goa and Uttarakhand despite visible signs of 'anti-incumbency'; and its almost complete disappearance from the politically important state of Uttar Pradesh and offered gratuitous advice to the party. Journalist Saba Naqvi who was reporting from the state till March 7 and writing about a 'surprise' performance of the coalition led by Samajwadi Party tweeted soon after the results were clear: "Dear Rahul Gandhi, Occasionally, you make nice speeches and your ecosystem praises you. Do you want to stay and campaign for the BJP n 2024 or let go and allow others to lead the Congress? Please note the furious fight put up by other parties, victory or defeat and then look at Congress....[4] As suggested in Saba Naqvi's tweet, there was much discussion devoted to the unexpected victory of the BJP in four states where it was in power and retained it, leading inevitably to debates about its prospects for winning a third successive term. A large chunk of time was justifiably devoted to the spectacular victory of the AAP in Punjab where it steamrolled over its rivals. Virtually the entire top leadership of the traditional ruling parties, the Congress and the Akali Dal personally lost the elections and their own seats. This also triggered much debate about the remarkable rise of the AAP as a successful political start-up and its openly stated ambitions of replacing the Congress as the natural alternative to the BJP. Much time was devoted to how a tsunami of 'anti-incumbency' sentiments swept away the old ruling establishment in Punjab.

But barring a few analysts here and there, there was hardly any attempt to analyse the four 'pro-incumbency' verdicts. That's the gap this book aims to plug in subsequent pages. But some more recent history first.

The 2021 Verdicts

Less than a year ago in 2021, when the second wave of the Corona pandemic was ravaging and rampaging across India, three dramatically different personalities from across India had cause for muted celebrations as the pro-incumbency magic had worked yet again. The chief minister of Kerala demolished five decades of pontificating punditry by winning a second successive assembly election with a huge mandate. This kind of thing had not happened in God's Own Country since the 1970s. In faraway Kolkata, the election strategist Prashant Kishore who had become a kind of personal advisor to chief minister Mamata Banerjee looked smug by the afternoon of May 2, 2021 when his 'brave' prediction that the BJP would not cross 100 seats in an assembly of 294 seats looked to be coming true. Kishore had struck his neck out and predicted the same much before the election results were announced. By riding a tsunami of support (though losing her own seat), the former Congress leader, the brash, belligerent, bellicose and mercurial had won a third successive term. It doesn't happen very often, but both Prime Minister Narendra Modi and Home Minister Amit Shah looked humbled and humiliated. They won a consolation prize though: the BJP won a second consecutive term in Assam by defeating the formidable Congress-AIUDF combine. Another former Congress leader Himanta Biswa Sarma who made the dog Pidi famous by publicly stating that Rahul Gandhi seemed more interested in feeding biscuits to his pets than listen to the grievances of party leaders, became chief minister. It was yet another victory for pro-incumbency.

It is not as if people have completely ignored this phenomenon. For years, scholars and academics have been observing the emergence of this phenomenon in the 21st century. But somehow, their observations and their attempts to analyse the factors behind the rise and rise of pro-incumbency have not percolated down to media pundits who dominate the so-called prime time TV 'debates'; write copious lines of hindsight masquerading as insight or populate digital platforms with their sclerotic and nakedly partisan and polemical prose. Back in 2013, Milan Vaishnav of the Carnegie Foundation had written about this in a co-authored paper: But in India, years of scholarship and popular commentary have argued that voters there prioritize factors other than good economic performance when evaluating incumbent governments. Namely, Indian voters are said to put more stock in patronage, populism, or parochialism. As the saying goes, in India voters do not so much cast their vote as they vote their caste... India has witnessed the rise of a cadre of popular state chief ministers who have been both highly touted for their economic achievements and richly rewarded by voters. This lineup of CEO chief ministers cuts across party and regional lines, featuring BJP leaders such as Modi, Raman Singh (from Chhattisgarh), and Shivraj Singh Chouhan (from Madhya Pradesh); the Indian National Congress's Sheila Dikshit (who, until recently, governed Delhi); and the regional party bosses Naveen Patnaik (Odisha) and Bihar's Nitish Kumar.[4]

A Colourful Cast of Characters

Look at the cast of characters (some of them are no more with us) who have led the pro-incumbency march as generals. There is the fiery 'street fighter' (in her own words) Mamata Banerjee who won a third successive term in 2021. In sharp contrast, there is the genial, erudite, ever polite and polished Naveen Patnaik who has won a staggering five successive terms as chief minister of Odisha. By next year, he will break the record set by the late Jyoti Basu as the chief minister with the longest continuous stint of a major state. There was the haughty and almost goddess-like late J. Jayalalithaa who won a second successive term in 2016, apart from two previous stints. In contrast, there was the smiling, loveable late Sheila Dikshit who won three successive terms as Delhi chief minister. There are Dr. Raman Singh of Chhattisgarh and Shivraj Singh Chouhan of Madhya Pradesh who won three successive terms before 'anti-incumbency' finally caught up with them in December 2018. Of course, Shivraj Singh Chouhan is back as chief minister since early 2020 thanks to many leaders elected on Congress tickets 'suddenly' feeling that the Congress party was not 'serving the masses' and following Jyotiraditya Scindia into the BJP. All is fair in love, war and politics, after all. There was the combative Jat leader Bhupinder Singh Hooda who ruled as Haryana chief minister for two successive terms with the 'help' of independents. His successor Manohar Lal Khattar is another study in contrast. Looking mousy and meek compared to Hooda, Khattar of the BJP is serving his second successive term as chief minister, albeit with the 'help' of allies. In Maharashtra, after three successive terms of the Congress-NCP government, the BJP and Shiv Sena formed an uneasy alliance after the 2014 assembly elections and the young and energetic Devendra Fadnavis of the BJP became the chief minister. He actually won a second successive term as chief minister by leading the pre-poll BJP-Shiv Sena alliance to victory. But the red carpet was literally pulled from under his feet as the Shiv Sena joined hands with old foes the Congress and the NCP. All is fair in love, war and politics, after all. Gujarat is a different ball game altogether. The BJP has been ruling the state continuously since 1995 and if it wins the elections again scheduled for December 2022, it would have ruled the state continuously for 32 years when assembly elections are due again in 2027. The Left Front ruled West Bengal continuously for 34 years. But Gujarat, to an extent like Maharashtra and Assam is different because barring Narendra Modi and Tarun Gogoi of Congress (who won three successive elections in Assam), the many other BJP chief ministers of the state have not been towering personalities like, say Naveen Patnaik and Mamata Banerjee. One peculiar example of a 'pro-incumbency' beneficiary is Bihar Chief Minister Nitish Kumar. When he won his second term in 2010, Nitish Kumar was immensely popular in the state. Since then, he has switched allies twice and won two more terms, making it four consecutive terms. But most surveys show his popularity has waned considerably and it is the allies which keep him in the chair. Still, winning four successive terms is no joke. And lastly, who can forget the proverbial joker in the pack Arvind Kejriwal. When the BJP swept all the 7 Lok Sabha seats in 2014, Kejriwal and his Aam Aadmi Party looked like a meteor that had streaked through the Indian political skies. How wrong the pundits were. He has won two successive monstrous mandates in assembly elections in Delhi.

The leaders are all so different from each other that it would be foolish to look at similarities that could explain pro-incumbency. The only similarity is their almost mystical ability to win, again and again. The accompanying graphics shows these pro-incumbency beneficiaries with the total number of years as chief minister.

Now, its Pro-Incumbency with a Difference

Look at the map of India as on mid-March 2022 where states with pro-incumbency and re-elected governments are marked in blue, while states where anti-incumbency seems the norm in this century are marked in red. It appears like a sea of blue with an occasional splash of red. For distinguished and respected geriatrics, even the occasional splash of red was an aberration in their day and age. For them and for a majority of voters in that era, the Congress was the party that gave independence to India. For them, Prime Minister Jawaharlal Nehru was not only Prince Charming, but also the King of all he surveyed. Even his critics have

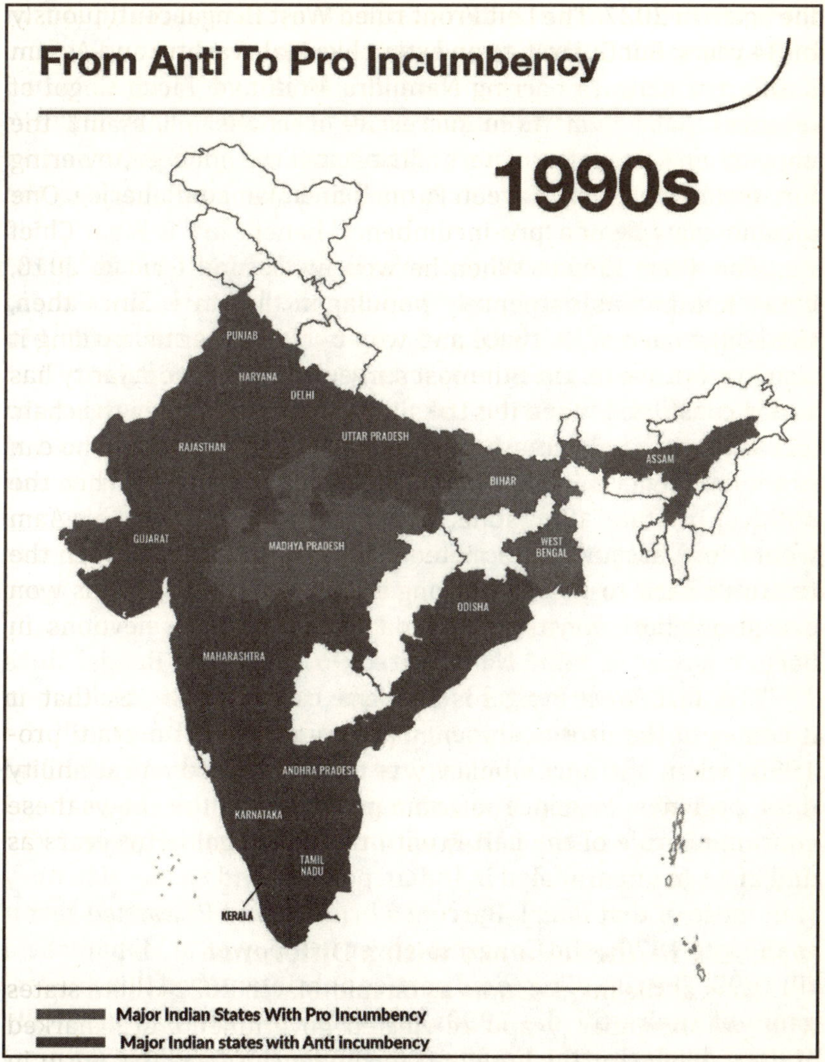

to admit that for all his faults, Nehru did not allow his immense popularity with the masses to become a demagogue and then a de facto dictator as many leaders of countries newly freed from colonial rule did. For the first twenty years since independence, the term 'anti-incumbency' simply did not seem to exist in the Indian political vocabulary as the Congress made it a habit of winning elections. The only splash of red appeared in 1957 when the Communist Party of India became the first Communist party in the world to win truly 'free and fair' elections, though it was to the Kerala assembly. The government did not last very long as Nehru revealed that he was as human as all of us after all, by unfairly, unjustly and undemocratically dismissing the state government. But since this is not a treatise on Nehru, we come back to the incumbency phenomenon.

The year 1967 was the one in which 'anti-incumbency' became fashionable in India. The Congress led by Indira Gandhi eked out a narrow Lok Sabha victory by Congress standards, but also lost ten states after the assembly elections in that year. That was the last time when the Lok Sabha and assembly elections to all states were held simultaneously. That also marked the end of pro-incumbency as a kind of musical chairs game began in Indian politics. In state after state, beginning in 1967, the Congress would lose assembly elections to an opposition coalition only to storm back to power during the next elections. There were exceptions both ways, of course. The Congress has never come back to power in Tamil Nadu since 1967 and West Bengal since 1977. In fact, West Bengal is a unique case study in itself when it comes to the pro-incumbency phenomenon. In an era till the 1990s when anti-incumbency was the buzz word and electoral data provides evidence of anti-incumbency, the 34-year-old continuous rule of the Left Front in West Bengal between 1977 and 2011 in unparalleled in Indian political and electoral history (but more of that later). Barring a brief Sharad Pawar-led revolt in the late 1970s, the Congress never lost power in Maharashtra till 1995. The rise of regional parties only intensified this musical game of chairs till the 1990s, by when the BJP had gradually started displacing the Congress as the most formidable political force in national politics. The regional parties, except perhaps the Asom Gana Parishad which won assembly elections in 1985, have never gone away since then. But the dominant political narrative till the 1990s was anti-incumbency. It is strange how pundits still keep harping on 'anti-incumbency' even today in TV debates and newspaper columns despite clear evidence to the contrary.

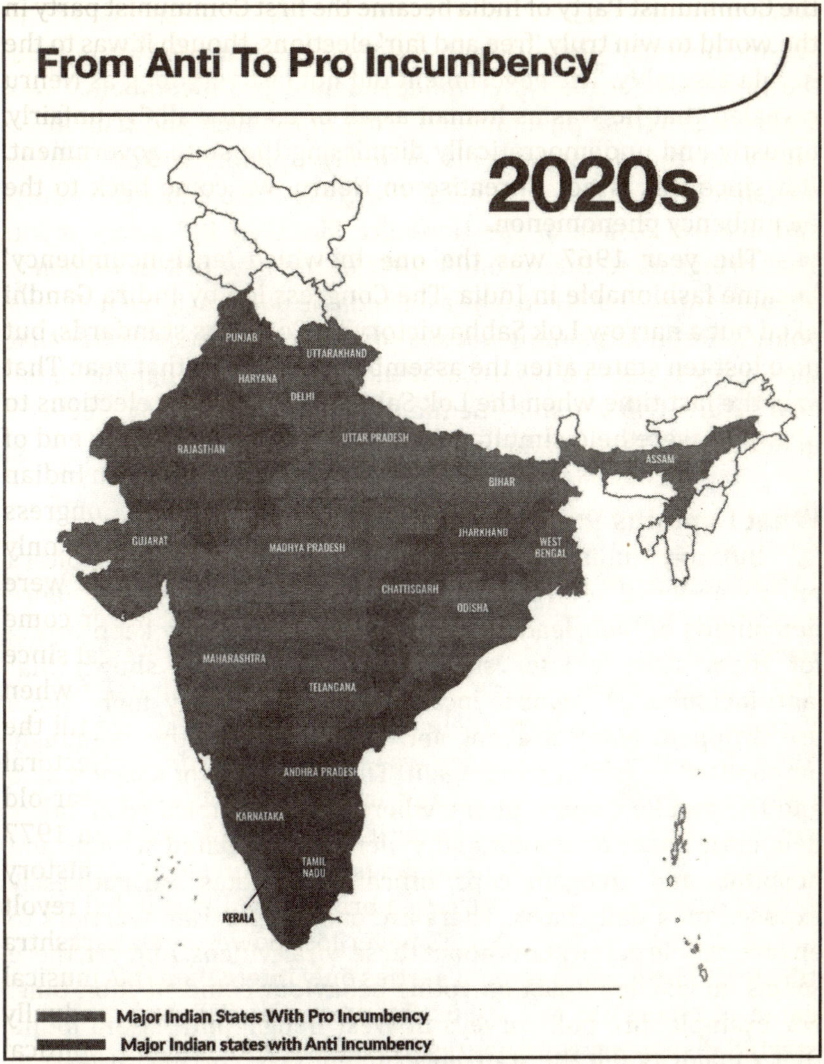

Beginning the mid-1990s, the era of anti-incumbency started fading when Lalu Prasad Yadav won a second consecutive term as chief minister in Bihar. He was sent to jail on corruption charges and forced to resign. Lalu installed his barely literate wife Rabri Devi as chief minister and his party won a third successive mandate in 2000. The BJP won Gujarat in 1995 and has kept winning since then. We have already discussed the other 'pro-incumbency' torch bearers in brief. What makes the pro-incumbency phenomenon different this time is twofold: for the first two decades after independence, pro-incumbency was a purely Congress phenomenon. That era is well and truly over, except in the desolate souls of many opinion writers whose nostalgic love for the old, 'liberal' Congress era matches their deep and visceral dislike of the Narendra Modi-led BJP government. That brings us to the second aspect of the new pro-incumbency phenomenon. The BJP maybe a formidable political force in Indian politics. But it has simply not acquired the 'monopoly' status that the Congress once enjoyed. Nor does it look likely to happen in the near future. Can you imagine the BJP winning assembly elections in Kerala and Tamil Nadu in this decade?

What Explains Pro-Incumbency?

But any Indian interested even a bit in Indian politics must wonder: if voters are more literate, more aware and more demanding of their leaders and parties, why do they keep voting for them? Survey after survey across India has shown that 'anti-incumbency' against local MLAs is extremely high. Some are dropped. Many are not and the party and the seemingly 'unpopular' legislators win again. This is the age of social media and the mobile camera phone where every potholed road, many deliberate cases of assault and violence, dilapidated schools and hospitals and arrogant cops, officers and netas are ruthlessly exposed on a daily basis. There are enough partisan warriors to ensure people get to know about these 'viral' videos. And yet, there seems no visible impact on voting behaviour come election time. For example, pre-poll surveys in West Bengal and Assam found that a majority felt the state government was 'corrupt' at least to some extent and that they did not get benefits under the myriad welfare schemes offered by the state governments. Yet, the ruling parties were returned to power with thumping and comfortable majorities respectively.

In reality, except a lot of song and dance about state-of-the-art government schools and mohalla clinics that were backed up by massive expenses on advertising, the real benefit that Delhi citizens got was free electricity for up to 200 units every month, 20,000 litres of water and free bus rides for women. Otherwise, there has not been a significant improvement in physical and social infrastructure. Yet, Arvind Kejriwal won again with a massive majority. Was free electricity enough to sway voters his way? Or look at Maharashtra. Between 1999 and 2014, the Congress-NCP alliance was seen as visibly corrupt. The highest number of farmer suicides in the state happened during that period. Chief ministers were changed frequently, with some being forced to resign under a cloud of corruption charges. But the Congress-NCP alliance won three successive election victories, including one after the 26/11 Mumbai terror attacks. In terms of performance, Bihar chief minister Nitish Kumar rates extremely poorly compared to his peers for many years now. And yet he won a fourth successive term. There was a time when people laughed at Naveen Patnaik saying he doesn't even know how to speak the native language Odiya. Pundits felt that it was his alliance with the BJP that kept him in power. But he junked the BJP before the 2009 elections and has won three bigger mandates on his own since then.

The obvious question is: what explains this return to the era of 'pro-incumbency' elections, albeit with a range of parties and personalities benefiting, rather than the monopoly era of the Congress? The authors have identified three factors that explain this phenomenon. Pre- and post-poll analysis done by a range of organizations like C-Voter and CSDS-Lok Niti, to name just a few offer strongly credible data-based evidence that make these three factors stand out as pivotal, if not entirely complete and definitive explanations. Subsequent chapters of the book will analyse these factors in some detail. But this introductory chapter offers a brief synopsis.

The Personality Cult

Many commentators, journalists and even scholars have been arguing that Indian democracy and Indian elections are now firmly influenced by the personality cult and how elections have become increasingly 'presidential' in nature, referring obviously to the United States of America. To be sure, both Jawaharlal

Nehru and Indira Gandhi were towering personalities. But at the state level, barring some notables, the personality cult emerged first when the Congress decline started. Arguably, the first chief minister to leverage and take advantage of the personality cult was the late M.G. Ramachandran, Tamil movie superstar and multiple times chief minister till his death in 1987. The other movie superstar who also leveraged the personality cult was N.T. Rama Rao, who delivered a numbingly shock defeat to the Congress in assembly elections in Andhra Pradesh in 1983, within just a few months of forming his own new regional party Telugu Desam. Of course, since it was the 1980s, he lost the 1989 assembly elections badly because of anti-incumbency. J. Jayalalithaa is the third movie superstar with her own personality cult as chief minister. No other film star has been as successful as them, though many have tried.

It is not as if only film stars enjoyed the benefits of a personality cult in Indian politics. Once the magic of the Nehru-Gandhi brand name started waning, other political leaders developed their own personality cults. We had Lalu Prasad Yadav in Bihar. Jyoti Basu was already the Prime Minister India never had. Though Mulayam Singh Yadav was more politically powerful and electorally successful in Uttar Pradesh, it was Mayawati who enjoyed the perks of a personality cult. Then came Narendra Modi who has gone on to become Prime Minister. There is Nitish Kumar of Bihar who was conferred the title of 'Susashan Babu'. We have the street fighter Mamata Banerjee who has a visible personality cult. To some extent, even Shivraj Singh Chouhan, Dr. Raman Singh and Vasundhara Raje Scindia had their time and place under the sun within their states. And not all were controversial and polarising. Three-time chief minister Tarun Gogoi was affable; five times chief minister Naveen Patnaik is in a class by himself and three times chief minister Sheila Dikshit was one of the most liked politicians in the country. While the individual personalities differ, the pro-incumbency 'champions' do share some traits: personal popularity and ability to win elections, a connect with masses, being decisive and ruthless when required and sometimes bold gamblers.

Connect with Masses

This is a quality that is very difficult to measure and quantify. Yet it has been demonstrated in election after election for the last few decades that this 'connect' does affect electoral outcomes. It has been 25 years since Lalu Prasad Yadav was the chief minister of Bihar. And yet, not even his critics can deny the personal connect he has with his loyal supporters. This connect almost took his son Tejashwi Yadav to the post of chief minister in Bihar in the November, 2020 assembly elections, only to lose really narrowly to the NDA alliance though his party the RJD emerged as the largest one. Who knows, if the Assadudin Owaisi led AIMIM had not won five seats, split the Muslim votes in many other seats and the alliance partner Congress had not performed so miserably, Tejashwi Yadav would have been the chief minister of Bihar.

Similarly, the BJP was on a really shaky ground during the 2017 assembly elections. Close to 22 continuous years in power had made the voters weary. The Patel agitation that rocked the state in 2016 seemed to have alienated a large section of hitherto loyal voters. The sitting chief minister Vijay Rupani was described at best as lacklustre in both charisma and performance. Old rural voters seemed all set to go back to the Congress. Sensing defeat, Narendra Modi made emotional appeal after appeal to voters of Gujarat. It was his personal connect with the masses that saved the day for the BJP.

Traditionally, it has been considered that it is leaders who emerge after years and years of grassroots politics develop that personal connect with the masses. That is true to an extent. Lalu Yadav, Nitish Kumar, Mayawati, Narendra Modi and Mamata Banerjee among others are classic examples of this grassroots approach. But this is not a given thing in politics. Naveen Patnaik had no interest in politics. He mingled with the global jet-setting crowd and devoted most of his time to things literary and artistic. Till today, he can't speak fluent Odiya. And yet, who can deny the connect he has with the masses in Odisha? You don't become a five times chief minister by being a former jet-setter who just parachuted into local politics. Then again, J. Jayalalithaa hardly did any grassroots work before her mentor M.G. Ramachandran made her General Secretary of his party AIADMK. She remained arrogant, haughty, aloof and distant. But for voters in Tamil Nadu, she was and remains Amma even after her death.

Clean, Decisive and Ruthless Image

There is hardly a state government existing in India that voters consider to be free of corruption. Given the nature of our rent-seeking bureaucracy to exploit scores of rules and regulations that enable citizens to access services and given the greed for cash by politicians, it is impossible to not have corruption in this country. Earlier in this chapter, we mentioned how a majority of voters in Assam and West Bengal considered their state governments to be corrupt to some extent at least. But that is being nullified to a large extent by the personally clean images of chief ministers who keep winning. There have been allegations of corruption of course, by political opponents. But they do not seem to have convinced voters. Even in the case of J. Jayalalithaa who was convicted by the Supreme Court (indirectly) after her death on corruption charges, voters in Tamil Nadu were convinced she was punished enough for her excesses between 1991 and 1996 and turned a new leaf.

The other related factor is of appearing to be decisive and steel-willed while taking decisions. The chief ministers who keep winning enjoy this perception. Even the suave Naveen Patnaik is known to deal ruthlessly with opponents. Voters are aware of this. Strangely, it makes them like him even more. Mamata Banerjee is cut from the same cloth, though she doesn't waste time on being nice and suave. When chief ministers appear 'weak' or indecisive, then pro-incumbency goes for a toss. The biggest example is Raghubar Das, former chief minister of Jharkhand. He was accused of being corrupt. As we have seen, no big deal in India. His fatal weakness was appearing to be weak. That was one key reason why the BJP not only lost the state in the 2019 assembly elections soon after Modi's historic second triumph, but also the sitting chief minister losing his own seat. The seemingly weak Vijay Rupani almost cost the BJP the state of Gujarat. And despite virtually all opinion polls giving a handsome victory to the BJP in Haryana, the seemingly weak Manohar Lal Khattar survives as chief minister only thanks to a post poll alliance with a faction of the Lok Dal.

The chapter will analyse in more detail how this personality cult and presidential style politics works by looking at electoral and other data. It also attempts to analyse the 'mysterious' connect that these 'rock star' personalities have with masses and how it impacts electoral outcomes.

Welfare Means Loyal Voters

Perhaps one of the biggest failures of India as a democracy has been the inability of the State to provide basic, decent quality public education and health and basic physical infrastructure needs like roads, electricity, clean drinking water and toilets. Attention to this has enabled Asian countries that were once much poorer than India race miles ahead not just in human development indices, but also in sheer per capita income. Even the once basket case Bangladesh looks poised to surpass India in the near future on these parameters. Against this backdrop, 'welfare' has emerged as the biggest vote catcher in recent decades. Even his critics acknowledge that despite his weak performance when it comes to the economy, it was the massive implementation of 'welfare' schemes like free toilets, gas connections, zero balance bank accounts and free pucca houses that carried the day for Narendra Modi in the 2019 Lok Sabha elections.

Many chief ministers have been doing the same much before Modi or alongside him. We will not go too far back when 'mid-day meals' for school children were announced in Tamil Nadu in the 1960s. Let's stick to this century. Dr. Raman Singh became 'Chawal Wale' Baba for his scheme offering both free and heavily subsidised rice to poor voters. Similar efforts and schemes earned Shivraj Singh Chouhan the moniker of 'Mamaji'. Nitish Kumar became 'Susashan Babu' not just for vastly improving the law and order situation in his first two stints, but also earned the gratitude and votes of millions whose daughters were given free bicycles to go to school. Telangana chief minister K.C. Rao went one over Modi by offering substantial cash payments to farmers, as did Naveen Patnaik in Odisha. The free electricity model adopted by Arvind

Kejriwal in Delhi and now offered by his party in other states has become a pathbreaking and many say dangerously populist welfare measure.

Even when it comes to physical infrastructure, there is a race to build airports, metros, expressways, new electricity supply lines and what not. You may call it populism; but decades after independence, the Indian citizen is finally getting access to basic amenities. It is possible that the need for such basic amenities will be fulfilled in the not-too-distant future. For example, toilets and bank accounts now actually reach more than 85 per cent of the population. In such an event, new 'welfare' measures will emerge as new avenues to harvest votes. But there can be little doubt that such schemes have played a role in ensuring pro-incumbency sentiments.

This chapter will use actual data from welfare schemes and match them with voter behaviour to provide data-driven evidence of the electoral potency of this factor.

Weak Opposition Helps Incumbents

What was endemic during the era of Congress monopoly over power when a structurally and organisationally weak opposition played a very critical role in delivering pro incumbency has now become a sporadic affair confined to some regions and states; not the whole of India. And yet, it does play a significant role in helping incumbents win re-elections despite the presence of the fabled anti-incumbency. This chapter will analyse the various instances where opposition weakness has actually played a very important, if not critical role in ensuring pro-incumbency verdicts.

We highlight just two of them in this introductory chapter. In 2020, Nitish Kumar was no longer the much admired 'Susashan Babu' of Bihar; nor was he as popular as he was in 2010 at the peak of his political ascendancy. He had dumped the BJP as an ally in 2013 when Narendra Modi became the prime ministerial candidate, his ostensible publicly stated reason was he could not bear to share the same platform with a 'communal' leader like Modi. He teamed with old foe Lalu Yadav, whose alleged 'jungle raj' was his calling card during elections; won a big mandate in assembly elections 2015 and accepted the younger son of Lalu,

Tejashwi Prasad as deputy chief minister despite apprehensions raised even by his well-wishers about the danger of corruption and lawlessness of the RJD era making a comeback. When that actually started happening, Nitish Kumar dumped Lalu and joined hands with the 'communal' Modi. In the meanwhile, his prohibition policy was creating more problems than it could solve.

So when elections became due in November 2020, Nitish Kumar had a tough challenge to confront. To compound his woes, Chirag Paswan announced that his party LJP would put up strong candidates against JD (U) candidates across the state. As electoral data later showed, in 33 assembly seats, the loss margin of votes of the JD (U) candidate was lower than the number of votes won by the LJP candidate. How then did Nitish win a fourth consecutive term? Well, the 'Grand Alliance of RJD', Congress and Left parties allotted 70 out of 243 seats of Bihar to Congress. The Congress lost 51 of those 70 seats. The final electoral tally was: 125 for the Nitish-led alliance and 110 for the Tejashwi-led alliance. Imagine the possibilities if a weak Congress had not put up such a miserable show.

The Congress doing poorly is not a new, or surprising story this century. But the BJP doing pathetically is. Once upon a time, the BJP was the dominant party in Delhi. As expected, it won a majority in the newly constituted assembly of Delhi in 1993 when it became a state, albeit with curtailed powers and no power over the Delhi Police. But much to the dismay of its supporters, it has failed to win a single assembly election in the Capital since then. First, it lost three consecutive times to Sheila Dikshit and Congress and then it has lost three consecutive times to Arvind Kejriwal and AAP. That is indeed strange for a party that is so dominant that it has swept all seven Lok Sabha seats from Delhi in 2014 as well as 2019. But there can be no doubt that the state leadership of the party in Delhi has been uninspiring, if not worse. Hence the six consecutive cakewalks to rivals.

Economics or Identity?

We have already quoted Milan Vaishnav of Carnegie Foundation earlier in this chapter where he says: "In India voters do not so much cast their vote as they vote their caste." There can be no doubt that identity has played a major role in Indian elections since they were first organised in 1951-52. It persists even now. For example, an overwhelming majority of Muslims will simply not vote for the BJP and back a horse they think can defeat the BJP. This was reinforced in assembly elections in 2021 in West Bengal where most Muslim votes went to Mamata Banerjee and in 2022 in Uttar Pradesh when most Muslim votes went to Akhilesh Yadav. Mamata won and Akhilesh lost, but that is a different matter not related to the pro-incumbency hypothesis of this book. Similarly, despite winning just 1 out of 403 seats in UP in 2022, the BSP led by Mayawati managed a vote share of about 13 per cent. This is the core 'Jatav' Dalit vote bank that has remained loyal to Mayawati for three decades. Even in southern India, a part of the country about which lazy analysts think otherwise, caste plays a crucial role during elections. This is one reason why we have not added good economics as the fourth factor behind the contemporary phenomenon of pro-incumbency waves, though we were tempted to. But economics is an important factor nevertheless.

Good economics got a terrible reputation in the aftermath of 2004 and the reputation persists despite increasing evidence that it has started becoming a factor. In 2004, Atal Bihari Vajpayee the bold reformer with his India Shining campaign unexpectedly lost the Lok Sabha elections. Many analysts concluded that the India Shining campaign was like showing a red rag to a bull: the bull in this case being poor and underprivileged voters who punished Vajpayee for neglecting them. In the chapter, we provide conclusive evidence that this was not the case. But sometimes, myths persist despite facts to the contrary. Good economics received a 'body blow' in Andhra Pradesh in 2004 when N. Chandrababu Naidu, the reformist chief minister who was given the title of CEO of Andhra by large sections of Indian and global media, lost the assembly elections quite badly. For analysts as well as many politicians, reforms and good economics became almost taboo after that.

As the chapter shows, it is welfare schemes for the poor that have played a more decisive 'economic' role in sustaining pro-incumbency rather than good economic policies that have a long-term impact. For the desperately poor, a bird in hand is often more than half a dozen in the bush. But Indian voters are not myopic as some arrogant and disconnected analysts tend to presume. For example, a scholarship for a girl that starts at age five and continues with modest contributions for higher education till she becomes 21 years old is not a short-term, immediate cash transfer. It is a long-term benefit. And the poor mother of the girl is wise enough to understand the enormous value of this long-term measure.

The Spoilsports or Spoilers

In 2022, the Badal family became famous across India for reasons they will not be happy with. Both the family patriarch Prakash Singh Badal and his son Sukhbir Singh Badal lost the assembly elections from their long-held bastions. But 10 years before that, the Badal had acquired fame for scripting a different kind of history. Against all odds and breaking a long-held record (like Kerala in 2021 and UP in 2022), they retained power in the assembly elections. The pattern till then was anti-incumbency sentiments throwing the existing government out. This had been going on since the 1970s. There were strong allegations of corruption and an extravagantly luxurious lifestyle of Sukhbir Singh Badal. Whispers about the 'failure' of the government to check the drug menace were growing louder. And yet the Badals won a second consecutive mandate.

The reason, as discussed in this last chapter of the book, was a family feud and a revolt. Basically, Manpreet Badal, the first cousin of Sukhbir and the finance minister of the state had serious differences with him. By 2010, the differences turned into a bitter, public feud and Manpreet quit the Akali Dal and formed his own party. In the 2012 assembly elections, his party failed to win a single seat. But the vote share of about 6 per cent that it won took away enough anti-regime votes to leave a confident Congress stunned and stung by an unexpected defeat. In politics across the world, leaders like Manpreet are called spoilers. Raj Thackeray too played the role of a spoiler in 2009 for the Shiv Sena-BJP alliance by winning a good enough vote share to deny power to his estranged former associates and hand it over on a platter to a very unpopular NCP-Congress alliance in Maharashtra.

As the chapter goes on to explain, not all spoilers come from family feuds of political dynasties. They come in different shapes and sizes and have differing impacts on electoral outcomes, as the 2022 Goa elections have shown. But like side roles in Bollywood movies, spoilers are just support cast; they don't play a big a enough role to be considered as factor behind pro incumbency verdicts.

But this book would be incomplete without analysing the ultimate symbol of pro-incumbency in Indian politics: Narendra Damodardas Modi. He has already been the chief minister of Gujarat for 13 continuous years before moving to Delhi as the Prime Minister in 2014. And while it is foolhardy to forecast electoral outcomes, Modi seems in with an even chance of winning a third successive mandate as Prime Minister in 2024. Only Jawaharlal Nehru holds that record. Even if Modi fails to match the record held by Nehru, he stands out as a classic case of how and why pro-incumbency works. First, the personality cult. Most political observers including his fierce critics compare Modi with Indira Gandhi. Justifiably so because he has delivered election victories even in assembly elections just like Indira did. Then comes welfare. In this field, one can describe him as the Franklin Delano Roosevelt of India. FDR is the only President who won four successive Presidential elections. His single-minded focus on helping the poor with state funds started the welfare revolution in the developed West. In the last 8 years, Modi has done the same in India. In fact, FDR was famous for his fireside radio chats with American citizens that by passed traditional media platforms. Modi does the same with his Mann Ki Baat chat on radio. When it comes to the third reason for pro-incumbency verdicts that Modi has enjoyed, the book is full of examples of how a Congress in decline has helped Modi. And let's not forget economics versus identity. Even his critics grudgingly acknowledge that Modi—for various reasons—has been immensely successful in breaking the stranglehold of caste and class identities during elections. He has failed when it comes to religious identity as an overwhelming majority of Muslims still don't vote for the BJP. That's a final frontier he may or may not conquer. But like Nehru and Indira before him, Modi has found his perch in history.

Like life, nothing is permanent in politics. So will this sustained phase of pro-incumbency end? And by when? We seek answers as we dive deeper into data and insights in this book.

References

1. @sardesairajdeep.....10.21 PM. 10/03/22)
2. It Could Be Kejriwal vs Adityanath In 2029—by Sagarika Ghose https://www.ndtv.com/opinion/it-could-be-kejriwal-vs-adityanath-in-2029-by-sagarika-ghose-2814030
3. https://scroll.in/field/965591/what-kapil-dev-and-cos-historic-1983-world-cup-win-means-to-various-generations-of-indian-fans
4. @_sabanaqvi. 2.41 PM. 10/03/22
5. https://carnegieendowment.org/2013/12/19/does-good-economics-mean-good-politics-in-india-pub-53988

□

2
GUTS, GUMPTION, GAMBLING & GLORY

There is this story about the late J. Jayalalithaa. An almost 'superstar' level Tamil actress, this Brahmin lady was the co-star of the real superstar of Tamil movies M.G. Ramachandran and remained close to him even after he formed his own party the AIADMK and became chief minister of Tami Nadu. So close were they that Jayalalithaa was made General Secretary of the party at the age of 35 in 1983. By then, both detractors and supporters had started telling startling tales about her.

Amma

After MGR died in 1987, Jayalalithaa had a harrowing time for a while. In March 1989, ruling party DMK members assaulted her and one of them even pulled her saree that came apart at the shoulders as she fell to the ground. She then vowed to return to the assembly only when it was safe for women. Almost overnight, legends grew around the 'Puratchi Thalaivi'. Two years later, she had her revenge in 1991 by storming to power as chief minister. Yet another fable was then created around her supposed collection of jewellery, sarees and even shoes as serious charges of corruption flew thick and fast. Her fans, most of them are better categorised as devotees always seemed to ignore her idiosyncrasies and temperamental behaviour.

In 1998, she formed an alliance with the BJP which came to power at the centre under the umbrella alliance NDA. One year later, she felt ignored and insulted by Prime Minister Atal Bihari Vajpayee. Jayalalithaa met Sonia Gandhi for tea and abruptly announced she would support a no confidence motion against

Vajpayee. (Incidentally, another leader with a personality cult of her own Mayawati too promised she would support Vajpayee till the last minute before 'ditching' him, in a manner of speaking. But she has failed the pro-incumbency test and will therefore find no further mention in this chapter). The fall of the Vajpayee government and his return to power in a few months made no difference to Jayalalithaa's devotees in the state. She came back as chief minister in 2001. One of the first major decisions she took was to order the state police to arrest her predecessor M. Karunanidhi after midnight who was shown on live TV being literally dragged out of his room and then his house by the cops. Her devotees cheered rapturously.

When she launched the 'Amma' canteens in 2013 to offer cheap food at subsidised rates to the poor, her devotees behaved as if Jayalalithaa was the first person to think of welfare schemes for the poor. The fact is, it was the long dead K. Kamaraj of the Congress who was the first political leader to launch a meaningful welfare scheme when he introduced free mid-day meals for schoolchildren in Tamil Nadu, way back in the 1970s. But Amma was, Amma is and Amma will remain Amma for the legions of her devotees who were her devoted voters. It doesn't matter a whit that the Supreme Court of India found her guilty of corruption, albeit after her death.

The late Cho. Ramaswami, founder-editor of Tuglaq and arguably the most upfront Tamil media person of his times had a very classical love-hate relationship with Amma. He supported Jayalalithaa when she was absolutely down and out, and opposed her when she was at the peak of her glory days. One of the authors had a free-flowing conversation with him during the 2001 assembly elections at his Chennai office. He said: "Jaya's biggest strength is also her biggest weakness. She is kind of a loner and takes almost all her decisions singlehanded. It took her a long time to understand that for all the decisions that she takes, she can't really blame on others. And this includes decision on the company she keeps. But her strength is that her supporters like her and support her even with all her weaknesses...no matter what."

Just imagine. A deeply patriarchal state steeped in Dravidian angst against upper caste Hindus revering and virtually worshipping a corruption convict, temperamental, vindictive and Brahmin woman. This is what a personality cult is all about and we are seeing more and more of it across India. K.R. Manoharan of the Azim Premji University wrote a profile for the portal *The Wire* just before her death in 2016: "The intensity of adulation that Jayalalithaa receives from her supporters rivals that of any godman in the country. Elderly AIADMK leaders, including the ex-chief minister of Tamil Nadu, O. Panneerselvam, openly prostrating before her; local leaders sponsoring special offerings in temples on the occasion of her birthday; AIADMK cadres tonsuring their heads to pray for her victory and tattooing her name on their chests to prove their loyalty are common sights in Tamil Nadu...dismissing these displays of loyalty from the lower classes towards their leader as cynical calculations would be intellectual snobbery. The problem with Bonapartism is that it actually works."[1]

But to be fair to Amma, her re-election in her last electoral bout was against all odds and pretty much rooted in social welfare schemes and delivery of governance as well. When the C-Voter tracker predicted her pro-incumbent verdict in 2016 assembly election, everyone refused to believe saying it went against the history of pendulum swings in Tamil Nadu, without even realising that the penultimate election was neither pendulum nor swing. Even in her defeat earlier, she remained in the Assembly with impressive numbers and continued to humiliate the DMK government by consistently calling it 'the minority government' for a full five years as chief minister Karunanidhi did not have majority numbers on his own. TN is known to have huge spectrum coalition drama with either DMK or ADMK as the nucleus. All this changed in 2016 when Amma virtually forced each and every alliance partner to contest on the ADMK symbol of two leaves. She thought that coalition drama aside, people were actually voting in her name, not in the name of the Alliance. And she was absolutely right in her assessment.

The Personality Cult Exists in All Fields

Personality cults exist in every walk of life, and in every field. And they are often inexplicable at first glance. Look at what the tennis legend Novak Djokovic is doing. In 2021[2] when he won the Wimbledon title and his 20th Grand Slam one, equaling the record of Roger Federer and Rafael Nadal, it looked certain that he was destined for the all-time record as well the difficult to measure moniker of all-time greatness. One bad final at the US open and he missed his 21st record-breaking Grand Slam title. Never mind, said his diehard fans; he will do it in the Australian Open in January 2022. But there was and is a problem. Djokovic says he is not anti-vaccine but refuses to take the Covid vaccine saying it is his personal choice. He had to miss the tournament and Nadal won the final becoming the first to win 21st Grand Slam titles. Because of Djokovic's stubborn refusal to take the shot, it became possible for Nadal to win his 22nd Grand Slam title in the French Open.

From a commonsense perspective, Djokovic looks like a childish loser. But his legend has grown.

Sports journalist Christopher Clary wrote for *The New York Times* soon after Djokovic was deported from Australia: "We are talking about a player who became a champion despite growing up in Belgrade during the violent breakup of Yugoslavia, when NATO bombing forced him to interrupt tennis practices. He left home at 12 for a tennis academy in Germany as his parents and family borrowed and improvised to fund his training in the hope that the sport would be his route, and theirs, to better days...Djokovic's emotional loss to Medvedev in New York last year seemed to mark a shift in public opinion: a deeper connection and appreciation for his enduring excellence as he failed to complete his quest. But after Melbourne, the notion that he might, in the autumnal phase of his career, match the global popularity of Federer and Nadal seems far-fetched. Djokovic, a wizard at returning serve and shooting himself in the sneaker, has long been polarizing and, it seems, will remain so."

In a way, Djokovic and his controversial legend resembles that of many Indian politicians who are pro-incumbency stars. When it comes to coming from a humble and deprived background, Lalu

Yadav, Shivraj Singh Chouhan and to an extent K.C. Rao come to mind. When it comes to triggering intense dislike among a section of people, there is Narendra Modi. When it comes to 'courting' controversy like Djokovic, who else but Mamata Banerjee? And when it comes to taking big, seemingly foolhardy gambles with one's career, Naveen Patnaik did that by dumping the BJP before the 2009 elections. These are things you cannot measure statistically or quantify.

The First Rule Is Win Elections, And Keep Winning

When she stunned the pundits by leading her party to a majority in the 2007 UP assembly elections, the cult already being built around Mayawati became even more intriguing and fascinating. In just her first few months as CM, she sacked a powerful politician Anand Sen Yadav as minister when he was accused of raping a girl. It looked as if she meant business and kept packing off her own party men accused of sexual crimes to jail. Of course, to make the Dalit struggle for dignity and a fair share in power, Mayawati started the process of building huge statues of herself in Lucknow and the commercial hub Noida adjacent to Delhi using taxpayers' money. Who cared? After all, she deserved it all as 'Dalit Ki Beti'. By 2009, when Lok Sabha elections were due, Mayawati was a serious contender for the top post. The 'English medium types' elites sniggered at her Gucci bags, at the mountain of currency notes around her neck and body gifted by admirers during her birthday and much else. In her own uniquely elite way, Shobha De wrote a column in the *Hindustan Times* in March 2009 where it looked like she was defending and cheering for Mayawati: "Let's face it—Mayawati drives us mad. Us??? Who's 'Us'? Oh...us is us! People who count. Thought leaders. Opinion makers. Bull shitters. People still living in some la la land, imagining we are important. Get real, guys. Before you can say 'Kanshi Ram', Mayawati will be on that *kursi* in Dilli. The same one her foes are determined to keep her ample backside away from. And if perchance Mayawati's derrière does occupy the *gaddi*, God help those foes. Mayawati will whack their butts with that handbag of hers, whip their asses, and then the *asli* fun will start."[3]

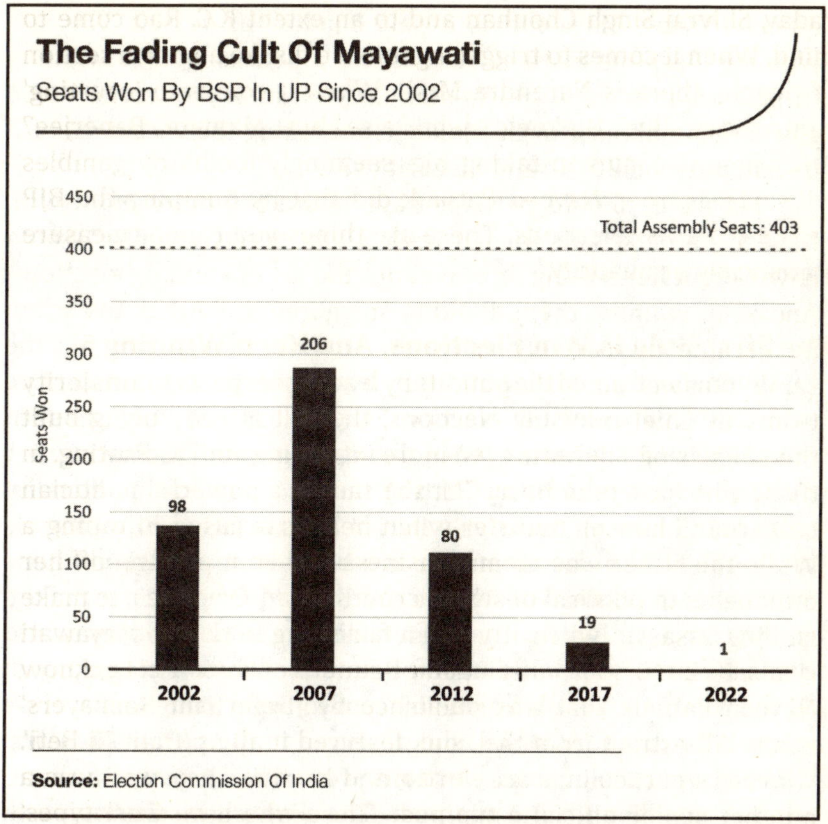

Whether Shobha De would have used terms like 'her ample backside' or 'Mayawati's derrière on other woman politicians is a moot point. But that's not the point this chapter or even this book trying to make. The fact is that Mayawati forgot to, or was unable to follow the golden rule: Win Elections and Keep Winning. She lost the 2012 UP assembly elections. Then came the shocker in 2014. The BSP drew a blank and failed to win a single Lok Sabha seat. Then came an even bigger shocker in the 2017 UP assembly elections. The 2022 assembly elections in UP, in which Yogi Adityanath was returned to power with a massive mandate a second time, making him the state's first-ever chief minister to be re-elected have been nothing short of a complete meltdown for the BSP. The once formidable party was reduced to a mere 19 out of 403 seats. The aura and the personality cult started fading quickly. Today, Mayawati is a pale shadow of herself. You see, winning elections matters. At least for a politician. Like winning trophies matter for a sports star. Do you think the world would give a damn about Novak Djokovic not taking the vaccine shot if he had not won 20th Grand Slam titles?

Mayawati should perhaps have interacted more often with Naveen Patnaik. This former 'elite Delhi based socialite' would have taught her a thing or two about the art of winning elections. And keep winning them. Pundits sniggered at Patnaik too when he became increasingly active in politics; though not for the same reasons as Mayawati. But by winning five consecutive terms as chief minister, Naveen Patnaik has not only silenced the sniggering Slytherins (with due apologies to J.K. Rowling for those who have read Harry Potter), but also created a personality cult around himself that rivals that of his late father Biju Patnaik. While the father was all macho and believed in bludgeoning his opponents to political death, the son has acquired the aura of the smiling assassin when it comes to dealing with opponents and rivals. In 2018, journalist Ruben Bannerjee wrote a biography of Naveen Patnaik that was published by Juggernaut Books. Here is a small extract from the book featured in the portal *The Wire*: "Naveen's gut feelings are strong and he relies heavily on them,' another senior official explained. Those who have worked with him closely say that Naveen hides his emotions well. He may have a very poor opinion of someone, but the person will never get to know that. On the contrary, it is more likely that the chief minister's warm hospitality would have floored him and the person may go away thinking he has made a good impression on Naveen."[4] One of the authors had a fairly detailed interaction with Naveen Patnaik in late 1998 in the form of an interview at Naveen Niwas in Bhubaneswar. The house, near the airport was stately and graceful, and yet not a patch on the luxurious monstrosities you can see in the legendary and notorious Mehrauli farmhouse area or Sainik Farms where politicians have their bungalows. The man was barely a year into active politics by then, and it was clear to the author that he could just about stitch together a sentence or two in his supposedly native language Odiya. Naveen Patnaik was courteous and graceful, but the author could see the glint of steel even in his affable and seemingly innocuous replies to even some tough questions. But the author also admitted he never had imagined in late 1998 that Naveen Patnaik would keep winning, and winning elections.

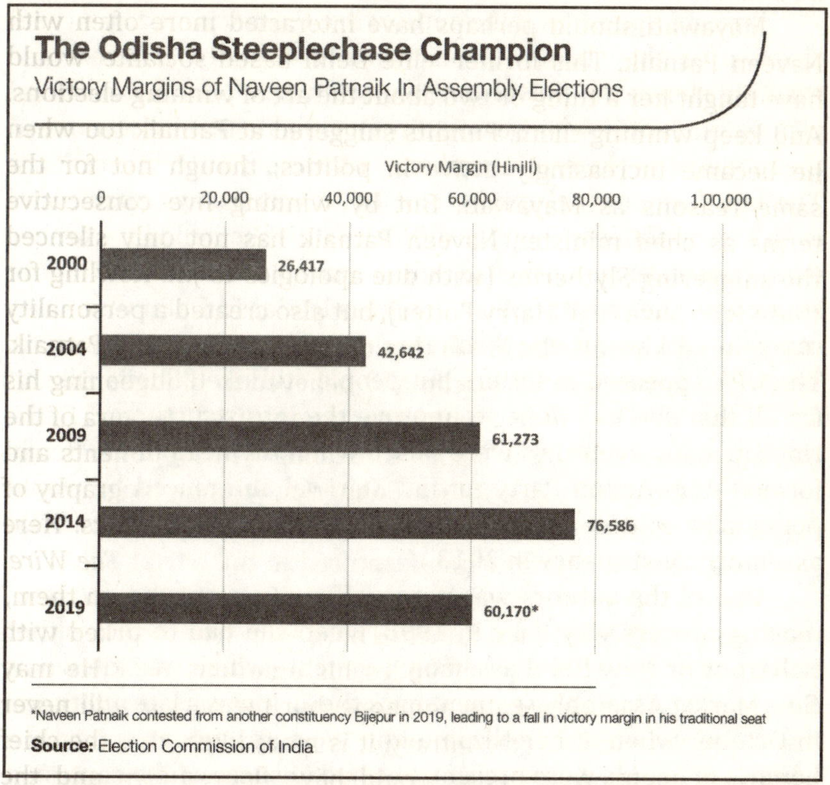

While they differ widely in temperament, style of working and even their public persona, all pro incumbency stars share one common trait: They keep winning elections and their parties keep getting voted back to power. During the 2020 Delhi assembly elections, Arvind Kejriwal was mostly sugar and honey (relatively speaking) when it came to targeting Narendra Modi and the BJP. And won another massive mandate. The next year, Mamata Banerjee was all bile and bravado when it came to targeting Modi and the BJP during the 2021 assembly elections. She won a bigger mandate compared to the previous election in 2016. Glaringly contrasting styles. But both won. As the late Chinese leader and reformer Deng Xiao Peng is reported to have said: "It doesn't matter what colour the cat is as long as it catches the mice".

Personal Victories Matter

It might appear as if the authors are too fascinated by Arvind Kejriwal as they bring up his name. Not guilty. But this one example shows the power and importance of personal electoral victories in launching a personality cult. Sheila Dikshit was one of the pioneers of the pro-incumbency phenomenon in this century. The late former chief minister of Delhi was always affable and even her opponents found it difficult to dislike her. She won her own constituency with handsome margins, leaving no doubt about who the most popular Congress leader in Delhi was. Then came the UPA scams, the Nirbhaya shock and an economy in crisis. The UPA appeared in tatters but people still liked Sheila Dikshit for all that she had done to improve the infrastructure of Delhi. Not too many eyebrows were raised when the head of the newly formed Aam Aadmi Party Arvind Kejriwal announced he would personally contest against Sheila Dikshit from the New Delhi assembly constituency in 2013.

One of the authors was personally witness to the decision-making process way back in 1998, when she had to pick either Babarpur or New Delhi assembly segment (which was known as Gole Market Assembly segment back then). It was a late afternoon in October when at her Nizamuddin West apartment and only a handful of people were present. She had unsuccessfully contested East Delhi Lok Sabha election twice and both times, the Babarpur assembly segment had given her a huge support against all odds. While New Delhi assembly segment was never a Congress stronghold to start with. One seat was offering her the cushion of almost guaranteed victory based on the Muslim support base. The other one was out of her comfort zone, but much more 'inclusive' to drive home the message. After deliberating she opted for the challenging one. And then retained that seat for 15 years. NCR Delhi was symbolic core of India and the New Delhi assembly segment was the ultimate symbolic core of that core. It became a

Congress stronghold for all practical purposes because of Sheila Dikshit.

Fast forward to 2013, Sheila Dikshit was expected to become collateral damage then, but definitely not the way it happened. Congress supporters were convinced Kejriwal was all bluff and bluster and was contesting personally against Sheila Dikshit just to get more publicity. There is no doubt that Kejriwal and his colleagues (most have either left him or been unceremoniously thrown out) and supporters then appeared like scarlet pimpernels if not Don Quixote and Sancho Panzas. But what a spectacular entry Kejriwal made into electoral politics. He actually defeated the sitting chief minister Sheila Dikshit in her own constituency by a massive (by Delhi assembly seat standards) margin of 25,000 votes. The cult of Kejriwal was created almost overnight after that and has not dimmed a bit in the last almost 10 years despite many electoral setbacks here and there. Losing her own seat to an 'upstart' by such a large margin was no doubt a personal setback for a politician like Sheila Dikshit who had largely ruled Delhi successfully for three consecutive terms. But it was clear to all that the Congress was anyway going down.

Her last electoral fight was the 2019 Lok Sabha elections, and to her credit, she actually made Congress the main challenger to BJP and pushed AAP to third position. Right before the 2019 election, in the same old Nizamuddin apartment, she told the author "I don't wish to contest, but if that is what it takes to take the fight back in enemy's territory, let it be...". And who was the enemy? At least she was damn clear about that. "Make no mistakes. I am under no illusion. We lost in Delhi because we allowed AAP to eat up our support base. If we have to revive back the Congress in Delhi, we have to first take back what AAP has taken away. We can handle the BJP later..." she said. Profound wisdom. True to the last word.

So Agonisingly Close, Yet So...

Losing her own seat to an 'upstart' by such a large margin was no doubt a personal setback for a politician who had largely ruled Delhi successfully for three consecutive terms. But it was clear to all that the Congress was anyway going down. In 2019, the BJP-led NDA government in Jharkhand was not very popular with voters who were also unhappy with the chief minister Raghubar Das. The NDA lost the assembly election; and Raghubar Das lost his own seat. This result too was not a surprise for political analysts. But sometimes a personal loss can cost your party a re-election as BJP leaders agonisingly realised in Uttarakhand in the 2012 assembly elections when sitting CM General B.C. Khanduri lost his own seat and Congress pipped the power race just by whisker.

After the humiliating Lok Sabha defeat in 2009, it looked as if the BJP was keen on political hara-kiri. B.S. Yediyurappa who built the BJP literally from scratch with his colleagues in Karnataka was compelled to resign as chief minister by the top leadership in Delhi because of corruption charges. He left the party in a huff, to come back only when Narendra Modi became the PM candidate in 2013. A kind of parody was being played by the BJP in Uttarakhand back then when it kept changing chief ministers (as it did in 2021).

In 2011, C.L. Manoj wrote for the *Economic Times*: "But the truth is that the BJP is in trouble. To many insiders, the problems are clearly identifiable: no clarity on leadership, confusion over political and ideological direction, and the inability attract allies to expand the almost defunct National Democratic Alliance. Credible solutions to these problems, many leaders say, are crucial for its fortunes in the 2014 Lok Sabha polls. The biggest problem is the seemingly intractable question: who is the BJP leader? In its 31 years of existence, the BJP is trying to lead a life without its two towering leaders: Atal Bihari Vajpayee and L.K. Advani for the first time; never mind Advani's yatra ambitions."[5]

A few months before assembly elections were due, the party brought back Major General B.C. Khanduri as the chief minister. Gen. Khanduri was extremely popular in Uttarakhand as an honest, incorruptible and efficient administrator. He was famous across India as the minister in the Atal Bihari Vajpayee government who not only implemented the ambitious Golden Quadrilateral project linking the four major metro cities of India, but also scaling up highway construction in a manner never thought possible before in India.

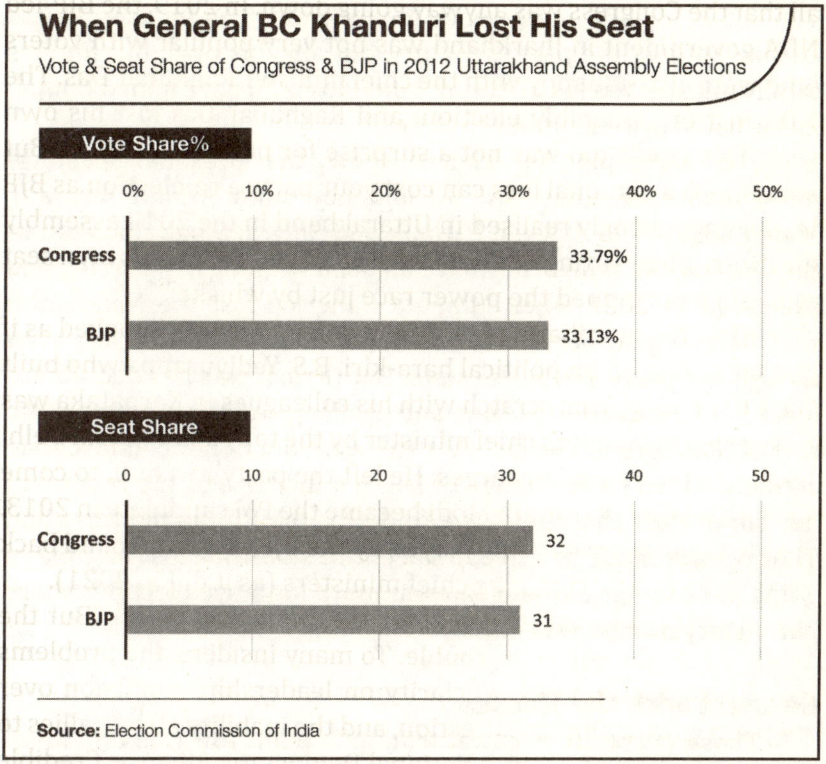

BJP supporters were very happy when Gen. Khanduri came back as chief minister. In 2009, they had been both baffled and disappointed when the leadership in Delhi had removed him as CM after the BJP lost all five Lok Sabha seats to the Congress in what could be described as a mini wave for the party. With Gen. Khanduri back, BJP supporters and workers were convinced they a good chance of winning again despite anti-incumbency. The election was a closely fought affair. In an assembly of 70 seats where 36 was the magic majority mark, the Congress won 32 seats. The BJP was just one step behind with 31 seats. Tragically for both Gen. Khanduri and the BJP, Gen. Khanduri lost his own seat. If he had not, it would have been 32 for the BJP and 31 for the Congress. BJP supporters claim senior colleagues of Gen. Khanduri deliberately sabotaged his re-election bid just to cut his larger-than-life figure to size. That doesn't matter anymore.

The fact is, for pro-incumbency to work, the chief minister has to ensure not just the party's victory, but also his own. But for this totally unexpected loss, Uttarakhand too could have joined Punjab in the list of pro-incumbency states.

The accompanying charts show the personal electoral performance of some pro incumbency stars Arvind Kejriwal, Mamata Banerjee, Naveen Patnaik and Shivraj Singh Chouhan in the last few elections. They have all been winning big, barring one exception in 2021 when Mamata Banerjee lost the Nandigram seat narrowly to her former confidante Suvendu Adhikari even though her party swept the state. But then, it was her decision to leave her home turf in Kolkata and challenge Adhikari on his home turf of Nandigram. The fact that she went out of her comfort zone actually added to her image of being a fighter and the resolve of her supporters that they have to defeat the BJP no matter what. That resolve made her sweep the entire state. She lost no time in going back to her old seat Bhowanipore for a bye election where her victory margin was massive.

Connect with the Masses

These personal electoral triumphs point towards one more crucial trait that the pro-incumbency champions have in common: a seemingly direct and personal connect with the masses, which often saves their party much embarrassment. This 'connect' cannot be measured or quantified, except through election results; but is there and people as well as honest political analysts feel and sense it on the ground.

Let's begin looking at this phenomenon of personal connect with two losing causes. In late 2018, there seemed to be a consensus among analysts and opinion polls that the BJP was losing assembly elections in Rajasthan, Chhattisgarh and Madhya Pradesh. Rajasthan was expected to maintain its anti-incumbency track record; Chhattisgarh and Madhya Pradesh had seen 15 continuous years of BJP rule and voters seemed to be in a mood for change. The analysts and opinion polls were right. The BJP lost all three states. But while it lost Madhya Pradesh because of agrarian unrest and voter fatigue, the connect that 'Mama' Shivraj Singh Chouhan enjoys with the masses ensured the loss was wafer-thin, with the Congress falling short of a majority mark by 2, winning 114 while the BJP won 109 seats. Interestingly, the BJP vote share at 41.02 per cent was higher than the Congress vote share of 40.89 per cent.

Surely a large part of the credit must go to Shivraj Singh Chouhan and his connect. In Chhattisgarh, Dr. Raman Singh too had developed a connect as 'Chawal Wale Baba' in the early phase of his tenure. But clearly he had lost the connect by 2018 and the BJP was routed. In Rajasthan, while popular and with her own personality cult, Vasundhara Raje Scindia never could connect with people the way her colleague Shivraj Singh Chouhan did. About a year or so after having lost, Chouhan was back as CM when Congress leader Jyotiraditya Scindia joined the BJP with a host of MLAs who resigned from their seats. In the bye elections that followed, along with the Scindia factor, the Mamaji magic worked and the BJP now has a comfortable majority.

Writing for the portal *Scroll*, Akash Bisht was not so sure of anti-incumbency against the CM as the major factor: "If these were the factors, how do you justify the BJP crossing the three-figure mark and making it such a close contest?" asked Bhopal-based political analyst Girija Shanker. "How do you justify the BJP winning in Mandsaur and Ratlam? The results were not like that of Chhattisgarh, where the chief minister had become unpopular among people."

APS Chouhan, who heads the political science department at Jiwaji University in Gwalior, agreed. Lauding Chouhan for a spirited performance, he said that it was the former chief minister's enduring popularity which had made such a close contest possible. "However, people were not so convinced with the performance of their MLAs," he added.[6]

One of the authors had personally interviewed Shivraj Singh Chouhan in 2015 in Bhopal and realised why people and voters of the state liked him. His office was jam packed with supplicants, sycophants and an assorted array of white kurta-clad folks who desperately wanted to look important. The author was extremely disappointed when the people in his office said the interview-cum-meeting which was supposedly confirmed was not pencilled in his appointments diary for the day. The officious babus and sycophants informed the author and his colleague grandiloquently to come some other time. There was a mad rush and lots of jostling when Shivraj Singh Chouhan arrived. He was supposed to leave for the airport in a few minutes to visit a village to check on some irrigation scheme meant to increase wheat productivity. The author's colleague, like a true journalist, along with the author barged in and told a startled Chouhan that we had flown down from Delhi to Bhopal only because we were given a confirmed time for the interview. His sycophants kept jostling around near his chair. His aide kept saying the chopper to take him to that village is ready. After looking puzzled and frowning for a few seconds, Chouhan told his sycophants that he will give us a ride in his own car to the airport and give the interview inside the car. He told the disappointed sycophants to come in some other vehicle. And the man did give a full-fledged interview, even bristling with anger when asked about corruption charges. But he was unfailingly polite and courteous.

Stumbling At The Gates of Pataliputra

In another chapter where we have mentioned how the structural and often persistent weakness of the opposition parties and leaders leads to pro-incumbency verdicts in states where the incumbent is no longer popular. Bihar and Congress were cited as a prominent example. To briefly give some other facts not given in that chapter, Nitish Kumar, a former colleague of Lalu Yadav and always a few steps behind Lalu in charisma and mass connect, became the chief minister of Bihar with the BJP as a junior alliance partner in 2005. So benighted and so pathetic was the state of Bihar after 15 years of 'Lalu Raj' that Nitish became a miracle man of sorts in his first tenure by merely improving the basic law and order machinery and infrastructure. He was returned as chief minister with a huge mandate in 2010 and became famous as 'Susashan Babu'—the leader who delivers good governance. By then, it appeared as if he was hit by what could be called 'sycophantisis', an ailment where you actually start believing what sycophants tell you.

Mama Ji Rocks

Victory Margins of Shivraj Singh Chauhan in Assembly Elections

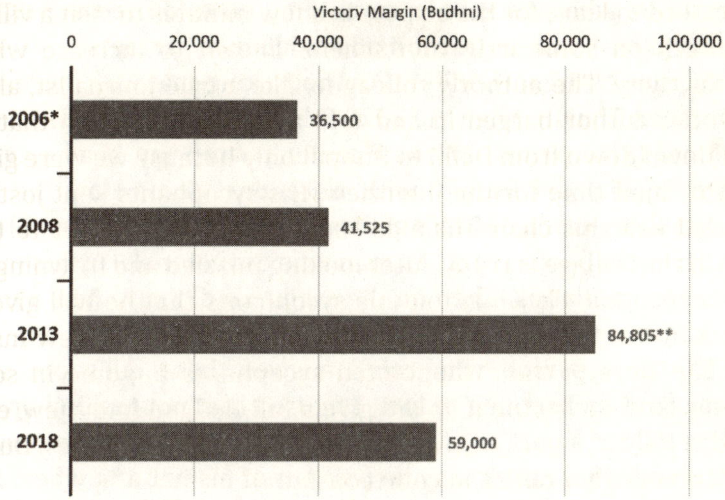

*Made chief minister in late 2005, Shivraj Singh Chauhan contested by elections in 2006
** He contested from another seat Vidisha in 2013

Source: Election Commission of India

Perhaps that disease made him snap his long-standing ties with the BJP in 2013 when Narendra Modi was made the prime ministerial candidate. His government in Bihar was saved and supported by the RJD led by Lalu Yadav. Both Nitish and Lalu, contesting separately, lost the 2014 Lok Sabha elections badly, but won a massive mandate to rule Bihar together in November 2015. Since Lalu was barred by law from either contesting elections or holding office, he virtually declared his youngest son Tejashwi Yadav as the inheritor of the Lalu legacy and personality cult by making him the deputy chief minister. Though Nitish was the CM, the RJD was the bigger party and everyone knew who was calling the shots in this regime. Corruption charges inevitably followed, as did whispers of the return of 'Goonda Raj'. In mid-2017, Nitish did another U-turn, dumped the RJD and came back to the NDA, happily accepting the man he used to excoriate in 2013 as the prime minister and his putative boss as the leader of the NDA. This saved the day for Nitish; along with the post of chief minister. But he was no longer the popular 'Sushashan Babu of 2010'. An increasingly large number of voters started thinking he was a rank opportunist who was keener on holding on to office than either ideals or a basic commitment made to alliance partners.

Charles Assisi of Founding Fuel had a long chat with journalist Sankarshan Thakur when the 2020 Bihar assembly elections were announced. He writes: "What I couldn't wrap my head around though is why did he ally with Narendra Modi? How did his socialist side embrace Modi's extreme right? The impression I got from Thakur's book is that of a man who cannot make up his mind and keeps vacillating. Then on the other hand, I have heard from others that not making up your mind is a strategy.

The only person who could answer these questions was Thakur. And on listening to him, I figured that not making up his mind is indeed a part of Nitish Kumar's strategy. His closest aides don't know what rabbit may he pull out of his hat and when. But what Thakur did make clear is that Nitish Kumar's graph looks to be on the downward spiral...Is that one of the reasons why you call Nitish Kumar amoral?" I asked him.

"Yes," Thakur said. "Nitish is amoral. His morality is about power. He is a creature of power."[7]

The rest of the story has been described in the other chapter. About how Nitish Kumar managed to cling on by the skin of his teeth. How the disastrous decision to trust Rahul Gandhi and his lieutenants and give them 70 seats to contest probably cost Tejashwi Yadav the chief ministerial chair. It seems the younger son Tejashwi is now shedding his spoilt rich brat image and trying to emulate his father Lalu Prasad Yadav who remains far more popular than Nitish Kumar despite five convictions for corruption.

Cowherd Who Loves Hema Malini's Cheeks

Tejashwi Yadav seems to be becoming a far more serious politician after the 2020 elections. But even his supporters doubt if he can ever match the mystique, the aura and the rambunctious personality cult of Lalu Yadav. In contemporary times, many politicians have used the cheeks of Hema Malini as a metaphor for good roads. They have been rightly called out for their downright sexist views and remarks. But somehow, even feminist scholars, journalists and commentators seem to indulge him with a smile even when he makes outrageous statements. Perhaps that's the result of long, hard years cultivating the image of a cowherd who was destined to empower the backward castes and communities in a society dominated by upper caste feudals. If a little bit of buffoonery helps along the way, why not indulge the gawking and gullible media folks from Delhi, and even New York and London.

The New York Times had an India Ink section about a decade ago that was probably abandoned around the time Narendra Modi became Prime Minister. The journalist Neyaz Farooqi who was born and brought up in Bihar wrote for India Ink in November 2012:

"He took on the high and mighty in bold letters. His other achievement was further erasing the word 'development' from the state's vocabulary and adding 'corruption', rather gloriously. Because of this, he was a source of both pride and ridicule.

But many Muslims, like my villagers, and Yadavs still preferred him, as no major religious riots took place in his kingdom. No one taunted any cowherd, at least to his face. Mr. Yadav made an alliance possible between two distinct communities, many a times at conflict with each other in past: the Yadavs, who have traditionally herded, prayed and protected cows, and Muslims, many of them having a diet that included cow meat as well.

In spite of all his shortcomings, he turned out to be the unifying force in a highly fragmented society like ours, and he would often say that even if he didn't provide *swarg* ('heaven' in Hindi), he gave the powerless sections *swar* ('a voice').

I grew up on the stories of his rise, his humour, his further rise. But more than a chief minister of the state, he was a character of folklore for us.[8]

When you talk, discuss or write about Bihar, it is best to let the words of journalist Sankarshan Thakur speak. He too is from Bihar, like Neyaz Farooqi, but doesn't write about Lalu like a fanboy. Here is the mystique and the personality cult of Lalu in Thakur's elegant prose in the newspaper *Telegraph* in 2017:

"Consider the odds Lalu has waded against these past decades, the most obstructive of which, quite certainly, is Lalu himself—a Goliath riven by fault lines of his own authorship, at once the conjurer of promise and its exterminator.

He arrives on the stage like a bolt in 1990 and turns Bihar to blight. Fifteen straight years in power. Fifteen fairly besmirched years—the absence of governance, near-zero development, personal and political scandal, dubious, often criminal, company, excessive nepotism, destructive populism, astounding chicanery and chutzpah. When the fodder embezzlement unseats him in 1997, he pulls wife Rabri Devi out of the kitchen and installs her chief minister. He is able to not only keep her in power the next three years, but also script an electoral return in 2000.

He is toppled from presidentship of the Janata Dal on revelation of fodder misdemeanour, he pulls out and pitches his own, and flourishing, tent—the Rashtriya Janata Dal (RJD). He is summoned to court by a trial judge. He sets out on an elephant, as if it were his baraat, followed by a sweeping fan-tail. He is charged with presiding over jungle raj; he uses the invective to inspire victimhood in his constituency and makes a virtue of alleged vice—"They are calling Bihar a jungle and that makes all Biharis junglees, they have insulted you!" That is how the election of 2000 was won....through his worst years, after losing power to the Nitish-BJP combine in 2005, Lalu remains a force to reckon with. His individual following has nearly always topped the Bihar charts, close to an average 20 per cent of the vote share. King, kingmaker, chief challenger—since Lalu entered the public arena nearly 30 years ago, he has either held power or hovered close to it."[9]

Does one really need to add more to describe and analyse the personality cult of Lalu? Perhaps one line upholding the spirit of partisanship that is necessary in politics: Delhi-based journalists must travel more often to the interiors of India, and more importantly, talk to real people instead of just local journalists, activists and resident experts.

Readers might well wonder why we haven't talked in detail about the mass and personal connect of pro-incumbency champions like Mamata Banerjee, K.C. Rao, Pinarayi Vijayan and Arvind Kejriwal. The answer is simple: the analysis and the descriptions would sound repetitive; besides, our aim is not to write a scholarly tome but a timely, contemporary book on a largely ignored phenomenon of Indian politics: pro-incumbency.

Tough Love Works

Journalist and author Sagarika Ghosh thought the session and the shoot would be a breeze. But destiny and the fiery temperament of Mamata Banerjee had other things in store for her that day. It was 2012 and Sagarika had flown down to Kolkata to host a special show for her channel CNN-IBN to mark one year of Mamata Banerjee as chief minister. A group of students had been invited to interact with her and ask her questions. The shooting began well as the 'Street Fighter' was lauded for ending the 34 years long Left rule which had become atrophied, corrupt and extortionate. But it all quickly went downhill when the questions became even mildly uncomfortable. One student asked her if the government had done the right thing by arresting a professor who had shared a cartoon of Mamata on social media.

The fiery lady fumed and launched a personal tirade against the poor professor, called him a Maoist and said there was a Maoist conspiracy afoot in West Bengal to finish her off. Sagarika made a gallant effort to mollify Mamata but all hell broke loose when another student politely pointed out that the leader herself had criticised the killing of a Maoist leader a few years ago by the Left Front government. Mamata launched another tirade and accused the students of being Maoists. They looked more gobsmacked than baffled. Mamata Didi then stormed out of the show.

By any standards, her behaviour that day, just one year after becoming chief minister, was petulant, childish and displayed an uncomfortable level of intolerance. But her fans, who also happen to be voters, loved it. They couldn't care less about berating hapless students who were corralled into a TV show. For them, Mamata Didi had shown that she is both tough and decisive. For large swathes of voters in India, being rough, tough and decisive, even when it borders on being cruel, is a trait worthy of admiration in a leader. Being tough and decisive has been one reason Mamata Didi has won three consecutive terms as chief ministers. Good girls, like good boys, often finish last.

Mercurial Mamata

Victory Margins of Mamata Bannerjee In Assembly Elections

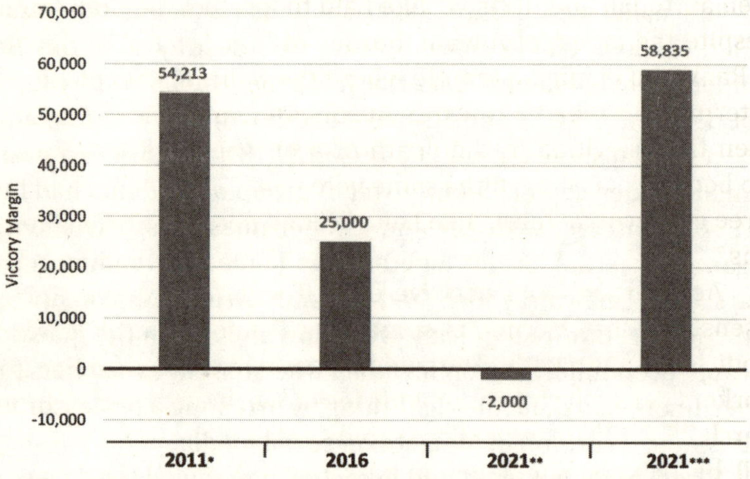

* She had not contested the 2011 assembly elections and opted for by elections after becoming CM
** She gave up her seat Bhowanipore and contested against former aide Suvendu Adhikari in Nandigram and lost
*** She went back to Bhowanipore for a by-election

Source: Election Commission of India

Two Hindi heartland leaders Lalu and Mulayam Singh Yadav too acted tough and decisive to earn the loyalty of more than a generation of vote asks. In 1990, L.K. Advani had launched the Ram Temple Rath Yatra from Somnath to Ayodhya to ostensibly counter the then Prime Minister V.P. Singh who had announced that the Mandal Commission recommendations asking for reservations in government jobs and educational institutions would be implemented. When the Yatra was started trundling across India on September 26, 1990, it became a war between Mandal and Kamandal that continues to rage till date.

Anyways, it was Lalu who acted 'tough and decisive' first by arresting Advani in Samastipur in Bihar, halting the Yatra in its tracks and packing off Advani to a distant guest house in a town called Dumka that now falls in Jharkhand. That one single 'tough and decisive' act has ensured that the Muslim-Yadav voter has remained loyal to him for more than 30 years. More importantly, that helped him defy the anti-incumbency phenomenon prevalent in the 1990s and win three successive terms. Mulayam was no spring chicken compared to Lalu then; nor was he afraid of being seen as 'tough and decisive' like Lalu to 'protect the Constitution'. Despite the arrest of Advani, hordes of 'Kar Sevaks' or devotees of Ram who wanted a temple where the Babri Masjid stood were determined to march towards Ayodhya. He ordered the police to open fire, resulting in the death of a number of Kar Sevaks. He too became a darling of the same vote bank. Though he didn't win three consecutive terms like Lalu, 'Netaji' became a legend for his fans.

Acting tough and decisive even if you are accused of being insensitive, if not cruel, is something Prime Minister Narendra Modi is familiar with. The sudden and shattering (for migrant workers particularly) nationwide lockdown announced by him on March 25, 2020 to prevent the rapid spread of the Covid pandemic will be debated for years, just as the demonetisation move is still being debated six years after it was announced. His critics called the lockdown as another proof of his tendency to impose draconian measures on the country. His fans, of course love that he acted in a strong and decisive manner. Some of the biggest victims of the lockdown were migrants from Bihar who often were forced hundreds of kilometres back home as livelihoods disappeared. They should have been furious with Modi for their upheaval and misery. It should have been reflected in the assembly elections held in Bihar in late 2020. It didn't. The BJP won 74 seats in the poll, just one less than the RJD and had the best strike rate in the state amongst major parties. Before the Gujarat assembly elections in 2007, many pundits had predicted the downfall of Modi. The reason was his 'strong and decisive' crackdown on the VHP and other right-wing outfits had begun to damage his image as a pro-business chief minister who meant business. The argument was: how could he afford to antagonise the core constituency of Hindu voters who had given him such a decisive mandate in the 2002 assembly elections after the infamous riots? In the end, they did and we won a comfortable second successive term as chief minister.

Is The BJP Going The Congress Way?

There is no space here to talk in detail to sociologists and psychologists to try and find out reasons for voters seeming to prefer strong and decisive leaders even if they are flawed. But if you match perceptions with electoral evidence, the link is very clearly there. Once Indira Gandhi had started installing puppet chief ministers across India, the terminal decline of the party in at least state elections had started. The dynasty seems to have continued this practice. The states where the Congress still does very well are states where it still has strong regional leaders: Captain Amarinder Singh in Punjab (till his recent unceremonious exit), Tarun Gogoi in Assam till old age and death; Ashok Gehlot and Sachin Pilot in Rajasthan, Siddharamaiah and D.K. Shiva Kumar in Karnataka and Harish Rawat in Uttarakhand. As of now, things are so bad for the grand old party that they seem to be the last remaining hands on the deck.

Some commentators seem to suggest that the high command culture, the imposition of leaders from Delhi and not nurturing strong regional talent, that proved so disastrous for the Congress is being repeated by the BJP. As for high command culture, there is no doubt whatsoever in anyone's mind who the Boss in the BJP is; and who the principal aide-cum-confidante cum sounding board cum 'hatchet man' is. Since the Lok Sabha victory of 2014, the two have ruled over the BJP with unquestionable authority; the elderly generation having been 'elevated' into a so-called advisory body called the 'Margdrashak Mandal'. More importantly, who will become the chief minister of a state if the BJP wins seems to be a decision now taken by the duo.

Mohammed Ayoob, Distinguished Professor Emeritus of International Relations at the Michigan State University wrote for the newspaper *The Hindu* in December 2020: "All indicators demonstrate that the Congress is suffering from a terminal disease. What is not so evident is that the Bharatiya Janata Party (BJP) is beginning to suffer from the same malaise....Earlier, even the tallest leaders of the party including Atal Bihari Vajpayee and L.K. Advani could not create a cult of personality around them thanks in part to the RSS's control. This has changed drastically under Prime Minister Narendra Modi. The fortunes of the party have become inextricably tied to the durability of Mr. Modi's charisma. Echoes of 'Indira is India' can be heard in the slogan 'Modi hai to mumkin hai (if Modi is there, it is possible)'... The BJP is slowly but surely turning it into a mirror image of the Congress. Just as the glue that held the Congress together for several decades was the allurement of power, increasingly the adhesive holding the BJP together is the appeal of office and the privileges that go with it."[10]

Well, we are not here to discuss the future of the BJP or the future of Indian democracy. Far better qualified scholars are already doing that. Our limited point here was the perception among voters of a 'strong and decisive leadership'. Two examples show how even brilliant political strategists and campaigners like Modi and Shah can stumble and blunder their way to defeat and near defeat. After Modi moved to Delhi as Prime Minister, Anandiben Patel was made the chief minister of Gujarat. She simply couldn't seem to handle the Patel agitation in the state and was replaced by Vijay Rupani, who exudes as much charisma discretion shown by the actress Kangana Ranaut. As described elsewhere in this book, it looked for a while that the Congress might finally upset the BJP applecart in the state. In the end, it was a close call with emotional appeals and the 'personal connect' that Modi enjoys with the voters of Gujarat that saved the day for the BJP. Rupani has been since replaced by Bhupendra Patel, a first time MLA, in September, 2021. Elections are due in Gujarat in late 2022.

'Weakness' Costs Votes and Elections

After almost four decades of being used to a cast f colourful, controversial and powerful characters as chief ministers, the people of Haryana were due for a 'shock' in 2014. They had become used to usually high-profile chief ministers like Bansi Lal, Devi Lal, Bhajan Lal, Om Prakash Chautala and Bhupinder Singh Hooda. When the BJP unexpectedly won the assembly elections in the state in 2014, they wondered who the BJP 'strongman' would be to lead the state. When the choice was announced, even many voters of Haryana were not familiar with the name Manohar Lal Khattar. The only positives he exuded, apart from being a lifelong dedicated 'pracharak' of the RSS, was being the exact opposite of a strongman. People in Haryana perceived him to be neither strong, nor decisive. This perception was amplified when a section of Jats in the state went on a rampage during an agitation demanding reservations. But the BJP top brass in Delhi seemed unperturbed. The Congress was crumbling and the Lok Dal once led by Devi Lal was disintegrating.

Another victory when elections came around in 2019 seemed a certainty. Opinion and even exit polls seemed to confirm this perception, giving a huge majority to the BJP. When the results were finally announced, all the pundits and virtually every poll turned out to be wrong. The indomitable Bhupinder Hooda, despite being largely ignore by his own 'High Command', succeeded in more than doubling the Congress tally to 31 seats in an assembly of 90. The BJP tally fell from 47 to 40, six short of a simple majority. It was a splinter group of the original Lok Dal named the Jananayak Janata Party led by Dushyant Chautala who saved the day for the BJP by winning 10 seats and forming a post poll alliance. You could say Haryana style that Chautala saved the 'honour' of both Khattar and the pro incumbency phenomenon. But the pro-incumbency doesn't just work in terms of seats that are won by the party. Sometimes the vote equation gets lost in the FPTP system that we borrowed from Westminster. Haryana happens to be probably the only example in 75 odd years of electoral democracy, where the leading party could not win a majority of seats even with almost 10 per cent lead in vote share. If we are looking at the votes, Mr. Khattar would be confused why exactly he did not win 2/3rd of the seats in Haryana. He might find the answers in the Gujarat verdict, where the much-debated photo finish was only in terms of seat share. In votes the BJP had a clear double-digit lead over the Congress.

Modi and Shah were not so lucky in Jharkhand. They had installed yet another virtually unknown and nondescript leader called Raghubar Das, a non-tribal, as the chief minister in a predominantly tribal state when the BJP led alliance won a comfortable victory in the 2014 assembly elections. This was a repeat strategy of Haryana where a non-Jat-Khattar was installed as the CM in a Jat dominated state. There were serious allegations of corruption against the government led by Das. As we have seen in the cases of Jayalalithaa and Lalu Prasad, corruption allegations do not become the decisive factor when the leader is charismatic and enjoys a connect with supporters and voters. Compared to Lalu and Jayalalithaa, Raghubar Das was a virtual non entity. The BJP paid a price in the 2019 assembly elections when it was down 12 seats to 25 in an assembly of 81 while the UPA alliance led by Jharkhand Mukti Morcha won a majority with 47 seats in the bag. The BJP was not decimated; but it sure was humiliated. Chief minister Das lost his own seat by a big margin. The message of Jharkhand was clear: if you give puppets as CM, at least make sure he/she is a corruption-free puppet who keeps the mouth shut and runs the government silently as you are asking him or her to do. Else, the puppet's stupidity and corruption will hurt the image of those hands that are seen installing the puppet. The message was originally given by Goa voters in 2017 elections when they defeated even the sitting BJP CM, but the leaders chose to ignore the message. Jharkhand voters underlined it with such clarity that BJP had to go for an immediate overhaul and bring back their estranged (yet most popular) leader Babu Lal Marandi back in the party and declare him the State unit head right away. Never mind the fact that they should have actually done this a decade back, or for that matter, never should have allowed to let an asset like Babu Lal Marandi to go away in first place.

Just Be Ruthless

Often, being tough and decisive and appearing to be so is not enough. Successful leaders, especially those who keep getting re-elected also have to be ruthless on many occasions. While being and appearing to be tough and decisive helps while duellist with other parties and their leaders, ruthlessness comes in handy when you have to ensure that no formidable rival emerges from within the party to challenge your supremacy, or at least your undisputed status as the first among equals. In dynasty-based parties, there is usually no dispute about leadership. For example, well before M. Karunanidhi passed away, everyone in Tamil Nadu knew the DMK Boss was M.K. Stalin, who is the chief minister now. In Bihar, Tejashwi Yadav has donned the mantle as the inheritor of Lalu Yadav despite occasional tantrums from his elder brother Tej Pratap Yadav; Akhilesh Yadav is the undisputed leader of his party in Uttar Pradesh and everyone knows K.T. Rao will succeed his father K.C. Rao in Telangana. On rare occasions, when there are many ambitious claimants to the mantle, the party tends to disintegrate, as we have seen with the Chautala dynasty formed by the late Devi Lal. Even in non-dynastic parties, there are times when there is never any doubt about who is the Boss. Narendra Modi since his Gujarat CM days, Jayalalithaa and Mamata Banerjee are classic examples. Others have to use every tactic and strategy taught in the art of ruthlessness to remain at the top and become undisputed leaders.

While his future as the undisputed leader of the BJP in Maharashtra is by no means totally secure, Devendra Fadnavis has displayed ample ruthlessness during his tenure as CM to continue remaking at the top of the heap even as the principal opposition leader. Destiny helped him a lot when the popular grassroots leader Gopinath Munde passed away in a road accident in Delhi soon after Narendra Modi became Prime Minister. Along with Nitin Gadkari, he was the name talked about as the future CM of Maharashtra. Gadkari was 'persuaded' that his talents are needed in Delhi to head a crucial infrastructure ministry. When BJP emerged as the single largest party in 2014 after having been forced to break its long alliance with Shiv Sena, Devendra Fadnavis, a Brahmin from Nagpur became the surprise CM in a state dominated by the Marathas. Gopinath Munde's daughter Pankaja Munde tried hard to emerge as a rival power centre who could eventually displace him. Astutely, and with a little help from Delhi, Fadnavis quietly cut her down to size. Eknath Khadse was another powerful leader who nursed ambitions of replacing Fadnavis. Not only was he a powerful backward caste leader, he was the leader of the opposition in the Maharashtra assembly between 2009 and 2014. His ambitions were dashed when Fadnavis was made the CM and he was given charge of many important portfolios to mollify him. Corruption allegations against him were once again 'handled' so astutely by Fadnavis that Khadse had no choice but to resign on 'moral grounds'. Systematically sidelined after that, he was denied even a party ticket to contest the 2019 assembly elections. Finally, after 33 years in the party, Khadse quit and is now a member of the NCP led by Sharad Pawar.

Kill Them All

We are not talking about actual murders here, but two contemporary pro incumbency champions have taught a lesson or two seasoned political leaders on how to be ruthless in weeding out potential rivals. Ironically, both come from non-political backgrounds. The first, Naveen Patnaik, does have a dynasty connection in the sense his father Biju Patnaik was a towering leader and chief minister of Odisha. But till he was more than 50 years old, Naveen had displayed less than zero interest in politics, happy to be a 'socialite' and a connoisseur of art, poetry, music and literature in the rarefied circles of Lutyen's Delhi. Soon after his father passed away in 1997, he made a sudden and unexpected decision to enter the minefields of politics. Folklore has it that powerful leaders of the party led by Biju Patnaik persuaded him to do that. The logic, in a repeat of the manner in which Indira Gandhi was preferred over Morarji Desai as prime minister in 1966 by powerful Congress chieftains, was that she being a relative neophyte in running a government could be 'managed'. Just like Indira Gandhi surprised, shocked, humiliated and then decimated the old powerful overlords of her party to emerge as a charismatic and popular leader across India with her own personality cult, Naveen Patnaik did the same to emerge as the most charismatic and popular leader of Odisha with his own unique personality cult. The leaders who fell by the wayside are many. But perhaps most readers would be aware of the name Baijayant Panda, one of the co-founders of the Biju Janata Dal. Perhaps the last remaining potential rival, Panda was suspended from the BJD in early 2018 and eventually quit the party and joined the BJP before the 2019 Lok Sabha elections. He had won two successive times from the Kendrapada Lok Sabha seat on a BJD ticket between 2009 and 2019. He contested again in 2019, this time on a BJP ticket. Though popular for taking good care of his constituency, Panda lost to a film star handpicked by Naveen Patnaik. This is the man who used to party with rock stars like Mick Jagger. The Baijayant Panda exit from the BJD is something one of the authors had never thought possible in late 1998 when he interviewed Naveen Patnaik. The author was working for the local TV channel promoted by Panda and had known him for about a decade before that. In his superbly designed and decorated house in a tony part of Bhubaneswar, Panda had unfurled his dreams and vision as he wanted the author to lead the local cable channel and transform it into a bona fide satellite channel. Panda had expounded on how he and some others had persuaded a seemingly reluctant Patnaik to the take the plunge. Panda himself was clear even back in Delhi that he would come to Delhi as a politician and preferably an elected one. He did become a Rajya Sabha and Lok Sabha MP. But did he have even a hint or an inkling that evening in 1998 that Naveen Patnaik would one day throw him out as a fully depreciated asset? But then, everyone underestimated Patnaik to their grief, including top BJP leaders!

Another non-politician who has displayed relentless ruthlessness in contemporary times is the AAP leader Arvind Kejriwal who is the chief minister of Delhi. Even when he was an Indian Revenue Service officer, Kejriwal dabbled in activism and 'social causes'. That was enough to earn him the Magsaysay Award in 2006. Kejriwal burst into the limelight in 2011 when he became the 'right hand man' of Anna Hazare who launched his anti-corruption agitation against the UPA government. Analysts say that the then massively popular movement led by Anna Hazare had many unintended (or intended?) beneficiaries, with the BJP being one of them. But there can be no doubt that the biggest beneficiary of that movement has been Arvind Kejriwal. Despite solemn promises and assurances not to get involved in 'dirty' politics, Kejriwal formed the Aam Aadmi Party in late 2012 with an unusual galaxy of characters to 'clean up the dirty politics of the system'. When the party was formed, he was just about the first among equals among with co-founders like lawyer-activist Prashant Bhushan, academician, author, farmer, psephology activist and politician among other things Yogendra Yadav, journalists Ashish Khaitan, Ashutosh and Shazia Ilmi part from popular Hindi poet Kumar Vishwas. This is not the full list. Initially, this bunch of 'amateurs' was scoffed at for its overtly idealistic rhetoric and antics. But the sniggers turned quickly into sneaking admiration when Arvind Kejriwal defeated the popular Sheila Dikshit in her own constituency in the 2013 Delhi assembly elections and became chief minister and resigned after a short stint.

After a brief flurry of ambition running amok during the 2014 Lok Sabha elections, the new party settled down and focused its energies on the Delhi assembly elections which were announced for February 2015. Narendra Modi appeared seemingly invincible. But Arvind Kejriwal created history when AAP won 67 out of 70 assembly seats in Delhi. That is when Arvind Kejriwal the activist turned a ruthless politician. Co-founders Prashant Bhushan and Yogendra Yadav were unceremoniously thrown out of the party along with the use of some colourful expletives. Shazia Ilmi had joined the BJP by then. One by one, his original colleagues either left (quietly or screaming loudly) or were eased out. Journalists Ashish Khaitan and Ashutosh decided politics was not their cup of tea and left. Perhaps the last man standing was poet Kumar Vishwas. He too was totally sidelined and now spends time throwing poetic barbs at Arvind Kejriwal. There is no doubt whatsoever in AAP anymore as to who is the boss.

In an article written just before the 2015 Delhi assembly elections for *rediff.com*, Somesh Jha and Archis Mohan wrote: "A senior Bharatiya Janata Party leader thinks Arvind Kejriwal is probably the best communicator in Indian politics today, better than even Narendra Modi in his ability to connect with the common man. The Aam Aadmi Party chief's opponents are far more charitable in their private assessment of him than several of his current and former colleagues. Anna Hazare is unable to trust Kejriwal, former diplomat and AAP founding member Madhu Bhaduri has slammed the party leadership as a bunch of 'misogynists', Kiran Bedi thinks Kejriwal is 'toxic' in his negativity, Yogendra Yadav has questioned his 'supreme' model of leadership and Shanti Bhushan feels he has gone astray...The epithet Kejriwal's detractors frequently use to describe him is 'dictatorial'—and this is what drives people away. Kejriwal's friends give a different spin to it. If they are to be believed, the departures are nothing but the weeding out of opportunists, fence-sitters and agents of other political parties. Kumar Vishwas, an old aide, says people like former Army chief V.K. Singh and Bedi were embedded into the India Against Corruption movement to 'misguide' Anna to part ways with Kejriwal. "Singh was a plant of the BJP and the Rashtriya Swayamsevak Sangh in the movement and he was successful in his attempt to finish it."[11] Wonder what poetic twist Kumar Vishwas would give to this display of trust in Kejriwal.

The lesson is: you will remain a Magsaysay Award-winning activist, and not a successful politician in contemporary India unless you are ruthless.

Gambles Often Deliver

He was perhaps the most unlikely 'gambler' in Indian politics. Many still don't consider him a politician the way Indian politicians are defined. And yet, the then Prime Minister Dr. Manmohan Singh decided to literally stake his post in a high stakes gamble in 2008. Derided even then as someone who worked under the shadows of the all-powerful UPA chairperson Sonia Gandhi, Dr. Singh was the last person one would classify as a gambler. But he did gamble big time. It was time to sign a historic nuclear deal with the United States of America, the culmination of a process that had started when Atal Bihari Vajpayee was the Prime Minister of India. Strangely, the BJP decided to oppose the deal in Parliament. Predictably, the Left Front with 54 Lok Sabha seats which literally propped up the UPA regime was hopping mad and threatened to withdraw support if Dr. Singh went ahead and signed the deal. Raconteurs of that era tell tales of how even Sonia Gandhi was worried about the survival of the government if both the BJP and the Left voted against it. But it seems Dr. Singh was firm, stood his ground and told Sonia Gandhi that he would rather resign than abandon the crucially important deal.

The deal went ahead and the government survived, albeit amid controversies and allegations of back room deals with bags full of currency notes. Less than a year after that, Lok Sabha elections were held and those who so vehemently opposed the nuclear deal were taught a lesson by the voters. The Congress surged to a totally unexpected high of 206 seats, the BJP slumped further to 116 seats and the most vehement and uncompromising critic of the deal the CPI(M) crashed from 43 to 16 seats, taking the Left Front down with it. All talk of a hung Parliament vanished into thin air as the UPA won a clear and decisive mandate. Sonia Gandhi had already declared in February 2009 that Dr. Manmohan Singh was the prime ministerial candidate. Many analysts ascribe three reasons why Indian voters voted for pro incumbency. The first was that they didn't like the hypocritical opposition of the BJP and were getting fed up with the Left Front. This was related to the second reason: a booming economy that seemed to have lifted all boats despite the 2008 Global Financial Crisis. And third: admiration for Dr. Singh for standing his ground and risking his post rather than succumb to 'blackmail' by the outdated Leftists.

Somini Sengupta filed a story for *The New York Times* soon after the 2009 verdict was announced where she wrote: The Congress Party's showing vindicates the prime minister's efforts to deepen a strategic partnership with the United States at a time when the Obama administration is deeply concerned about security in the region, chiefly in Pakistan and Afghanistan. A stronger government will also be better able to tackle issues of crucial importance to Washington, from economic reforms to climate change, although there is not necessarily agreement with the Americans on how to proceed."[12]

Modi, The Gambler

If Dr. Manmohan Singh was an unlikely gambler, Modi seems to be a habitual one. We have already mentioned how he risked offending 'Hindutva' voters prior to the Gujarat assembly elections by cracking down on increasingly strident and rhetorically divisive folks of the VHP and Bajrang Dal. Many of his supporters also thought he was taking needless risks. But perhaps Modi by then was already dreaming of the big prize. His gamble worked and the BJP won Gujarat effortlessly in 2007.

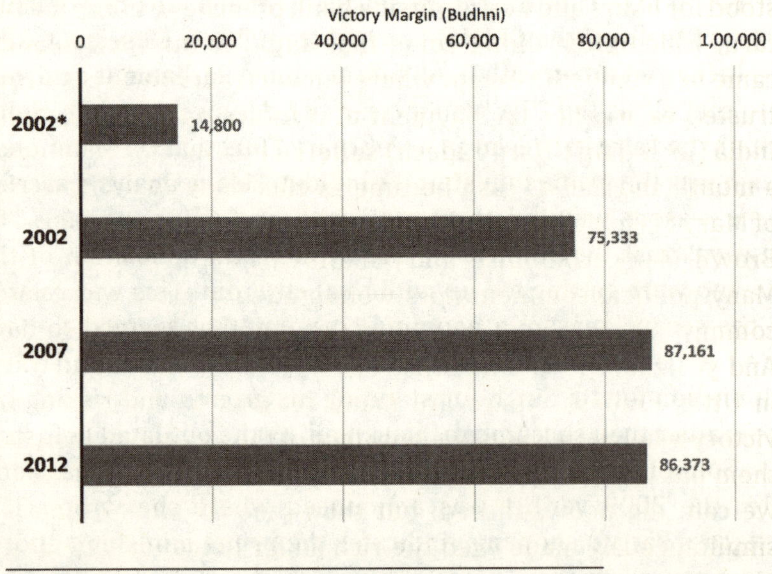

The King of Gujarat

Victory Margins of Narendra Modi in Assembly Elections

* Made chief minister in 2001, he contested by-elections in 2002

Source: Election Commission of India

It was as Prime Minister that he has taken the two biggest gambles of his political career. The first was demonetisation. In November 2016, just months before crucial assembly elections were due in Uttar Pradesh, Modi told a stunned nation at 8 PM in a television address that by midnight, all Rs. 500 and Rs. 1000 currency notes in circulation would become useless pieces of paper, declared as illegal tender. They would be replaced by a new series of Rs. 500 and Rs. 2000 currency notes. In a stentorian voice, he warned citizens of 'some discomfort' till enough of the new notes were printed. In an even more stentorian voice, he appealed to citizens to tolerate the discomfort for a while because he had no choice but to take this decision in the decisive fight against black money and corruption.

Mayhem would be a very mild word for what followed. Literally thousands gathered outside bank branches in every town and city to exchange their old notes for the new ones; of which there were not enough. The cycle rickshaw puller and the marketing manager of a multinational with a trademark tie both stood for hours and hours outside bank branches waiting for their turn, which often didn't come that day. The informal economy came to a standstill, except where known traders and consumers trusted each other for payment at a future date. People across India (including Uttar Pradesh) suffered horribly for well beyond a month and half as cash became as elusive as the alleged tomb of Mary Magdalene in the blockbuster novel *Da Vinci Code* by Dan Brown. Many economists and pundits called it an act of madness. Many political commentators wondered why Modi was bent on committing political hara-kiri in the forthcoming UP elections. And yet, the BJP won a monstrous mandate a few months later in Uttar Pradesh. There are many reasons for that incredible victory where Modi was the only face of the campaign. But one of them has been described far more elegantly by sociologists than we can: the poor suffered; but they cheered Modi because he simultaneously made even the rich suffer in his crusade against black money.

The other big gamble was Balakot in February 2019, when Lok Sabha elections were just round the corner. A Pakistani suicide bomber in Jammu & Kashmir killed 44 CRPF jawans on February 14. Indians were outraged and wanted retribution. Modi promised them one in his public speeches. But the consensus was that there could at best a Uri style incursion into Pakistan occupied Kashmir to kill a few terrorists. Even that seemed doubtful as the surprise element was gone and the Pakistani military would anticipate such a strike and prepare accordingly. Then, Indians woke up in the morning of February 27 to learn that a contingent of Indian Air Force jets had crossed deep into Pakistani airspace and territory the previous night in a surprise move and bombed a major terrorist training camp killing hundreds and returned back home safely before Pakistan could realise what was happening.

His critics accuse him to 'leveraging' Balakot to gain an upper hand in the 2019 elections. Could be. In any case, the consensus among sensible commentators is that it was his slew of pro-poor welfare policies that earned him another mandate. But look at the enormity of the gamble. What if the Indian Air Force jets had been shot down and pilots killed? That the Pakistan Air Force is no spring chicken was known the day after Balakot when their F-16 war planes came within a whisker of entering India and actually dropped bombs close to an Indian military base. If India had lost pilots on the night of Balakot, who knows how badly the gamble would have turned against Modi? We will never know. What we do know that Modi gambled big time, and he hit the jackpot.

The Regional Gamblers

By August 2018, the first chief minister of Telangana K.C. Rao, an astute politician who had risen the hard way through grassroots politics, could hear the distinct rumblings against his government. Assembly elections were next year to be held simultaneously with the Lok Sabha elections. He had started getting wary of the rising popularity of Prime Minister Modi in Telangana, though the BJP till then was an insignificant player in state politics. Erstwhile enemies Congress and the Telugu Desam seemed to be holding discreet parleys to form an alliance and oust him from power come 2019. He took and calculated risk, a gamble in other words. He resigned in September 2018 and fresh elections were called for late 2018 instead of the originally scheduled summer of 2019. As usual, there was no dearth of pundits who termed it a foolhardy decision that betrayed signs of nervousness and weakness. But the die was cast.

As if often happens with the pro-incumbency champions, the gamble paid off big time. In 2014, as the leader of the movement to form a separate state of Telangana, Rao and his party the TRS had won a majority of 63 seats in an assembly of 119. A majority yes, but by no stretch of imagination a big mandate. In the 2018 elections, the TRS tally shot up to 88. This was when Rao was confronted with a formidable alliance of Congress, TDP, CPI and a regional outfit, all of whom had a strong base and history in the state. His wariness about Modi too turned out to be true with the BJP doing unexpectedly well in the 2019 Lok Sabha elections. Today, the BJP is the principal rival of TRS as the bitter exchange of rhetoric between the two, which once cooperated in Delhi, clearly indicates.

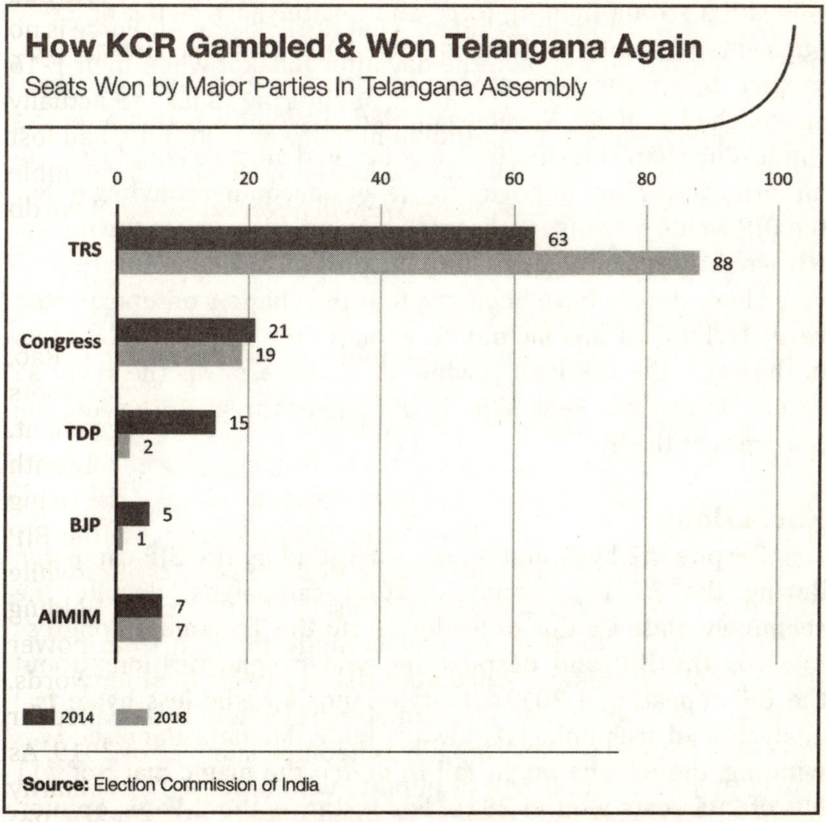

In another chapter, we have already talked about how the 2009 election verdict in Odisha was an 'unexpected' one that surprised many. Essentially, Naveen Patnaik dumped the BJP as an ally after more than 10 years of mutually beneficial partnership. And yet, he virtually single-handedly delivered a comfortable victory for his party the BJD. While it was an unexpected verdict for many pundits, it was a calculated gamble for the farsighted and vastly underestimated chief minister of Odisha. But it was not an easy decision. In the 2000 and 2004 assembly elections, both the BJP and the BJD had reinforced each other's strengths as they together defeated the Congress. In 2000, the BJD won 68 seats, the BJP 38 and the Congress 28. In the next elections held in 2004, both the BJD and BJP tallies slipped to 63 and 32 respectively while the Congress jumped from 28 to 38. Clearly, the Congress was still a strong fighting force and a vote share swing of a few per centage points could land the BJD in trouble. The alliance seemed to appear even more important as the 2009 elections approached. And yet, Naveen gambled. His logic was that after the Hindu-Christian riots in 2008, a continued alliance could risk the minority vote. More importantly, he was becoming convinced that the BJP would be a bigger threat to him and his party in the future. His gamble, or political assessment proved deadly accurate. The vote share details have been given in the chapter on unexpected verdicts. But just one factoid here: out of the 21 Lok Sabha seats in the state, the BJP won 8 while the Congress was the surprise winner in just one seat. Who is the bigger threat to Naveen, the Congress or the BJP?

Khela Hobe

Despite the hype and hoopla surrounding the BJP campaign during the 2021 assembly election campaigns; despite the seemingly mass exodus of leaders from the Trinamool Congress towards the BJP and despite the wild prognostications about the BJP repeating a 2017 UP style landslide, the less hysterical analysts and psephologists always knew Mamata Banerjee was winning, though she might fail to match the magic mark of 211 out of 295 seats won in 2016. For instance, the C-Voter opinion polls consistently indicated that the TMC would win a comfortable majority despite the BJP hype. But even our seasoned and battle-scarred pollsters were surprised when the results came in. Far from dropping well below the 211 mark, the TMC actually improved its tally. The BJP leaders realised that when Mamata

Banerjee sounded the bugle with her combative battle cry 'Khela Hobe', she really meant business.

As usual, analysts have analysed the reasons behind the triumph to death. Some ascribed it to the lack of a declared credible CM face against the mighty Mamata. Some argued that the huge influx of TMC turncoats being given party tickets to contest upset the old grassroots Sangh workers who had toiled hard for decades to make the BJP a party that could no longer be taken lightly. Some were convinced the welfare schemes worked wonders when the time came for voting. Others correctly argued that the Congress and Left vote completely collapsed. They did. But why did they go en masse to the TMC instead of the BJP? Some foolish commentators held forth that actually it was Prashant Kishore who deserves the credit for the famous victory.

Interestingly, both the newspaper *The Times of India* and the portal *Scroll* published pieces listing seven reasons why Mamata won soon after the results were declared. There were just two 'reasons' common to both the lists: The Muslim vote and the women's vote. The authors found one 'reason' provided by *Scroll* quite interesting, though we don't really know how big a reason this was. *Scroll* argued: "The Trinamool, by and large, did not have an ideological core till very recently. However, it was forced to change when confronted with the BJP—a party with possibly the strongest ideological core of any in India. To counter the party's Hindu nationalism, the Bengal-based Trinamool reached for an obvious choice: Bengali nationalism. In 2021, the Trinamool painted itself as a nativist force while the BJP was a party of *bohiragotos* (outsiders) and Borgis (as people in the state remember the Maratha raiders who led a destructive invasion of Bengal in the 18th century)."[13]

In their own ways, most of the reasons may be right. Sensible people were anyway expecting a Mamata victory. We think she might have gambled and lost a battle to win a bigger kingdom. We are referring to her sudden decision to contest against the BJP candidate Suvendu Adhikari in Nandigram. Now Adhikari was at the forefront of the Nandigram agitation that along with the Singur protests nailed the future of the Left Front. He was one of her closest confidantes and aides. Though not in the league of his mentor, he was charismatic and popular, with an extremely strong grassroots support base in Nandigram. She had never contested elections from Nandigram unlike Suvendu and his family members who seemed to lord it over the area, with Suvendu's father being a TMC Lok Sabha M.P. from the same area. Yet she Mamata chose to contest against him. When critics sniggered that she would anyway contest also from her traditional Bhowanipore seat, Mamata publicly made it clear that she would contest only from Nandigram.

This bold decision, or gamble electrified her supporters and the cadre base. Mamata was sending a clear message that she was so supremely confident of winning another mandate that it did not matter from where she contested. All speculation and rumours among wavering voters about her nervousness vanished. Mamata lost narrowly to Suvendu; a battle lost. But her gamble ensured she won the war and a bigger kingdom. Such is the stuff of political and electoral legends.

The Social Network

You might have seen the famous movie 'The Social Network' that is a kind of biopic on Mark Zuckerberg, the founder of the social media networking site Facebook. It's not a very flattering portrait. For many 'right wing' Hindutva advocates, the founder of Twitter Jack Dorsey is a man worthy of intense hatred for the seeming eagerness with which Twitter suspends or bans Hindutva handles. For most Indians, Google is associated with the homegrown Sundar Pichhai; most probably haven't heard of or have forgotten the names of the founders Larry Page and Sergey Brin. Many also don't seem to know that all of them are exercising an ever growing influence on Indian politics and elections.

The smart pro-incumbency champions realised the value and power of social media not just to create a personality cult but connect directly with the masses. Even the laggards who till recently believed that the heat and dust of road shows, rallies, door-to-door visits and public speeches were more than enough to communicate with the voters have widened up. They have all learnt from the 72-year-old Narendra Modi who was one of the, if not the, first leading politicians in India to use extensively use these platforms to build his own 'Social Network'. So pervasive is the presence and influence of these social media platforms, particularly among the younger voters that even Mayawati and her party the BSP used social media quite widely during the 2022 Uttar Pradesh assembly elections. Why Mayawati, even the Marxists who love to hate all things spawned by 'that' imperialist and exploitatively Capitalist America have fallen in love with these 21st century tools of communication.

And why not? It is without doubt the most cost-effective and efficient way for a politician and a part to reach of out to the asses without actually investing time, energy, money and boots on the ground zero painstakingly take you message door to door. Nor do you have to grudgingly reserve large sections of your electoral war chest for advertising in radio, newspapers and magazines. Just create a meme, preferably with a funny video either praising your leader or lampooning her rival. It costs literally nothing except some vivid imagination and the basic ability to shoot and upload a short video. Then post it on all social media platforms. Your 'friends' will share the meme and the message and members of the WhatsApp groups you belong to will forward it to members of their WhatsApp groups who will then...Sometimes, either because the meme conveys the political message very powerfully or touches a chord or some reason that only sociologists and psychologists can explain, the meme goes viral and gets tens of thousands of 'likes'. Even mainstream media outlets pick up the 'story' as it goes 'viral' on social media. All this at a fraction of the cost of hiring an advertising agency with their smart brains to come up with PowerPoint presentations on the range of tools that can be deployed to hammer the central message home.

In an insightful yet pithy analysis of the growing influence of social media on electoral and overall politics, Anuradha Rao who teaches at the Singapore Institute of Technology wrote for the online version of the venerable *Economic & Political Weekly* in December 2019: "Social media played a prominent role during the 2019 Indian general elections as political parties, politicians, and supporters (real or otherwise) used it extensively for political campaigning and communication. Following the global trend, social media has been increasingly used by Indian political actors for routine political communication between elections to provide unmediated and direct communication to connect leaders and citizenry, and to re-energise the political landscape in the country. While the recent general election has provided the most visible manifestations of this shift, social media platforms have been integrated into routinised political communication since the 2014 general elections, which swept the Bharatiya Janata Party (BJP) to power. This shift builds on Prime Minister Narendra Modi and the BJP's extensive use of social media in the run-up to the 2014 elections and during his first term in office...It was Modi's phenomenal success in the 2014 general election that made other political actors in India to sit up and take notice of the game-changing nature of social media. With other political parties jumping on the social media bandwagon, the landscape of political communication in India has never been so heterogeneous, inclusive, fragmented, energetic, chaotic, creative, and equally polarising at the same time."[14]

Main Bhi Chowkidar

Other leaders and parties are fast catching up; but they have a lot of hard yards to pound because of the head start enjoyed by Narendra Modi. Back in 2009, when social media platforms were tiny tots in India, it should have been he young, next generation leader like Rahul Gandhi who should have kick started the widespread use of social media by successful and ambitious political leaders. The authors think, his father the late Rajiv Gandhi certainly would have. It was a provincial politician from humble roots whose English was at best functional who first saw the future of social media and promptly became 'active' on these platforms. Since the 2002 Gujarat riots that killed almost 1,000 people, Modi has been reviled and become the symbol of a resurgent and yet malignant version of 'majoritarian Hindutva' by large sections of liberal media both in India and abroad. In 2005, he, as the constitutionally elected chief minister of Gujarat was denied a visa to visit the United States. So Modi realised during the infancy of social media that he now had a tool to bypass the traditional media (that hated him anyway) and connect directly with his actual and potential supporters in 2009. In no span of time, he literally opened the floodgates. Initially, his followers were hundreds of thousands of Hindus who strongly felt the elitist Delhi based media not only looked down upon these 'country bumpkins' even if they were IIT graduates, but also instantly branded anything 'Hindu' as bad for India. They not only became avid Modi followers on social media and in real life politics, but also launched a furious assault on 'Lutyens Delhi'. Contrary to what pundits still stubbornly and one might say foolishly insist, the early followers of Modi were not wild eyed, tilak spouting, ashes smeared fanatics. Many were sober and measured commentators of Indian politics, albeit with a world view that refused to bow down to the diktats of Lutyens Delhi that almost completely controlled mainstream media. In 2010, the 'right wing' journalist who is not given to either hyperbole or hysterics (like so many Lutyens Delhi mavens do) used his Twitter handle to send a simple post: '@bhupendrachaube. India will embrace Modi as PM. I shall remind you of this tweet the day NaMo takes oath as PM. Promise'.[15] This was during a friendly banter with senior journalist Bhupendra Chaube. For liberal media, even many BJP leaders laughed at this seemingly wild forecast. But the Modi army of followers 'believed' and started creating a cult around him even as they sought to change the 'narrative'.

So powerful was this new tool in the ideological war that liberal media folks were taken aback by the ferocity of the assault launched by Modi Bhakts. What started off as a largely volunteer driven and chaotically inorganic and spontaneous outpouring soon morphed into a well-oiled machine. The liberal media in India simply did not have any answers except single out the abusive and lander out social media posts amongst the torrent of otherwise sober and reasoned revolt against their monopoly over 'narrative'. They derisively termed these social media warriors as 'Internet Hindus' far from feeling humiliated, tens of thousands, maybe more openly became Internet Hindus. Very little is spoken about

How Rahul Lost the Plot

Votes Won By Rahul Gandhi & BJP in Amethi Lok Sabha Elections

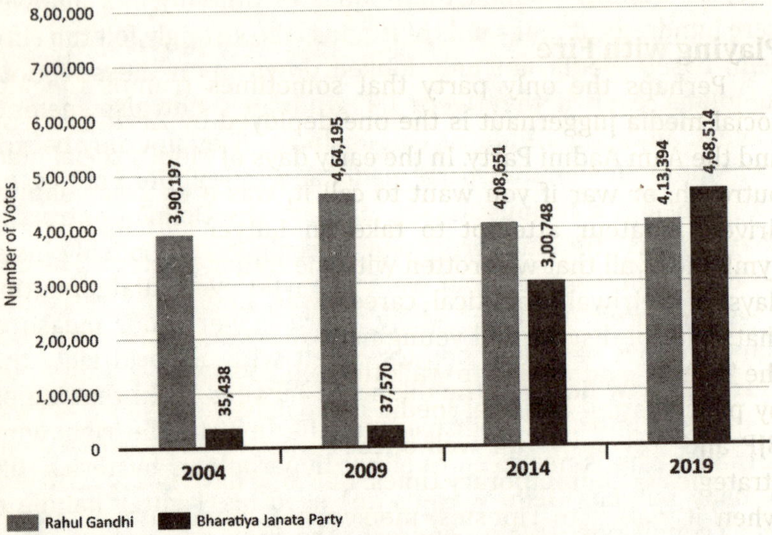

* Smriti Irani contested against Rahul Gandhi & lost. She defeated him in 2019

Source: Election Commission of India

this, but the mainstream media behaved in the most 'illiberal' manner during this period. Many actually asked for controls on social media to check 'abuse'. And virtually none complained when social media handles of journalists like Kanchan Gupta and Shiv Aroor were blocked under instructions of the UPA regime. But the Modi social media juggernaut rolled on becoming an integral part of a grand strategy to capture power in Delhi. The volunteer followers were still there, but an IT Cell became the hub of communications strategy and tactics. After 2014, it almost mirrored a sleek corporate mission. But Rahul Gandhi was still no match for Modi. He had been accusing Modi of corruption in the fighter aircraft Rafale deal with France in the run up to the 2019 Lok Sabha elections. It looked like the Gandhi family scion had hit the nail on target when he pronounced during a rally referring to

Modi: 'Chowkidar Chor Hai'. The nail turned out to be a boomerang. In no time at all, Modi added the words 'Main Bhi Chowkidar' to his social media handles. The entire Union Cabinet followed suit, as did hundreds of t hounds, if not millions of followers.

Playing with Fire

Perhaps the only party that sometimes trumps the Modi social media juggernaut is the one deployed by Arvind Kejriwal and the Aam Aadmi Party. In the early days of Modi's social media outreach, or war if you want to call it, was a chaotic volunteer driven, amateur attempt to take on Lutyen's Delhi that was symbolic of all that was rotten with the Indian 'system'. The early days of Kejriwal's political career was something resembling that: a lot of disgruntled young men and women disgusted with the 'system' and willing to walk the talk, at least in a limited way, by participating in social media campaigns. Of course, both the BJP and AAP now run well-oiled, corporate style social media strategies in contemporary times. But they have not lost the edge when it comes to ripostes, memes and humorous comebacks. Kejriwal had resigned as chief minister of Delhi in early 2014 after 49 turbulent days in office during his first term. In some Lok Sabha election rallies, Modi used to taunt him as AK-49 without taking his name. But everyone knew whom he was referring to. When the 2015 Delhi assembly elections were announced; the social media team of AAP actually came up with memes with the catchword: AK-49 or sometimes simply AK is back. It worked.

Sometimes, frequent and active users of social media amongst Indian politicians get brutally attacked at their attempts at humour. Shashi Tharoor is a suave and sophisticated politician who was won three consecutive terms as Lok Sabha MP from Trivandrum in Kerala. He is also an active social media user with 8.3 million Twitter followers. In late 2021, when the winter session of the parliament, Tharoor sent out a tweet that had a selfie with some lady MPs from various parties. He wrote the following words tongue firmly in cheek along with the selfie: "Who says Lok Sabha isn't an attractive place to work?"[16] As it usually happens in social media, there was a lot of outrage and Tharoor had to say sorry.

Mamata Banerjee carries her cult of bellicose belligerence in her social media avatar too. In 2022, apparently fed up with the constant criticism by the Governor of the state Jagdeep Dhankar, Mamata used Twitter as the preferred platform to 'excommunicate' him. She announced to the media: "Every morning and evening he [Governor] tweets accusing and attacking us. As if he is the only supreme and we are bonded labourers. I cannot take it. I have blocked him today on Twitter." But some social media posts by politicians are so disgracefully sexist and slanderous that far from chuckling, you feel like throwing up. During an interview, senior journalist Rajdeep Sardesai tried to ask Smriti Irani about Modi supporters being abusive and sexist. When she showed him this tweet by the Youth Congress president, even the ever talkative and argumentative Sardesai was rendered speechless for some seconds.

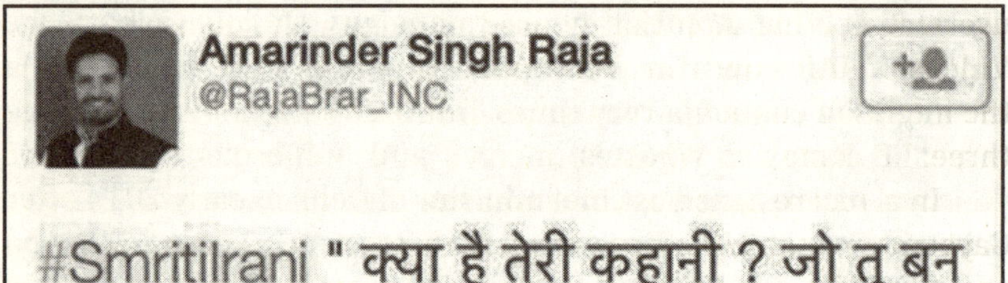
Amarinder Singh Raja
@RajaBrar_INC

#SmritiIrani " क्या है तेरी कहानी ? जो तु बन बैठी इतनी जल्दी #BJP की महारानी , क्या कला दिखाई जो मोदी हुए दिवाने - तु सुनादे तेरी ज़ुबानी। "

Translate from Hindi

5/29/15, 9:01 AM

103 RETWEETS 80 FAVORITES

But the real danger to Indian democracy doesn't come from these cheap and disgraceful remarks by politicians. Even as some successful pro-incumbency stars have strengthened their personality cults by using social media smartly; its misuse threatens Indian democracy because it has the power to subvert elections and electoral outcomes. And there can be no doubt that the biggest danger comes from the team led by Mark Zuckerberg. Twitter in India is a lot of bluff and bluster in India with just about 25 million users. The posts there get a lot of attention because apart from politicians, a lot of intellectuals, liberals and journalists are active on it. You Tube is a powerful medium with close to 450 million users in India. Well-made short, or long, You Tube videos pack a real punch and reach millions even if they are not very rigorous about facts. Facebook is also extremely powerful with about 430 million users in India and Instagram too is growing exponentially with a user base now of about 225 million Indians. But the killer in India is WhatsApp with about 550 million active users. It is WhatsApp that is used to eventually make You Tube Videos, Twitter and Facebook posts and a lot also finally reach the intended target via WhatsApp groups. Zuckerberg controls all three: FB, Insta and WhatsApp.

In a recent blog post in a website 'rest of the world', lawyer Gayatri Khandhadai argues persuasively: "It may seem that social media is a boon for democracies—it enables greater participation and access to information. While this is true, a closer look is warranted. At the heart of democracy is the possibility of exchanging ideas, concerns, and possible solutions. But as several reports have pointed out, social media platforms and the way in which their algorithms are deployed result in the creation of deep echo chambers, where individuals are repeatedly shown similar narratives and content that confirm their preexisting biases. In these echo chambers, voters lose exposure to varied thinking, ultimately leading to polarization and intolerance. While all of the blame should not be placed on algorithms, the challenge remains in relation to the lack of transparency on how they are developed and deployed. Recent revelations by a Facebook whistleblower about the company's decision to prioritise profit over human rights point to the platform monetizing hate at the cost of user safety. This confirms concerns raised by activists in India over the past few years. In India, research shows that Facebook has been a vital platform for the spread of hate speech, misinformation, and calls for violence against Muslims and other minorities."[18]

So what needs to be done to what is threatening to turn into a Frankenstein's Monster? Well, the scope of this book is limited to analysing the pro-incumbency phenomenon in India politics and elections. People with far more brains, experience, insights, opinions and actual power are already seriously debating this. We will therefore leave it at that. But the fact is: even when (not if) regulations are imposed on the unrestrained use of social media platforms, successful politicians with positive messages will keep enhancing their personality cults.

Before we conclude this chapter, it is important to reassert what was mentioned in the introduction. Elections in India are increasingly becoming presidential; more American-style than British-style. Personalities seem to matter more than parties. India has had towering personalities in the past who led presidential-style campaigns. But that was at the national level and perhaps only Indira Gandhi fits the bill with may be Jawaharlal Nehru being the second example. In the 21st century, this has steeped across India into states. A typical response from a Delhi voter during a poll conducted by C-Voter in 2019 provides a telling glimpse of this. When asked: whom will you vote for in the coming Lok Sabha elections, the instant answer was: Modi. When asked: whom will you vote for in the assembly elections due a few months later in Delhi. An equally instant answer from the same respondent was: Kejriwal. The same trend was observed by C-Voter trackers in 2018 round of Assembly election in Rajasthan, MP and Chhattisgarh. However, a big section of media was willing only to pick up the data of Vidhan Sabha voting preference from the C-Voter Tracker. They just ignored, or rather declared null and void, the data on the Lok Sabha Voting preference in the same elections. It did not fit their narrative. The same set was writhing in disbelief when Rajasthan sent a verdict of 25-0, Chhattisgarh 11-0 and MP 27-2 in favour of BJP within six months of the so-called 'Honeymoon Period' that the same set of journalists have been selling to set the narrative. The election verdicts confirmed the profound validity of the response. Scholars bemoan that Parliament and the assemblies are becoming rubber stamps of the all-powerful executive. A debate on that is beyond the scope of this book.

But don't for a moment think that the Indian voter is now so swayed by the pro-incumbency rock stars that she leaves good sense behind at home while going to the polling booth. She is still concerned about issues just as she was during the first elections held in independent India in 1951-52. It is just that in her considered judgement laced with a touch of emotional connect, she seems convinced in a vast majority of states that the incumbent is more capable of delivering what she needs and wants than the challenger. The pro-incumbency rock stars don't have a common list of rules and traits. Do you think the belligerent war cries of Mamata Didi in any way are similar to the suave finesse of her 'neighbour' Naveen Babu?

References

1. https://thewire.in/politics/deconstructing-jayalalithaas-cult-of-personality
2. https://www.nytimes.com/2022/01/16/sports/tennis/novak-djokovic-australian-open.html
3. https://shobhaade.blogspot.com/2009/03/ferragamo-handbag-for-mayawati.html
4. https://thewire.in/books/naveen-patnaik-biography-ruben-banerjee
5. https://m.economictimes.com/news/politics-and-nation/bjps-problems-no-clarity-on-leadership-confusion-over-political-direction-and-inability-to-attract-allies/articleshow/9937964.cms
6. https://scroll.in/article/905476/if-it-was-not-anger-against-shivraj-singh-chouhan-government-what-accounts-for-bjp-s-loss-in-mp
7. https://www.foundingfuel.com/article/the-amorality-of-nitish-kumar/
8. https://india.blogs.nytimes.com/2013/11/29/in-bihar-village-an-enduring-love-for-lalu-prasad-yadav/
9. https://www.telegraphindia.com/7-days/the-bane-and-boon-of-being-lalu/cid/1315862
10. https://www.thehindu.com/opinion/op-ed/is-bjp-going-the-congress-way/article33439197.ece
11. https://www.rediff.com/news/report/delhi-polls-how-to-lose-friends-the-kejriwal-way/20150131.htm

12. https://www.nytimes.com/2009/05/17/world/asia/17india.html
13. https://scroll.in/article/993899/cash-transfers-votes-from-women-and-muslims-7-reasons-why-mamata-banerjee-crushed-bjp-in-bengal
14. https://www.epw.in/engage/article/how-did-social-media-impact-india-2019-general-election
15. @kanchangupta. 12.33 PM. 22/05/2010
16. @ShashiTharoor. 11.41 AM. 28/11/2021
17. https://indianexpress.com/article/cities/kolkata/mamata-banerjee-blocks-governor-jagdeep-dhankar-twitter-7749956/
18. https://restofworld.org/2021/social-media-india-democracy/
19. https://www.thenewsminute.com/article/never-got-tn-wrong-aiadmk-will-win-no-positive-swing-dmk-c-voter-43446)

□

3
WELFARE

Two television images and stories come to mind when we discuss the term 'welfare' in the Indian electoral context. One is from Delhi in 2012 and relates to then eternal rebel Arvind Kejriwal. The other is from a village in Amethi parliamentary constituency during the 2019 Lok Sabha campaign featuring the pioneer of opinion polls and private sector TV journalism in India, Prannoy Roy interacting with a poor Dalit lady. Both the images and the stories tell us a lot about how political leaders and voters understand 'welfare' and how it has been used as a successful weapon in their arsenal by successful pro-incumbency champions when they go to war to get re-elected.

The 'Bijli Chor'

When the first series of images were flashed across TV screens and followed up the next day, the Aam Aadmi Party was about to be born. According to Arvind Kejriwal, high electricity bills were symbolic of how the government in cahoots with private sector capitalists was looting the ordinary Indian. In October, 2012, his outfit India Against Corruption organised a Delhi-wide protest where he was seen allegedly cutting the lines of a 'faulty' electricity meter. Like almost every other media outlet, CNN-IBN featured a story: "Activist Arvind Kejriwal will carry on his crusade against the Delhi government over inflated electricity bills for the third day in a row. He has planned to protest outside the office of the Delhi Electricity Regulatory Commission on Monday. Since Saturday, the IAC member and his associates have been burning electricity bills and personally fixing power connections as a mark of protest. On Sunday, they visited the house of a person who died of heart attack after DISCOM officials raided his house suspecting power theft". A day after launching his 'bijli-paani satyagraha', Kejriwal started Sunday's protest by visiting the house of 65-year-old Kailash Chand, who died of a heart attack following the raid at his house in Najafgarh. Kejriwal said the household had an electricity bill of very low amount due to which officials suspected Chand of committing power theft. "Even though he had paid his bill, the officials entered his place through back door and cut off his power supply," Kejriwal alleged.[1]

A lot of folks in not just the so-called Lutyens Delhi, but also the rest of the country either smiled indulgently or scoffed at the 'antics' of Arvind Kejriwal who had by then let out enough signs that he was electoral politics despite his vehement denials. But the mocking has given way to grudging admiration. Kejriwal and his party not only got elected on a plank to remove the nexus between corrupt politicians and crony capitalists, they also actually delivered free electricity as promised. One of the key reasons for the massive mandate given for a second successive time to Arvind Kejriwal was free electricity, apart from water. Any household that used less than 200 units of electricity per month was totally exempt from paying any bill. More than 5 million consumers of electricity were directly benefited by this scheme. Add the consumers along with their family members and you get the majority of Delhi voters in your pocket. Fiscal prudence and such fancy terms be damned. Welfare schemes and freebies help you win elections and virtually every pro-incumbency champion realises this instinctively.

Modi in Amethi

The images and conversations from 2019 bordered on the eerily haunting. Prannoy Roy and his team of reporters at NDTV have been covering elections for decades. He also leads a motley group of journalists, columnists, think tank members and even bankers called 'Limousine Liberals' who actually travel across India in fancy cars and SUVs (by Indian standards) to gauge the mood of the Indian electorate during Lok Sabha elections. One of those pit stops was a typically unknown and unkempt village of mostly poor Dalit families in the Amethi Lok Sabha constituency represented by Congress President Rahul Gandhi. Prannoy Roy, in his halting Hindi, was trying to strike up a conversation with a Dalit woman in front of her brow and weather-beaten house that looked distinctly dilapidated.

His constant companion during election debates Dorab Sopariwala, whose Hindi is far worse than that of the 1990s Sonia Gandhi, hovered around trying to make sense of the conversation. Without getting into all the details, the gist is: the poor Dalit woman proudly pointed towards a relatively newly built structure and announced with a hesitant smile that it was the new family toilet. She had no hesitation who had built the toilet for her and her family: Modi. The Prime Minister not only won a bigger mandate in 2019, but the Congress President Rahul Gandhi was personally humiliated, losing his family pocket borough. The Balakot air strikes, Hindutva masquerading as nationalism and outright jingoism are reasons ascribed for the re-election of Modi. But even his staunchest critics, unless they are blinded by irrational personal hatred, will agree that welfare schemes played a big role in Modi getting a bigger mandate. Now, you can't really accuse Prannoy Roy or NDTV being Modi fans. But the channel did feature the programme.

Voters Don't Want Justice i.e., NYAY

It is not as if Rahul Gandhi and the Congress didn't offer 'welfare'. In fact, he announced the mother of all welfare schemes NYAY which offered Rs. 6,000 a month in cash to 20 per cent of the poorest Indians. Former Prime Minister Dr. Manmohan Singh gave an interview to PTI that was featured in NDTV: Dr. Singh said the Congress's NYAY scheme (of minimum income for poor) would usher in a new model for social welfare and prudent economics, as economic benefits would lead to a rise in consumption levels, resulting in kickstarting economic growth.

"We think that spending 1.5 per cent of GDP for 20 per cent of the population is absolutely fair and just. The Congress party is also committed to fiscal discipline. Our nearly USD 3 trillion economy has the fiscal capacity to absorb this expenditure. There

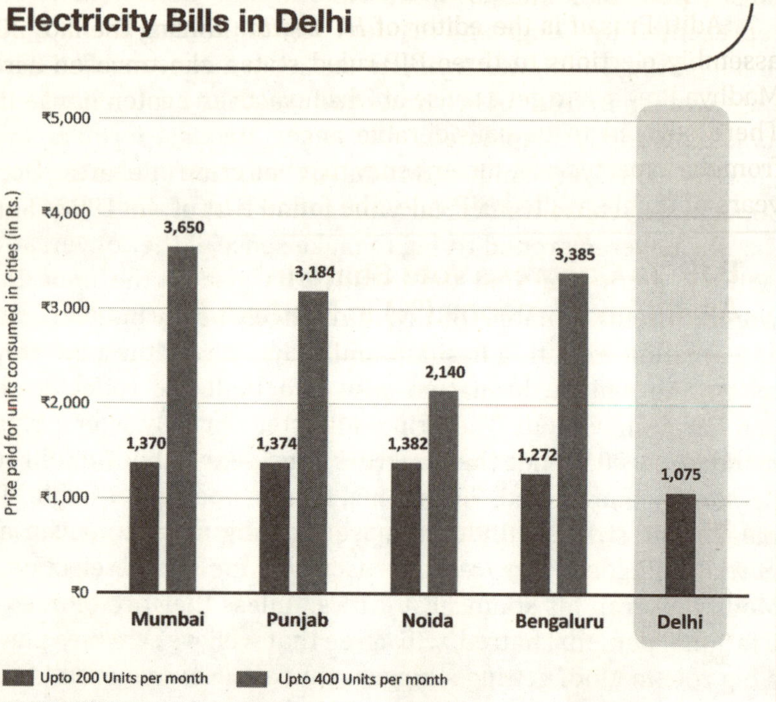

Source: Delhi Dialogue Commission

will be no need for any new taxes on the middle class to finance NYAY. Only those who have no compassion for the poor will oppose NYAY," he said.[2] Why the poor Indian voter refused to buy the promise of a cash transfer of Rs. 6,000 a month is beyond the remit of this book and for scholars to debate, discuss and argue. But the authors can probably think of only one reason: trustworthiness. If the Congress was really so keen of NYAY getting implemented, and if this was practically possible to do so, well, they had 10 long years of UPA to do the needful. The fact that they didn't, probably explains that this is not really sustainable. People voted for the 6,000 rupees that Modi transferred in their account in one full year, than the 6,000 rupees that Rahul Gandhi promised to transfer every month. If your promise of 6,000 every month compared to 6,000 every year given by Modi cannot get you votes; then issue is not the scheme but the trustworthiness on who can actually deliver on the schemes.

Mamaji Finally Loses, And Yet

Aditi Prasad is the editor of *HT Digital*. During the late 2018 assembly elections to three BJP-ruled states, she travelled across Madhya Pradesh to get a sense of what exactly the voter was feeling. There seemed to be considerable anger amongst farmers, apart from the expected anti-incumbency that had crept in after almost 15 years of uninterrupted BJP rule. She found a lot of anger no doubt,

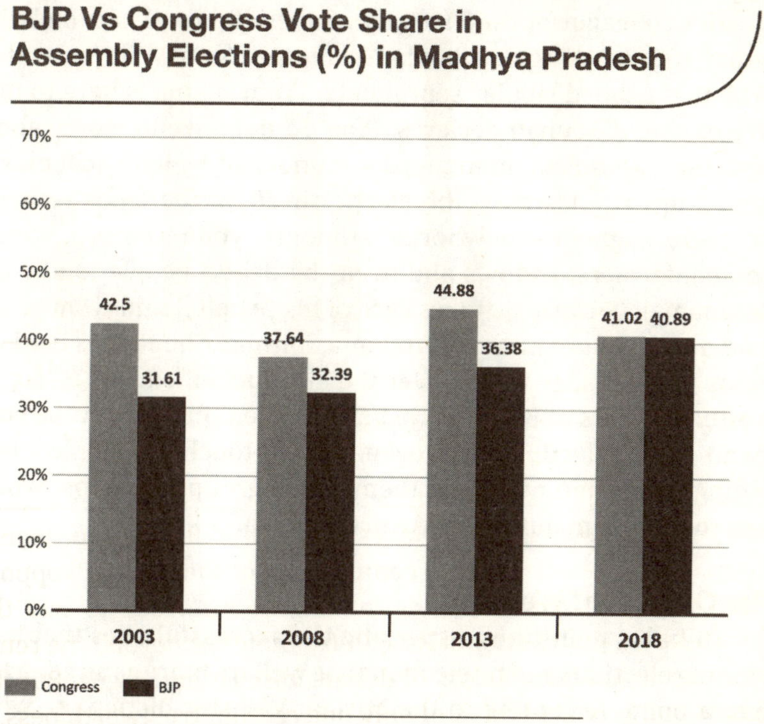

Source: Election Commission of India

particularly in the areas where the farmers agitation had taken a violent turn. She sensed after talking to voters in cities, towns and constituencies that perhaps the winning streak of the BJP in Madhya Pradesh was coming to an end. "But what astonished me was the personal goodwill and popularity that the chief minister Shivraj Singh Chouhan enjoyed even among critics of the BJP government. Except some diehard Congress supporters, I rarely found anyone saying anything harshly negative about him. Most agreed he deserved the moniker 'Mamaji' because of the numerous welfare schemes launched by him for the poor and the women", she says. The BJP did lose, by the narrowest of margins, got a higher vote share than the Congress and denied even a simple majority to its rival. That too after 15 years of incumbency in a state which was pretty much a swing state between BJP and Congress till phenomenon of Mamaji happened. In about a year, Mamaji was back as chief minister.

Her colleague at the *Hindustan Times*, Kumar Uttam had filed a story after tracking the Chouhan campaign for a while in October, 2018 that echoed similar sentiments: "Your mama is here to take care of you," Chouhan declares. "You do not have to worry about anything."...Chouhan announced a number of welfare schemes in the run-up to the last assembly election in 2013. There was a scheme for every segment—newborns, students, young entrepreneurs, women, farmers, widows and even the dead. "People fondly call him mamaji because he takes care of his people," said women and child development minister Archana Chitnis...Chouhan is banking on his mama image to tide over the anti-incumbency that has set in after 15 years of BJP rule. He has travelled throughout the state ahead of the elections on November 28, touching people's feet, folding hands and waving at them. Small groups of people would wait to greet him during his Ashirvad Yatra."[3]

The Origins of Welfare

In India, politicians, especially the successful ones that keep winning elections and re-elections use welfare more as an adjective than a bond. According to the Miriam Webster dictionary, when the word welfare is used as a noun, it means: "the state of doing well especially in respect to good fortune, happiness, well-being, or prosperity". Of course, a second interpretation of the word welfare as a noun is something any politician would prefer: "aid in the form of money or necessities for those in need or an agency or program through which such aid is distributed" But when it is used as an adjective, it means exactly what successful politicians do: "of, relating to, or concerned with welfare and especially with improvement of the welfare of disadvantaged social groups."[4] To go back in history, after the Industrial Revolution in the West, the landowning feudal aristocracy gradually surrendered power to a breed of aristocrats called robber barons by the late 19th century. The term "robber baron" as defined by Encyclopaedia means: "term for one of the powerful 19th century American industrialists and financiers who made fortunes by monopolizing huge industries through the formation of trusts, engaging in unethical business practices, exploiting workers, and paying little heed to their customers or competition."[5] By the early 20th century, even supporters of capitalism felt that robber barons were giving a bad name to capitalism and many of their monopolies were dismantled. But welfare economics, rather welfare politics, was yet to emerge. A lot of citizens were either legally not allowed to vote or 'discouraged' from doing so (booth capturing is not unique to Indian politics, you see.).

It was the Great Depression of 1929 that first hit America and then the rest of the world that led to the emergence of welfare as an economic tool and more importantly, as a weapon in politics to win and keep winning elections. A Democrat from a wealthy, aristocratic family Franklin Delano Roosevelt won the presidential elections in 1932 and took oath in January, 1933. The American economy was in state of virtual collapse. Industrial production had almost halved between 1929 and 1933 and unemployment was estimated at 25 per cent, though what is now called 'disguised unemployment' (where masters' degree holders drive taxis since they can't find jobs) was probably as high as 50 per cent. Whatever his reasons (and we are not really into detailed history here), FDR unveiled an economic package called the New Deal. Welfare economics and welfare capitalism were formally born. The New Deal essentially meant the government launching massive spending programmes to help the unemployed earn at least a liveable livelihood. Money was spent even to dig ditches to ensure people had some work and some income (shades of MNREGA?).

The First Pro-Incumbency Champion

Almost a century after the New Deal, economists are still debating its merits and flaws. That's their job. Our focus is political. FDR became the first politician to use welfare economics and politics to become a pro-incumbency champion. The poor and the unemployment were so grateful for even the meagre handouts that they are elected him in 1936. His spending binge on welfare schemes continued and FDR won a third successive term as President in 1940. By then, the Second World War had started, which America joined in late 1941. Breaking all records, FDR won a fourth successive election in 1944 and died as President in 1945. We have no doubt that FDR and legions of successful politicians that followed him in democracies understood a simple thing far better than pundits do: more poor people vote than the better-off ones during elections, and well designed and executed welfare schemes for them often tends to beat 'anti-incumbency' sentiments.

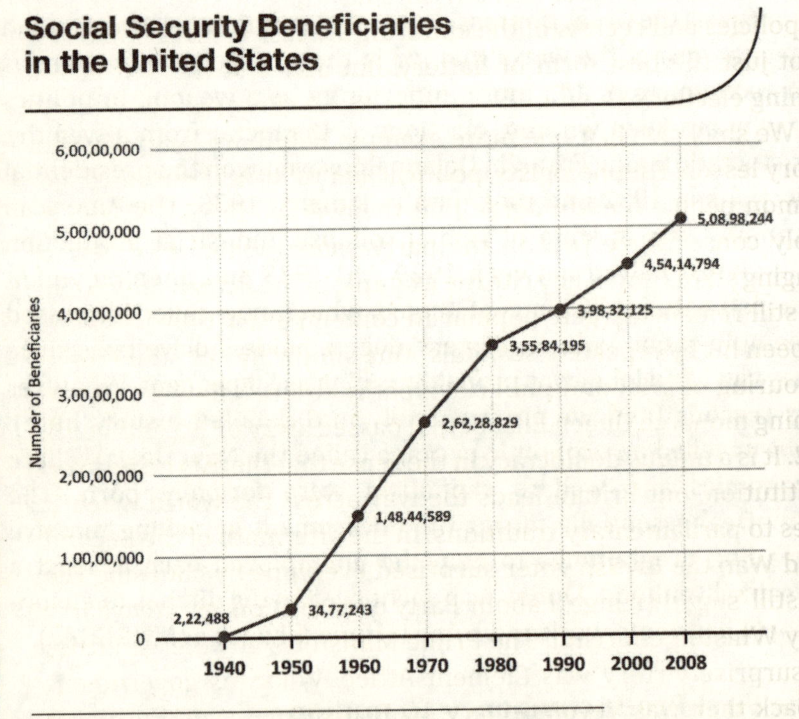

Source: www.ssa.gov

To quote the official National Archives of the country: "The New Deal focused on three general goals: relief for the needy, economic recovery, and financial reform. During the One Hundred Days, Congress enacted 15 major pieces of legislation establishing New Deal agencies and programs....One of the ways FDR chose to accomplish this was through the radio, the most direct means of access to the American people. During the 1930s almost every home had a radio, and families typically spent several hours a day gathered together, listening to their favourite programs. Roosevelt called his radio talks about issues of public concern 'Fireside Chats'. Informal and relaxed, the talks made Americans feel as if President Roosevelt was talking directly to them."[6] The numerous welfare schemes for the poor since 2014 and the trademark 'Mann Ki Baat' radio talk given by Narendra Modi reveals that either he or one of his close aides and advisors has toughly researched the life, policies and secrets of the enduring success of FDR. Imitation is not just the best form of flattery, but also a strategy to keep winning elections.

We shall give just one more example before we conclude the history lesson. Psephologists, political analysts and even so-called common people tend to agree that the average British citizen is deeply conservative (not in the party sense) when it comes to changing status quo. They cite the example of the British monarchy that still remains largely popular in contemporary times when it has been hit by repeated 'scandals'. One simply has to witness the outpouring of grief and public sympathy when Britain's longest-reigning monarch Queen Elizabeth II passed away on September 8, 2022. It is a unique democracy in the sense that there is no written Constitution, but Britain leads the way across the world when it comes to parliamentary traditions. In the aftermath of the Second World War, the British voter surprised everyone by choosing the then still 'slightly fringe' Labour Party over the Conservative Party led by Winston Churchill. The Prime Minister who emerged from this surprise victory was Clement Attlee. What his government did back then was 'revolutionary' by British, and even European standards. He established the first modern 'capitalist welfare' state in Europe, if not in the world. Virtually the whole of Europe follows those tenets of welfare capitalism till date. So once again, don't for a moment think that 'welfarism' is something smart Indian politicians discovered to lure voters.

When Chief Ministers Pre-Empt and Out-think Modi

What Modi does as the Prime Minister, regional leaders have demonstrated they can go a few steps ahead when it comes to welfare schemes. Take K.C. Rao who has won two successive terms as chief minister of Telangana, a state that was formed in 2014. Almost a year before followed suit with a nationwide scheme for farmers, K.C. Rao launched the now famous 'Rythu Bandhu' scheme for about 6 million landowning farmers in the state. Under this scheme, perhaps the first direct cash transfer scheme for farmers, irrespective of the size of land owned, beneficiaries were promised Rs. 8,000 a year per acre. This was like manna from heaven for 86 per cent of the 6 million farmers of the state who own up to 5 acres or just about a hectare of land. Look at what happened overnight to a small farmer with three acres of land in Telangana. Thanks to the Rythu Bandhu scheme, this farmer would suddenly get Rs. 24,000 a year in his bank account. That maybe small change for the urban puppie, but was a huge bonanza for the family of the farmer. The average per capita income of Telangana is a relatively high Rs. 2.57 lakhs a year; though estimates suggest per capita income of small farmers would be Rs. 1.5 lakhs a year at best. To add a sweetener, Rao also announced the 'Rythu Bheema' insurance scheme that offered Rs. 5 lakh to all farmers between 18 to 60 years who died either naturally or accidentally (read suicide, which is widely prevalent in the state). The economics was simple.

The politics was even simpler. In the previous chapter on personality cults, we discussed how Rao played a big gamble by preponing the assembly elections by almost half a year. Behind the gamble that paid off handsomely was the political calculation that voters led by grateful and happy farmers would forgive all and give him a second successive term. And why not? Telangana had 2.8 crore or 28 million voters in the 2018 assembly elections. Even if you assume each farming family had just two voting members, 12 million of the 28 million total voters had been given

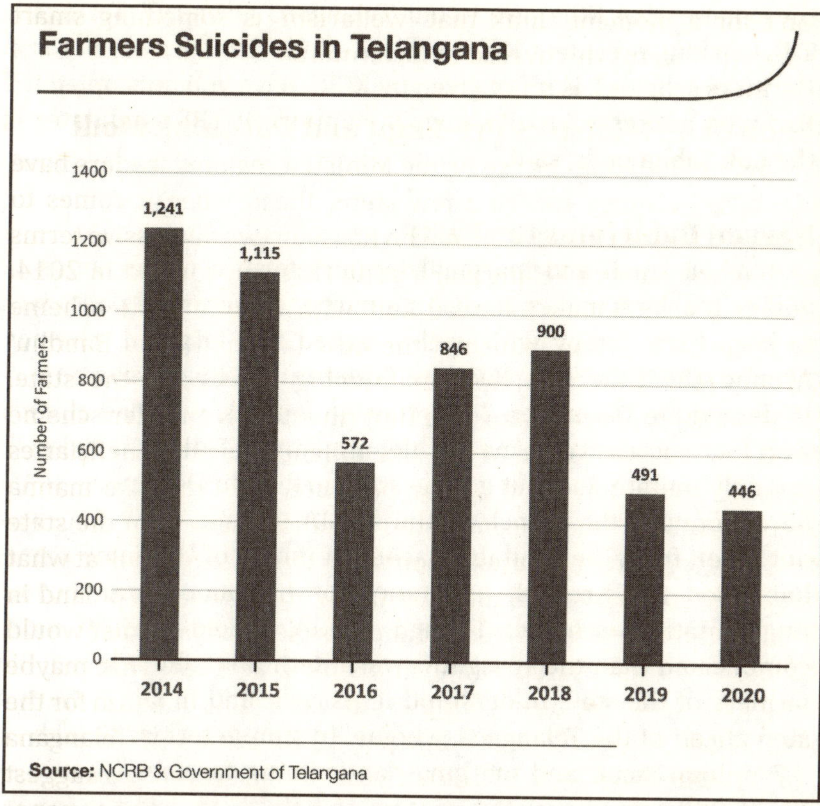

an unexpected welfare bonanza. Is it a wonder that Rao and his party TRS won 88 out of 119 seats when anti-incumbency was emerging as a strong factor before he announced these welfare schemes? Soon after his famous re-election, Rao had to face Lok Sabha elections. Modi being Modi, the Prime Minister indulged in his usual election rhetoric while campaigning for his party in Telangana about others copying his party's welfare schemes. According to a report filed by the Press Trust of India towards the end of march, 2019, TRS lost no time in giving it back to Modi by indulging in some chest thumping of its own: "Yesterday, he (Modi) came (to Telangana) and said about our Chief Minister that, he (Rao) claimed my (Modi) schemes to be his. I am asking Modiji, where did the idea of Rythu Bandhu come from? Is it not from KCR (Chief Minister K. Chandrasekhar Rao)? Is it not from the scheme that KCR gave to our Telangana farmers?" Telangana TRS working president K.T. Rama Rao said. "The idea of PM Kisan (farmers scheme), is it not given by KCR? Have you not copied it?" Rao who addressed road shows in support of TRS candidates in the Lok Sabha polls, said.[7]

Naveen Babu Joins the Party

When small and marginal farmers form a major chunk of voters, it always makes sense for smart and successful politicians to keep them happy with well-designed and targeted schemes. Around the time K.C. Rao was celebrating his re-election in Hyderabad in December, 2018, Naveen Patnaik, who had already won four successive terms as chief minister of Odisha, decided to not only imitate Rao, but go one step further. In December, 2018, he announced the launch of the KALIA scheme. Now that was not taken from the Amitabh Bachchan movie of the same name, but stood for 'Krushak Assistance for Livelihood and Income Augmentation' scheme. Though KALIA looked slightly more complicated than the straightforward Rythu Bandhu scheme, the farmers of the state understood it all right and in fact it went a step ahead of the Telangana scheme. In simple terms, 37 lakh or 3.7 million small and marginal landowning farmers would get Rs. 25,000 spread over five seasons to help them invest in inputs plus labour if required. In addition, 5 lakh or 0.5 million landless cultivators and workers were to get Rs. 12,500 to invest in any livelihood activity of their choice. This was again, perhaps the first time that landless cultivators and workers got cash from their government; a no small change by Odisha standards. For a state with a per capita income of just about Rs. 1 Lakh a year, one can well imagine what the average annual income of a marginal farmer or landless labourers would be. For them to get Rs. 25,000 over five sowing seasons and a direct transfer of Rs. 12,500 respectively was a huge deal.

No doubt Naveen Patnaik cares for the poor and takes care of them, as all successful politicians do. But they also have their eyes focused on re-election. In the chapter on weak opposition, we have seen how the seemingly terminal decline of the Congress in the state has lent a helping hand to the BJD as the BJP struggled to emerge as a viable opposition alternative. By early 2019, the BJP was more confident than it was in 2009. It also looked better prepared having built a strong grassroots base. And then there was the Narendra Modi factor. But the Modi factor worked to some extent in the Lok Sabha elections which are held simultaneously with assembly elections in Odisha. The BJP won 8 out of 21 seats. In contrast, it won just 12 out of 147 assembly seats. People generally talk about the phenomenon of 'split vote' from Delhi (which, by the way, was coined by one of the authors of this book in 2004, ironically explaining that the lack of split vote phenomenon has resulted in the unexpected verdict as people voted in federal elections as if they were voting in state elections) considering that Delhi being a highly educated and high-income urban centre would understand the concept of split vote better. But the fact is that even with much lower literacy and income indices that Delhi, the electorate of Odisha was way ahead in the progressive thought process of split vote, years ahead of Delhi cycle of differential verdicts.

It is not as if the BJP had weakened in Odisha. Even in the assembly elections, it won a reasonably high 34 per cent plus of the vote share. But thanks to KALIA and numerous other schemes, the BJD won almost 46 per cent of the vote share. Game, set and match for Naveen Babu. In an interview to *The New Indian Express* soon after he won his fifth consecutive term as chief minister, Naveen Patnaik responded to schemes like KALIA and if they were adversely affecting the finances of the state, Naveen Patnaik said: "Well, you see, our annual budget is more than Rs. One lakh crore and only 5 per cent of that is spent on these programmes which are called doles. For us, these are not doles, these are tools of empowerment...We will certainly improve it (KALIA) over the next five years. It is a programme not only for normal farmers but also for the share-croppers and the landless."[8]

Perception and Trust Matters

We all know how the Narendra Modi regime at the centre announced the Kisan Samman Yojana whereby Rs. 6,000 is transferred every year directly to the bank accounts all farmers across India. But as we have just seen; at least in this case; Modi was the follower rather than the pioneering leader. Farmers have always been a powerful vote bank and 'cultivating' them has always been a priority for politicians who are really interested in winning elections in India. In the past, they have been showered with heavy subsidies on fertilisers and seeds; the MSP for food grains has been consistently increased and many states have even provided free electricity to farmers. But this has largely benefited the minority of large farmers as more than 80 per cent of them own one hectare or less of land. Even the overwhelming share of money paid through the MSP goes to farmers in Punjab, Haryana and western Uttar Pradesh. For small and marginal farmers, direct cash transfers were the political master-strokes that reinforced pro incumbency.

The natural question that one would ask is: if cash transfers can so dramatically affect voter behaviour, why did the Indian voter not opt for Congress president Rahul Gandhi in the 2019 Lok Sabha elections when his party offered the lip-smacking NYAY package that promised an annual cash transfer of Rs. 72,000 to 20 per cent of India's population which is deemed very poor? They should have flocked to the polling booths to make Rahul Gandhi the Prime Minister, isn't it? Well, as we have explained in other chapters, mere promises don't make the voter change her mind unless the promise sounds credible and doable. Clearly, the Indian voter did not find the extravagant promise of Rs. 72,000 a year made by Rahul Gandhi neither credible, nor doable.

In a column for the portal *The Print* in October, 2019, Shivam Vij wrote: "The opposition today suffers from a credibility crisis and a trust deficit among the masses, as the Lok Sabha election results showed. Part of the reason for the failure of NYAY in the Lok Sabha elections was the trust deficit between the Congress and a large number of swing voters. There are many reasons for this trust deficit, one of which is that the opposition comes across as being interested in nothing other than winning elections. Modi, on the other hand, believes in permanent campaigning giving the impression that he thinks about people's welfare every single day."[9] The authors agree with Shivam Vij about the lack of trust in the ability of the Congress. But we are not very sure about the second conclusion where he effectively says voters think the Congress is just Hungary for power while Modi constantly thinks about their welfare. Reason being just six months before the 2019 verdict, the same set of voters did give a mandate for Congress in three critical states of MP, Rajasthan and Chhattisgarh. And about a year prior to that, in Modi's home state of Gujarat, the Congress literally scared BJP by almost touching 80 seats. It was only a matter of 10 odd seats flipping and the BJP might have lost power in Gujarat. So, the crisis of credibility seems less against the Congress as an institution or its regional leadership, but more against the central leadership of the GOP.

That also presumes the Indian voter is naïve enough to think that Modi is not chasing electoral victories. Anyway, to each columnist her opinion about the Indian voter! And anyways, to each party supporter her own share of delusions. There are still many Congress supporters and fierce Modi critics who think the only reason Modi came back to power in 2019 was the Balakot air strikes after the suicide attack in Pulwama that galvanised the whole country in a temporary bout of nationalism. Perhaps, but that presumes voters of Tamil Nadu, Kerala and Andhra Pradesh, not to speak of Telangana, West Bengal, Odisha and Punjab were somehow spared the bouts of nationalism after Balakot. Or that they lack good, decent qualities like patriotism. The delusions of Modi Bhakts are not very different. When the BJP lost the West Bengal assembly elections badly in 2021, one reason offered was that virtually the entire Muslim vote, which is a considerable 28 per cent of the electorate, shifted lock, stock and barrel towards Mamata Banerjee. So, though the BJP jumped from 2 seats in 2016 to 77 in 2021, the hostile Muslim voters 'ganged up' against Modi and the Hindus, as usual, didn't consolidate behind one party like the Muslims do. If that were so, how did the BJP win a second successive term in Assam where a 'hostile' 34 per cent of the voters comprising Muslims ganged up against the saffron party? This too, when the man who became chief minister, Himanta Biswa Sarma publicly stated in rallies and meetings that he doesn't need the 'miyan vote to win Assam'.

More often than not, simple answers can be the most profound ones when trying to analyse seemingly surprising events or even electoral outcomes. But there is a world of difference between being simple and simplistic. The Indian voter may be simple; but she is not a simpleton as she has repeatedly demonstrated since the first elections were held in India in 1951-52. Unfortunately, too many pundits, commentators and scholars still fail to make this 'simple' distinction while analysing election results and voter behaviour.

Chawal Wale Baba

After 15 years at the helm and three successive terms as chief minister, Dr. Raman Singh lost the Chhattisgarh assembly elections of 2018 that even Congress supporters had not expected the scale of their victory. His compatriot from the neighbouring state Madhya Pradesh Shivraj Singh Chouhan also lost, but not as badly as Raman Singh. And yet, even in his loss (who knows, he might come back as CM when elections are next held in late 2023?), the legacy of Raman Singh as the 'Chawal wale baba' will linger on and endure. Pratyasha Rath of *Swarajya* magazine travelled to Chhattisgarh soon after the elections to talk to ordinary citizens and wrote this: "What is the name of the Chief Minister", I asked a group of tribal women in Mahasamund. It was my first field trip to Chhattisgarh and I was a rookie with one year of experience in the development sector...I do not know his name, but 'chawal wale baba' is what we call him"... For the next couple of hours, I went on to talk of a lot of things, but what dominated the discussion was how the women in the village zealously monitor the fair price shops and how this 'chawal wale baba' is doing some good work for them...And importantly, his PDS success story has been the one which exhibits what true political will can achieve even in the face of immense odds. This could very well have been the end of his stint as the CM of the state, but the road from Raipur via Bastar may just lead to New Delhi."[10]

Now, *Swarajya* magazine is known to 'lean' towards the BJP. But despite that, even development economists of all ilk today agree that the polices adopted and efficiently implemented by

How Chattisgarh Dramatically Improved
(% of Stunted & Underweight Children)

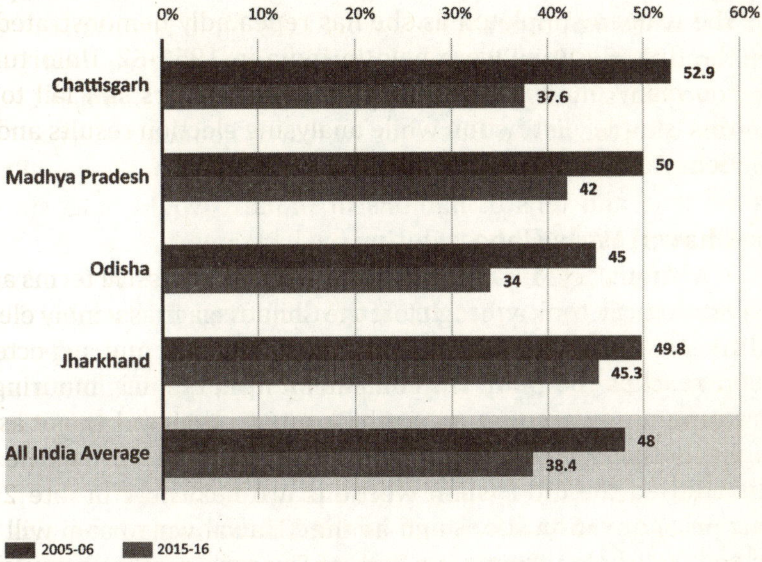

Source: Ministry of Child & Women's Development

the Raman Singh government to improve and upgrade the public distribution system is a rare case study of good economics co existing with good politics. Chhattisgarh, as most of us know, was carved out of Madhya Pradesh in November 2000. For three years, the controversial 'tribal' leader Ajit Jogi ruled as the chief minister anointed by the then Congress president Sonia Gandhi. The BJP won the first elections held in late 2003 and Dr. Raman Singh became chief minister, a post he held continually till late 2018. Like Odisha, Madhya Pradesh, Jharkhand, Bihar, Uttar Pradesh and Rajasthan, the tribal and scheduled caste heavy Chhattisgarh was marked by extreme poverty, malnutrition, hunger and the existence of welfare schemes only on paper. Dr. Singh, it seems, decided that it was impossible to do everything and yet keep voters happy. He focused on ensuring that subsidised food reached the poor for whom it was originally intended.

In today's world of JAM, i.e., Jan Dhan bank accounts, Aadhar cards and Mobile phones, such mundane things like distributing free or subsidised food to the poor has become incredibly smooth compared to the last. Just imagine, if JAM was not operational or not working properly, how would the Modi government have ensured that 800 million poor Indians received free food grains for two years during the Covid pandemic? As Dr. Nilanjan Ghosh, senior director at the Observer Research Foundation says: "The very worst that the western media writes about India would have come true and tens of millions of Indians would have starved because of lost livelihoods during the lockdown"

Without JAM and without any other 21st century technological tool, what Dr. Singh achieved in backward and illiterate Chhattisgarh in not only ensuring free and subsidised food reaches the poor without being siphoned off, but also in creating an awareness among citizens to demand these basic rights without having to pay bribes is a milestone. He completely dismantled the old system where private 'contractors' ran the fair price or ration shops and handed them over to community-based self-help groups to run to minimise corruption and diversion. He introduced a new hologram-based ration card that eliminated anywhere between 3 lakh to 5 lakh fake cardholders over time. This dramatic turnaround was one of the key reasons for his re-election in 2008 and 2013. Despite the 'chawal wale baba' moniker, there was no personality cult around him like in the case of a Mamata Banerjee or Arvind Kejriwal. Nor was he blessed with a weak opposition like his neighbour Naveen Patnaik in Odisha. Even when it lost three successive assembly elections, the Congress remained a powerful force in the state. Welfare of the poor was the success mantra for Dr. Singh's pro-incumbency verdicts. In an interview given to the *Hindustan Times* one year before the 2018 assembly elections, Dr. Singh had singled out his most significant achievement: "Our food security scheme is the most popular. It not only provides food security, but nutritional security and covers about 65 lakh families. There is not a single complaint in seven years, it is a transparent system."[10]

A large number of us leading cocooned urban lives fail to understand the power of Rs. 8,000 an acre to a small farmer. Similarly, a lot us worried about reducing calorie intakes, especially of greasy fast food, cannot understand the importance of a simple food item like rice bringing about a transformational change in the quality of life of poor people. When Chhattisgarh became a new state, the infant mortality rate was 78 per 1,000 which means 78 out of every 1,000 children born died very soon after birth. By the time Dr. Singh completed his third successive term, it had declined to 41. Lack of nutritious food is usually reflected in 'stunted' children, meaning kids who are underweight for their age. Under his tenure, this declined from 53 per cent to 37.6 per cent between 2005 and 2015, according to the National Family Health Survey, 2015-16. Similarly, the per centage of malnourished women has declined from close to 43.5 to about 27.5 in the same time period.[11] Chhattisgarh has gone beyond Madhya Pradesh, Jharkhand and Bihar in these quality-of-life parameters under Dr. Singh. Not a bad achievement at all for a poor tribal state ravaged by Maoists, among other problems. And wonder he won three successive terms as chief minister, despite the Congress being such a formidable political opponent?

Food, Education and Health

Through the example of the 'Chawal wale baba' phenomenon in Chhattisgarh, we have seen how crucial are efficient delivery of welfare schemes to the poor for politicians. Apart from food, education and health are two more 'public goods' that have a long-term and long-lasting impact on the population of a country. India is ranked a lowly 141 out of 184 countries in the latest available UNDP annual Human Development Index Report. The reason is simple. For the first five decades after independence, India failed spectacularly and miserably to invest in public goods like education and health. The result is pathetic literacy rates, health outcomes and life expectancy compared to other Asian countries that were far poorer with inferior quality of life compared to India till the 1960s. Investment in such public goods takes a generation or two to show actual results. It happened exactly that way with

Asian peers that started off poorer than India when colonialism was giving way to new and independent sovereign nations. Today, India is so far behind its Asian peers in terms of literacy rates, life expectancy and even per capita income that it is downright embarrassing. (See charts)

The modern-day godfather of welfare economics (the original one would remain John Maynard Keynes for those who follow economics) Amartya Sen expressed an individual opinion in an interview in 2013 that he had personally interacted with Rahul Gandhi and thought he would make a good Prime Minister. We all know what the views of the venerable Amartya Sen are when it comes to the Congress as compared to the BJP, and particularly Narendra Modi. Yet, that hasn't prevented him for indicting past governments (mostly Congress) for failing to invest in education and health. On June 30, 2014, the Economics Nobel prize winner Sen delivered a speech at an Asia House gathering and gave an interview to Naomi Canton about Modi and what his policy priorities should be as the new Prime Minister of India. In his own words: "He was not my favourite candidate, people know that, but he has now won. India is a democracy and so he has the right to govern. He has not yet announced his policies, so we will have to examine them and if we have some critical things to say on that, then that should be based on understanding of what he is announcing that he will do, rather than expectation of what he will do, as that would be very unfair to him....I don't think there is only one thing, but basically there is an approach, namely the approach has to be, that there is nothing as important both for spreading the fruits of economic growth and making it sustainable and to enhance it, than the development of human capability and that requires educational expansion and healthcare, both of which are in a mess in India..."[12]

Such has been the pathetic state of India for decades when it comes to even basic necessities that their provision becomes a weapon to win re-elections. Great leaders aspire to leave behind legacies that history will mark as transformational. We don't know if history will judge Narendra Modi as a great leader. But if you ask anyone who is not a victim if ideological bias what the biggest achievements and legacy of Modi between 2014 and 2024 would be, the answer would be: Toilets, one-room houses, subsidised gas connections and cylinders, piped water connections and bank accounts where your balance can be zero. Is that an 'achievement'? Well, in India it does appear to be so, simply because half a century of Congress rule did not cover these necessities, to an extent that for majority of Indian households they started looking like a luxury. Cash and food lead to such instant and immediate beneficiaries that they are promptly reflected in electoral behaviour. But 'welfare'-oriented investments and expenditure on education and health take much longer to make a material and substantive difference. Hence you will rarely hear voters say "I voted again for her or him because the literacy rate and life expectancy in my state has improved". To give credit where due, the AAP government in Delhi did manage to campaign out of better schools, not just in Delhi, but also in recently concluded Punjab elections. We are not sure if people voted for AAP in Punjab due their education policy in Delhi or it was sheer cumulative explosion of anger against the status quo of SAD and Congress rules, but to see Delhi Sarkari Schools in the AAP campaigns of Punjab was an incredible change of narratives for sure. Hopefully, the investments in these public goods that really started in earnest only in the 21st century will take another generation to fruitily so that poor voters don't chose leaders with male voters electing purely on the basis of cash in their accounts and female voters expressing their gratitude for the government ensuring her child is not sleeping on an empty stomach.

Nari Shakti

Way back in 2010, the newspaper *Deccan Herald* featured a story done by the news service IANS from Bihar. It was about a girl named Khushboo who had come second in the Bihar board exams. Coming from a family of modest means, Khushboo became an icon and celebrity in her own village; so much so that the Darbhanga branch of IGNOU made a documentary on her struggles and success. You might well ask: tens of thousands of girls have been doing well in studies in India for ages. What's so special about

Khushboo? Well, she was a beneficiary of the Cycle Yojana for girls launched by chief minister Nitish Kumar in 2007 under which about 8,70,000 bicycles were given free of cost to school-going girls in Bihar between 2008 and 2010.

The story quoted Khushboo and then added more information: "I simply pedalled five KM every day to the school thanks to the cycle provided by the government," Khushboo, a teenaged resident of Bagaun village in Katihar district, told IANS over telephone. The chief minister was so impressed with her success that he personally visited the village, congratulated Khushboo and gifted her Rs. 25,000 on behalf of the state government. Nitish Kumar couldn't help gushing about his two pet schemes that gave free uniforms and cycles to school-going children. According to the story, "Nitish Kumar also claimed that the Poshak Yojna (Uniform Scheme) and Cycle Yojna for schoolchildren had helped turn around education in the state. The attendance of girls has shot up from less than 1,70,000 to 4,90,000 in just three years. He said the scheme is 'very close to my heart'. He felt it has changed the face of Bihar with hundreds of thousands of schoolgirls riding bicycles to reach their schools every day."[14] Like K.C. Rao and Naveen Patnaik were undoubtedly concerned about the welfare of small farmers, Nitish Kumar too was concerned about girls going to school and getting educated. But all three also shared another thing in common: they wanted to be re-elected as chief minister. In 2010, Nitish Kumar won a massive mandate to remain chief minister. Apart from improving basic law & order and roads, free bicycles for girls was a big hit with voters. Fortunately or unfortunately for him, the moniker 'Cycle wale baba' was not given to him like 'Chawal wale baba' to Dr. Raman Singh. But while this was not the first, Nitish Kumar opened the doors to a new 'vote bank' for politicians that too spread across two generations: happy young girl students and their mother full of gratitude.

Mamaji's Ladli Laxmis

When Nitish Kumar was focusing on empowering girls via free school uniforms and bicycles, Madhya Pradesh chief minister came forth with an even more ambitious and far-reaching scheme for girls. *The New Indian Express* carried a detailed story written by Anurag Singh with actual case studies in November, 2021 to highlight the enduring success and impact of this scheme. According to the story: "This is the story of three girls from different parts of Madhya Pradesh whose flagging career goals saw a turnaround due to the timely intervention of the Madhya Pradesh government's Ladli Laxmi Yojana (LLY), a flagship scheme to uplift the girl child. Vedika Vaishnav harboured the dream of becoming an income tax officer, which came crashing after her father passed away in 2018; Neha Patel from Jabalpur

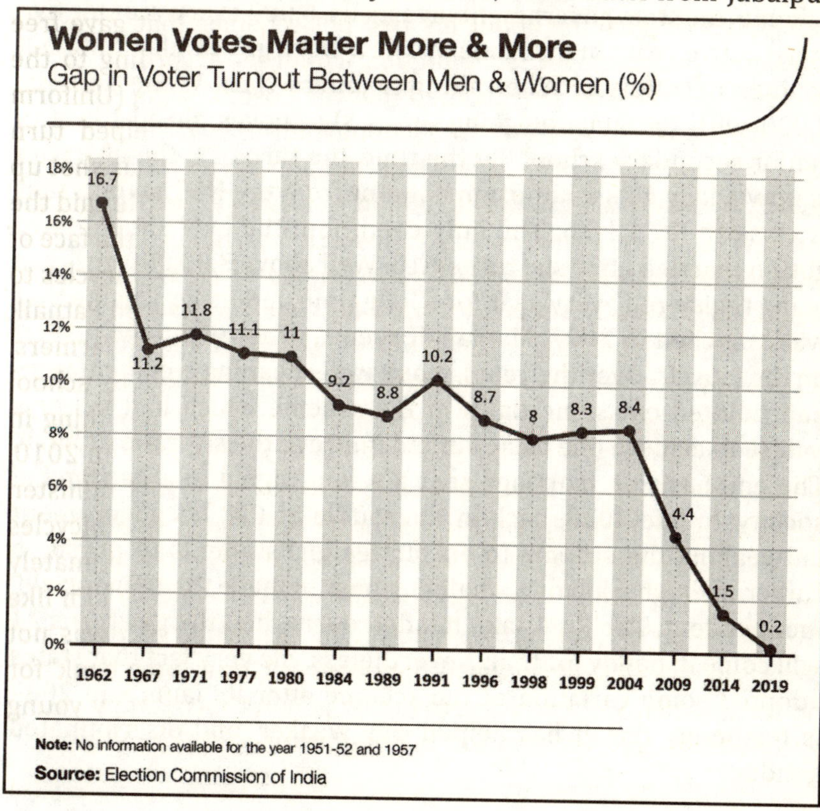

Women Votes Matter More & More
Gap in Voter Turnout Between Men & Women (%)

Note: No information available for the year 1951-52 and 1957

Source: Election Commission of India

aimed to be an Indian Police Service officer till her father's death in 2018 foiled this plan; and Prachi Kori stared at a blank future after she and her mentally challenged mother were abandoned by her father three years. But today, the three girls are reliving their ambitions, courtesy LLY... "My husband died in 2018 from a heart attack, a few months after the private company he worked for in Pithampur Industrial Area as an electrician shut down. My parents looked after me and my daughter, Vedika. Without the LLY, I could not have arranged for Vedika's Class 11 studies. Her ambition of becoming an IT officer would have just remained a dream," said Vedika's unemployed mother, Taruna Vaishnav."[14] The story goes on to highlight the other examples.

What is the 'Ladli Laxmi Yojana' that made Shivraj Singh Chouhan an even more popular Mamaji for voters? Under this scheme, the state government invests Rs. 6,000 every year for five consecutive years in the name of a new-born girl child in National Savings Certificates. When the girl enters class V, she gets Rs. 2,000 with the amount going up as she moves ahead towards senior secondary school. By the time she turns 21, the girl, who is now a lady gets a lumpsum amount from the NSC savings that is close to Rs. 1 lakh. The only condition; the lady should have gotten married after she turned 18. Well above 3,00,000 girls are being registered every year for a long time under the scheme that was launched in 2007. Mamaji, it seems, is not willing to just sit on the laurels. Over the years, many well-meaning commentators had pointed out some flaws in the scheme which had led to a failure to achieve one basic aim: to improve the sex ratio at birth. The emphasis on marriage sent a wrong signal to a patriarchal society. In late 2020, back in the saddle as CM, his government is tweaking the scheme to encourage girl students to pursue a career through a job or a small business to make them financially independent. The Rs. 1 lakh handed over when the girl turns 21 will come in handy for that. Nevertheless, the very fact that states adopted some variation of the scheme after its launch in 2007 is testimony that it has helped the 'weaker' and discriminated gender.

If Mama Can, Why Can't Mamata?

Two media outlets—*The Times of India* and the digital portal *The Scroll* published stories soon after Mamata Banerjee and her party TMC won a landslide third successive victory in the West

Bengal assembly elections in 2021. Both gave seven reasons why Mamata triumphed. Only two were common to both the lists: Women and Muslims. *The Scroll* wrote: "While Muslim support for the Trinamool Congress gets a lot of media attention, actually its biggest 'vote bank' is not a community but a gender. In 2019, according to a post poll survey done by Lokniti at the Centre for the Study of Developing Societies, the Trinamool Congress was the only party to have more women voters than men. Cut another way, 47 per cent of Bengal's women voted Trinamool while only 38 per cent went with the BJP...Unsurprisingly, Mamata Banerjee has sharply concentrated on wooing women using welfare, with a host of schemes designed to directly transfer cash to female hands. In return, clearly those hands have chosen the Trinamool's twin-flower on the EVM machine."[15] *The Times of India* had something similar to say about the female vote proving to be decisive in the elections.

And don't for a moment think women preferred Mamata over Modi when it came to ruling the state just because she is a woman. When it comes to their wellbeing and welfare, women don't care if the leader giving them something concrete is a man or woman. Look at the popularity of Nitish Kumar and Shivraj Singh Chouhan. In contrast, look at how Vasundhara Raje Scindia keeps losing every alternate election and how Mayawati seems to have lost the plot. During the abrasive, often abusive and high-pitched election campaign where rhetoric seemed to triumph over ground realities, most forgot the slew of female-centric welfare schemes that Mamata Banerjee had launched in the state. For instance, the 'Kanyashree Prakalpa' scheme offers Rs. 1,000 a year as scholarship to girls going to school when they turn 13 and a lump sum payment of Rs. 25,000 when they turn 18. The caveat is: the girl should be pursuing higher studies or a livelihood option when she turns 18 and should not be married. Then there is the 'Rupashree Prakalpa' scheme whereby poor families get a one-time cash grant for the marriage of their daughter provided she is above 18 years. Mamata didi also borrowed from Nitish Kumar and launched a 'Sabooji Sakthi' scheme in 2015-16 to give free bicycles to girls going to class 9th to 12th in the state.

The Swachh Bharat Factor

Of course, when we talk of women as a vote bank, you only have to look at the 2019 Lok Sabha elections to see how the female voter perceived the incumbent Narendra Modi as compared to the challenger Rahul Gandhi. It was a no contest. Breaking an almost seven-decade long gender gap, the voter turnout for women at 68.68 per cent was virtually the same as the voter turnout among men at 66.79 per cent. Can there be any doubt that toilets, gas

How Open Defecation Declined Post Swachh Bharat Mission

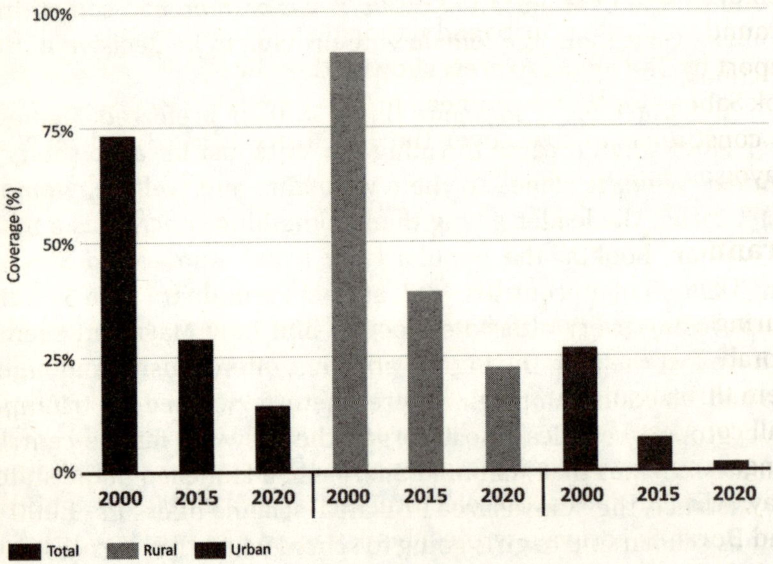

Source: Swachh Bharat Mission, Government of India

connections and cylinders and direct benefit cash transfers to bank accounts of women played a big role in the BJP crossing the magical tally of 300 Lok Sabha seats on its own in the 2019 elections? There persists a perception that the Balakot air strikes enabled Modi to turn on the 'nationalist' pitch at full blast which mesmerised voters who might not have opted for the BJP. Perhaps, there is no doubt Modi used Balakot in his public rallies. But those who followed his campaign which started at least a year before the elections will have to admit that there was virtually no rally, public meeting or some inauguration function where Modi didn't keep hammering the point about how toilets had given dignity to women and how gas connections had improved their health because it is a clean cooking fuel compared to kerosene, firewood or coal.

The CNBC TV 18 portal pointed out soon after the election results were announced that the expert view that primarily national security issues carried the day for Modi may be partly correct at best: The results are a resounding endorsement of Prime Minister Narendra Modi's popularity, his government's achievements in the last five years and his campaign, which centred around national security and nationalism, according to experts. A report by *The Indian Express* showed that the BJP-led NDA, in this Lok Sabha elections, was ahead in 71—or over 60 per cent—seats in constituencies that cover the 115 districts identified by NITI Aayog as 'aspirational'.[16]

Prannoy Roy Speaks

Once upon a time, the only 'private' and 'independent' voice during elections was that of Prannoy Roy. He and fellow pollster Dorab Sopariwala still religiously cover elections and discuss item threadbare in the TV channel NDTV. Though one of authors still considers him as the final word, another one insists he is no longer the only, or even the last word on elections anymore. Either way, what he says about electoral trends still carries weight. He and Dorab Sopariwala wrote a book named *The Verdict: Decoding India's Elections*. Edited excerpts were published in the magazine *Significance*: "The current high level of women's participation has been a major development in India's democracy. In 1962 the turnout of women was only 47 per cent, yet by 2014 it had shot up to 66 per cent—up by 19 per centage points. Meanwhile, men's turnout grew by only 5 per centage points (from 62 per cent to 67 per cent) over the same period...The rise in women voter turnout is even more pronounced in State Assembly elections. In fact, for the first time in India's electoral history, women's turnout was higher than that of men in the State Assembly elections of 2017–18. This represents an inflection point when annual quantitative improvements have finally led to a qualitative change in the gender underpinning of India's democracy. This speaks of social churn and it is not surprising that today political parties focus much more on woman's issues during their campaigns than before...period.

Women's turnout in villages is now 6 per centage points higher than in towns and cities. This is a huge change from 1971 when the turnout of women in rural areas was 8 per centage points lower than in towns. In addition to the focus on needs of woman voters, the rising influence of long neglected rural women voters is becoming a new and more important focus of electoral strategy."[17] The book talks all about what we have already discussed above about cycles, cash transfers gas connections et al.

Women and Alcohol

Folklore has it that in a deeply conservative and patriarchal society like India, the women of the family usually opted for the choices of their menfolk when it came to voting for leaders and parties. There is no empirical evidence to suggest this has actually been happening because the 'secret ballot' ensured that the men could never double check whom 'their' women voted for. Till 1967, all this didn't matter because when it came to ruling either at the centre or the states, the Congress had a virtual monopoly. In such a scenario, women and men would vote for the same leader, except on occasions when an 'independent' voted differently without telling her family about it. Again, there is no empirical evidence to back up these claims.

South Asia is indeed a funny region. Virtually all major countries have had really strong-headed women at the top executive post of the country. Starting with our own Indira Gandhi to Benazir Bhutto in Pakistan and Sheikh Hasina in Bangladesh or Bidhya Devi Bhandari in Nepal for that matter, all were part of this phenomenon started by none other than Sirimavo Bhandarnayake in Sri Lanka who on 21st July, 1960 created history by becoming the first woman Prime Minister in the world. And to think we have not even discussed the Nobel-winning, and still struggling, Aung San Suu Kyi who is simply known as 'The Lady' in thoroughly patriarchal Burma. We will keep a chapter in another book on the folks celebrating a certain Kamala Harris in the fountainhead of democracy, arriving centuries late on the scene what the nascent South Asian democracies did with ease 60 years back.

Coming back to the main subject of this book, and yet, it is taking so long to move away from deeply entrenched patriarchy. Some leaders thought they had discovered the magic formula to ensure women do vote independently of men and exercise their own choice. The magic formula was alcohol. We are not talking about the free distribution of liquor that still happens during elections. Rather, we are talking about prohibition where the sale and consumption of alcohol is virtually completely banned in a state.

To pay tribute to Mahatma Gandhi who was against alcohol, the then Bombay province of newly independent India totally banned alcohol except for some 'special' cases. The puritan Morarji Desai, who eventually went on to become the Prime Minister was the chief minister when serious agitations and protests for a separate state of Maharashtra mushroomed all over and many died in police firing on the protesting crowds. Eventually, in 1960, the two separate states of Maharashtra and Gujarat were created. Prohibition continues till date in Gujarat while starting in 1963, Maharashtra has gradually lifted all restrictions. In fact, you could order online your favourite bottle of tipple to be delivered at your doorstep during the pandemic.

Alcoholism is a serious issue in India, like in most countries. While the rich and the profligate die of liver cirrhosis causing grief to family members, alcohol has destroyed poor families because the man of the house polishes off the entire family income on booze if he is an alcoholic. For such women—and there are hundreds and thousands, if not millions of them in India—alcohol is an object of hate. The old Congress veteran Bansi Lal who was a strongman during the Emergency unexpectedly became chief minister of a coalition government in 1996, and kept his poll promise of imposing prohibition. In two years' time, the same government had lifted it. In 1994, N.T. Rama Rao imposed prohibition in

Andhra Pradesh as promised by him during the election campaign. By 1997, his son in law N. Chandrababu Naidu had deposed him and lifted all restrictions on alcohol. Currently, apart from Gujarat (where being a 'business friendly' state you can witness a parallel economy on booze evolved to different level of sophistication altogether by the enterprising Gujaratis and which can deliver you any brand of your choice under the sun at a 'premium'), Bihar is the second state under total prohibition. Again, it was imposed to fulfil a poll promise made in 2015 by Nitish Kumar. By all accounts, Nitish seems to be losing this battle and if history is any guide, he will lose the war against alcohol.

As Rohan Pandiarajan wrote for *The Indian Express* in 2010: "Demands for prohibition slowly gave way to temperance as the negative effects of prohibition included wide-scale sale of spurious and cheap liquor which can cause health problems and deaths, the rise of organised crime and bootlegging due to the growth of a black market for alcohol. Apart from this, the resultant loss of jobs to people working in breweries and vineyards was another stumbling block." Clearly, prohibition is no longer taken seriously by politicians as a way to lure women voters. It has proven to have short-term gains at best. For now and the future, politicians will focus on cash, scholarships for the girl child, reservations for women in jobs and elected bodies and similar things. And what about a share in real power, ask feminists. The authors completely agree with the contention of serious activists and thinkers that patriarchy will not change till the time women get a fair and real share in power, not just in politics, but also corporate offices and households when it comes to decision making. But that is beyond the remit and scope of this book which is limited to the pro-incumbency phenomenon in Indian politics. For instance, if 'welfare' schemes like reservations for women in elected bodies like panchayats (half the seats are already reserved) or jobs (like 30 per cent of police jobs reserved for women in some states) had materially and directly affected the re-election prospects of leaders, we would have analysed it. At this juncture, all we can say is that at least for the sake of winning and winning elections, politicians and political parties are no longer treating women like cattle to be herded into the polling booth during elections. At least that is a good start; no matter what the real intentions of the political leaders are.

Psst...What About The Gods?

Himanta Biswa Sarma is one politician who speaks his mind and never shies away from controversies if his words and actions trigger slugfests. A fellow Assamese journalist going by the name of Arnab Goswami had already triggered a tsunami of jokes revolving around Rahul Gandhi after that 'notorious' interview before the 2014 Lok Sabha elections where the Gandhi family scion literally kept chanting 'women empowerment' during answers to every question asked of him. When that interview was aired, Himanta Biswa Sarma was a 'loyal' Congress leader locked in a power tussle with his own chief minister Tarun Gogoi who had won three successive assembly elections but was ageing and beginning to ail.

The fight was a simple one: it seems Sarma wanted to be the future Congress chief minister of Assam while Gogoi wanted to promote his son Gaurav Gogoi who was a Lok Sabha MP and one of the 'dynastic' young Turks like Jyotiraditya Scindia, Sachin Pilot, Jitin Prasad, Sushmita Dev, R.P.N. Singh and Milind Deora, to name a few. As the succession battle in the Congress in Assam headed for a status quo kind of stalemate, Sarma, like a 'loyal' soldier of the party, "sought an audience with the High Command". (You will be surprised by media exports still write these words when they report on a Congress leader wanting to meet any member of the Nehru-Gandhi dynasty). In any case, after much effort and persistence, Sarma got to meet Rahul Gandhi. Nobody, except Sarma, Gandhi and his pet dog who also attended the crucial meeting knows exactly what happened. But soon after that, Himanta Sarma quit the Congress and joined the BJP and is today the BJP chief minister of Assam. It is Sarma who made Pidi (the pet dog of Rahul Gandhi) famous by stating publicly after quitting the Congress that his decision to quit came when he saw the young Gandhi seemed keener on feeding biscuits meant for Sarma to Pidi rather than listen to the travails of leaders like Sarma.

Assam Says 'No' To Gods

The lines above do not really have a connection with what we have to say here. But since we will be talking about the 'welfare' of gods, people can choose circuitous paths to reach God. So have we. In any case, Himanta Biswa Sarma, who was 'technically' the number two BJP leader in Assam after chief minister Sarbananda Sonowal announced in October 2020 that the state government would henceforth stop funding madrasas and Sanskrit schools that were government aided. About 550 madrasas and 100 Sanskrit schools would be affected though their teachers would be absorbed into normal schools. The amount involved was laughably small: about Rs. 4 crore or Rs. 40 million a year. But the symbolic significance, when assembly elections were not very far away was significant.

Almost all media outlets featured the story filed by IANS. Allow us to quote from the website of News18: "The Assam government will close down all state-run madrasas and Sanskrit *tols* (schools) as it can't afford to teach religious scriptures with public funds, state Education and Finance Minister Himanta Biswa Sarma said on Friday. "Our government's policy we had announced earlier in the state Assembly. There should be no religious education with government's funding," he told the media. "We have nothing to say about privately-run madrasas and Sanskrit tols," he added.

Following the government's announcement, All India United Democratic Front (AIUDF) chief and perfume baron Badruddin Ajmal said that if the BJP-led government shut down government-run madrasas, his party would re-open them after coming to power in the next year's Assembly elections. "Madrasas cannot be closed. We would reopen these 50-60-year-old madrassas if this BJP government closes them forcibly," said Ajmal, also a Lok Sabha member."[19] Badruddin Ajmal will probably have to wait till at least the next round of assembly elections due in 2026 before he can re-open those 500 odd madrasas with government funds because the BJP won a second successive term in 2021 and Himanta Biswa Sarma is the chief minister.

So, what would you call this: 'welfare' or 'religious war'?

India is indeed a lovably paradoxical place. Political leaders of all hues swear by the Constitution in public platforms and denounce mixing religion with politics. But so deeply embedded is religion in the Indian psyche and society that the same political leaders keep mixing religion with politics. In fact, so powerful is the 'perceived' influence of religious symbolism over voter behaviour that even diehard 'secular' politicians turn to the gods for electoral salvation. Rahul Gandhi with his fabled dimples couldn't resist a series of temple runs in 2017 in Gujarat when there was a feeling that the BJP is vulnerable and could be defeated. Subsequently, when he was accused of being disdainful towards Hinduism, he promptly wore a 'janeu' (sacred thread) over his jacket to proclaim himself as a 'proud' Hindu Brahmin and some courtier of his dynasty even came up with the 'gotra' that he belonged to. In the case of Rahul Gandhi, his electoral track record suggests that God helps only those who can help themselves. But you can't say the same about another 'secular' political leader who has successfully found electoral salvation among the pantheon of Hindu gods and goddesses, with token gestures to other religions to maintain the 'secular' balance.

The God of Aam Aadmis?

We are talking about the redoubtable Arvind Kejriwal who is now riding high on a horse of 'national' dreams. There can be little doubt any more that when it comes to winning elections or emerging as a formidable and serious player, the newbie Kejriwal is streets ahead of leaders like Rahul Gandhi who controls a massive 130-year-old party or a Mayawati who once ruled Uttar Pradesh like a queen. In 2012, when Arvind Kejriwal launched the Aam Aadmi Party with idealism dripping from his bespectacled face, he heaped scorn on traditional politics, politicians and political parties. He solemnly promised a new era of citizen-driven politics where caste, creed, community, ethnic identity and religion will have no role to play; apart from being totally free of the taint of corruption. After a brief spell of idiosyncratic madness in 2014 when he dreamt of winning a large number of Lok Sabha seats, Arvind Kejriwal the idealistic anti-corruption activist started getting gradually replaced by Kejriwal the politician who wanted to keep winning elections and become a pro-incumbency champion. His day under the sun came in 2015 when AAP won 67 out of 70 seats in the Delhi assembly elections. When 'idealists' like Yogendra Yadav who is a psephologist, intellectual, anti-corruption activist, columnist, TV debater, author, political leader, farmer leader and human rights crusader rolled into one soft-spoken package and the perennial multi-millionaire rebel lawyer Prashant Bhushan who files a PIL at the drop of a hat complained about dubious characters getting AAP tickets, they got the proverbial kick on their backsides and were thrown out. He then came tantalisingly close to winning Punjab in 2017 before stumbling badly during the last mile of the race. But perseverance matters, and AAP did create history by sweeping Punjab in the 2022 assembly elections. To give credit to the man, he doesn't waste time brooding on lost opportunities.

In 2018, Kejriwal decided to become a full time 'politician'. Welfare schemes like free electricity up to 200 units a month and free water had already made him immensely popular among Delhi voters. But Kejriwal apparently thought it would be wiser to buy insurance by supplications before the gods. He launched free pilgrimages for Delhi residents above 60 along with one adult attendant to 13 religious sites including Rameshwaram, Puri, Dwarka and Vaishno Devi. Ayodhya was added in 2021. To cement his 'secular' credentials, the Sikh holy shrine of Kartarpur was added in late 2021; elections being due in Punjab in February 2022. To make it a 360-degree all-purpose welfare scheme for all faiths, he added the famous Velankanni Church in Tamil Nadu. It is a different matter that his party was a serious contender in the Goa assembly elections. In just one year after the launch of the scheme, 36,000 elderly residents of Delhi had used this welfare scheme. However, 'God' or China (depending on your perspective) intervened in the form of the Covid pandemic in 2020 and the pilgrimages were suspended for almost two years. They have resumed with a vengeance now and pious Delhi folks are happy; as is Arvind Kejriwal.

There are many states offer this scheme to some category of citizens or the other. In 2017, perhaps to reflect the 'aspirational' mood of India, the Rajasthan government announced pilgrimage trips that included free air tickets along with local travel, lodging and boarding expenses. The race to offer free pilgrimages sometimes results in situations that embarrass one party that runs governments across many states. The Gujarat government under the BJP has been providing a subsidy of Rs. 20,000 to each pilgrim who goes to Kailash Mansoravar. When Yogi Adityanath became the BJP chief minister of Uttar Pradesh, the monk turned politician upped the ante by offering Rs. 1,00,000 to each pilgrim. This became an issue in Gujarat where assembly elections were due and anti-incumbency sentiments against the BJP were actually running high after 22 years of continuous rule. This was added to the laundry list of grievances that voters in Gujarat had against the incumbent government that had already seen two chief ministers since Narendra Modi went after a 'promotion' in 2014 to Delhi. A shaky BJP regime was saved massive embarrassment by Modi, and perhaps God.

The Haj Subsidy

The genesis of offering free pilgrimages as a welfare scheme goes back to 1932 when the British still lorded it over India. A Haj Committee Act was passed by the government that demarcated then Bombay and Calcutta as the embarkation points for Haj pilgrims and created a body to facilitate the pilgrimage. No explicit mention of any subsidy or cash grant as a welfare measure was specified in that Act. In 1959, the government of an independent and sovereign country India with Jawaharlal Nehru as the Prime Minister amended the British era 1932 Act. A new Haj Committee was formed for supervising and helping out with the pilgrimage with the Port of Bombay becoming a monopoly of sorts. A provision was also sneaked in to create taxpayer funded Haj Fund. In 1973, the real subsidies and the real welfare started when the government of India with Indira Gandhi as the Prime Minister abandoned the sea route for Haj and gave a monopoly to Air India to fly Haj pilgrims; which soon became a duopoly with the official airline of Saudi Arabia, Saudi joining the arrangement. In the early years of this welfare scheme, not too many pilgrims availed the benefits because the logistics of travel even within India to Bombay from the interiors was not an easy task for illiterate and poor Muslims. But that started soon as the Bombay monopoly was removed and Haj pilgrims could now board flights for Jeddah in Saudi Arabia from almost all major regions of India. The airports also launched and operated separate Haj terminals to make things even easier for the pilgrims. In 2018, a record 1,75,000 Muslims from India went for the Haj pilgrimage. So many Muslims from across the world now want to go for Haj that Saudi Arabia has imposed country wise quotas to manage the ballooning inflow of pilgrims.

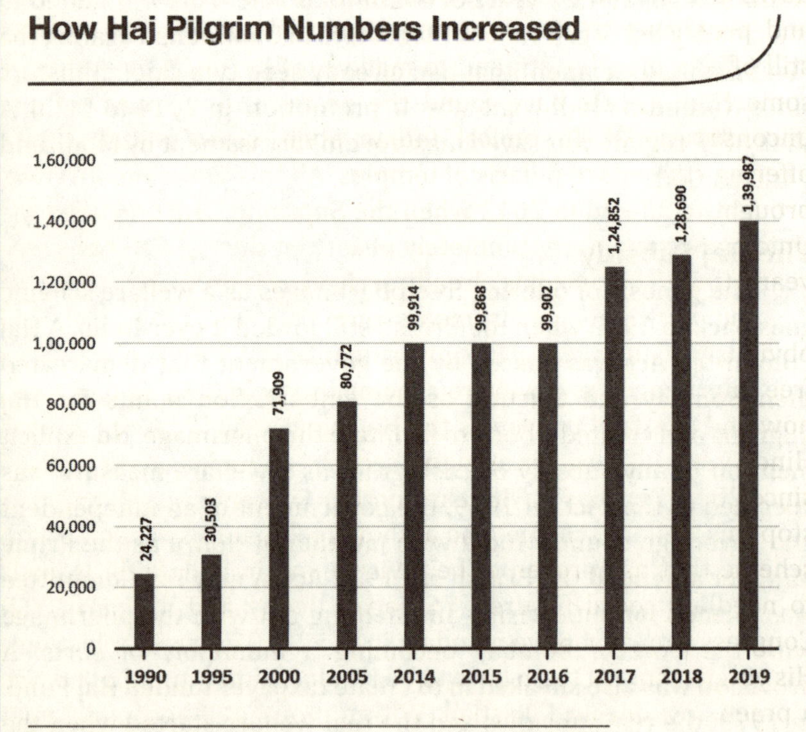

Source: hajcommittee.gov.in

The Haj pilgrimage started becoming a controversial point of debate in the 1980s when the handling of the Shah Bano alimony issue and the opening of the locks of the Babri Masjid in 1986 by the Indian government led by Prime Minister Rajiv Gandhi triggered a new round of religious polarisation in India. 'Aggrieved' Hindus complained that subsidy to Muslims to fly for pilgrimages with fully decked up facilities at Haj centres in big cities and Haj terminals at airports while Hindus got nothing was another example of Hindus becoming 'second class citizens' in their own homeland. During the 1990s, the religious polarisation deepened after the demolition of the Babri Masjid and communal riots. While 'Hindutva' politicians and outfits started demanding the abolition of the Haj subsidy or the provision of similar subsidies for Hindu pilgrimages, secular politicians doubled down and started becoming even more 'ultra-secular' by offering and promising to more welfare sops to Muslims. Many states still offer a monthly stipend to maulvis of mosques even though some High Courts have found the practice discriminatory and unconstitutional. In typical Indian style, some states started offering stipends to pujaris of temples. All this noise and fury was brought to an end in 2012 when the Supreme Court ordered the Union government to completely phase out the Haj subsidy in ten years' time. The time has already arrived as it is 2022.

But yes, state governments one after the other, the lead obviously being taken by BJP governments, started offering Hindus free pilgrimages as a welfare scheme. No politician or party will now end this facility even as the Haj subsidy has come to an end. Hindu votes also matter, as many 'secular' politicians have realised since 2014. Perhaps it will take another Supreme Court verdict to stop this welfare scheme. The authors feel that this is one welfare scheme that has proven to be divisive and in bad 'faith'. It leads to needless social fissures. Y.S. Jagan Reddy and his party YSR Congress won a massive mandate in the 2019 assembly elections. His voters, most of them have to be Hindus, didn't care that he was a practising, devout Christian. Within months of becoming chief minister, his government announced that it was doubling the free cash assistance to Christian pilgrims wishing to visit Jerusalem and other holy sites to Rs. 60,000. It triggered a huge controversy. He wants to be a pro-incumbency champion when elections come calling in 2024 and there are veritable gold mines of all-inclusive welfare schemes that provide benefits irrespective of religion. Why pick a divisive one?

Was Indira Gandhi Insensitive Towards The Poor?

This is a rhetorical question asked in a metaphorical way. Many top BJP leaders still taunt the Congress for the famous slogan 'Garibi Hatao' that propelled Indira Gandhi to a big nationwide mandate in the 1971 Lok Sabha elections and enabled her to vanquish her rivals and opponents within and outside the Congress in a decisive manner. The fact is, for most of the remaining part of the century, poverty remained stubbornly high, while per capita GDP, literacy and life expectancy moved up in a sluggish manner. Does it mean that Indira Gandhi and the legion of popular leaders before and after her in the 20th century were so selfish and callous that they never bothered about the welfare of the poor? Or, are the pro-incumbency stars of this century an entirely new breed of politicians who genuinely care for the poor and their wellbeing? Answers to both questions are: Hogwash. Politicians across the world were the same, are the same and will remain the same. They might claim they are in it for 'service' even as their supporters go about gathering voters and telling them that their 'Neta' can render service only if she has the 'power' to do so. The difference between then and the 21st century can be explained in another single word: money.

In the year 1991-92, the first year of the dramatic economic reforms unleashed by Prime Minister P.V. Narashima Rao with Dr. Manmohan Singh as the finance minister, the total Union Budget was Rs. 1,13,000 crores. During her Budget speech delivered on February 1, 2022 finance minister Nirmala Sitharaman allocated Rs. 2.35 lakh crores for direct transfer to bank accounts of farmers after buying the Kharif and Rabi food grains output at the Minimum Support Price. That's just a part of the total Union Budget of Rs. 39.45 lakh crores, almost 40 times the size of the budget three decades ago. Take another number to get more ideas. The total revenue receipts of the Union Budget in 1991-92 was Rs. 80,000 crore. In 2020-21, the Union Government collected more than Rs. 4.5 lakh crores from just taxes and chess on petrol and diesel. Even accounting for inflation, that's a big rise in the money that the Union Government is spending. Then you have states with their own budgets and expenditures.

How Tax Revenues Increased

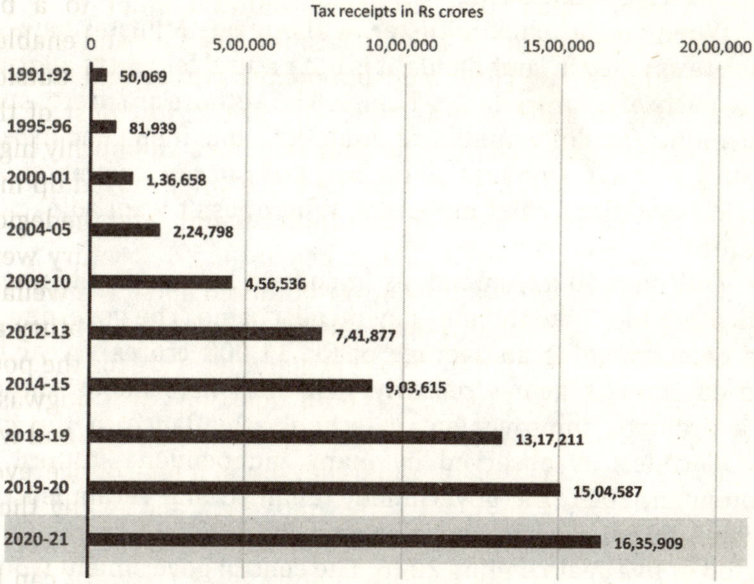

Source: Reserve Bank of India

This has happened despite a fall in both direct and indirect tax rates in the last three decades. The natural question is: but how did this happen? This book is about pro-incumbency stars and not a treatise on the fiscal situation of the Indian economy. So, we will be as brief as possible. First, the income of the country, both collectively and individually has risen dramatically in the last few decades. India's GDP was $ 266 billion in 1991-92; it will be $ 3,000 billion this year. India's per capita income was $ 300 in 1991; it is $ 2,000 this year. It is but natural that when income grows, tax revenues will also grow. That's exactly what has happened, particularly in the 21st century. The second is the widening of the tax net as well as base. Once again, we will not get into details. But as the economy has become more 'formal' and as digital records are maintained, it is not so easy any more to avoid paying taxes. Of course, as long as human beings are human beings, tax evasion and black money transactions will never go away. But they are not as rampant as they were in the glorious days of socialism.

When you, as chief minister or the Prime Minister have so much tax money in your hands, it is but natural for you to allocate large parts of it for welfare schemes. The authors are pretty sure that Indira Gandhi would have done the same if she had access to such massive amounts as tax revenues in her command. As would have many chief ministers. Who doesn't want to get re-elected?

This has had a tremendous impact on human development indicators too. Take the mid-day meal scheme. The government has been spending an average of Rs. 11,000 crores a year on mid-day meal schemes recently. Just this one scheme has led to a dramatic improvement in school attendance in the last two decades, as observed by many independent studies. In September, 2021, the government renamed and revamped the scheme to PM Poshan and allocated Rs. 1,30,794 crores for a period of five years ending 2026. The central government would give cash worth Rs. 54,000 crores and spend an additional Rs. 45,000 crores on the purchase of food grains. The balance would be provided by state governments. Of course, as long as there are governments and policies, there will be critics. Dilip Sinha wrote for the digital portal *The Wire* soon after the revamped scheme was announced: "What raises the suspicion that this announcement of a 'new' scheme might just be a damp squib is the financial outlays that have been provided. The release states that the financial outlay of the Union government for the for the five-year period 2021-22 to 2025-26 will be Rs. 54,061.73 crore. The equivalent budget allocation for the mid-day meal scheme for 2020-21 was Rs. 11,000 crore and for 2021-22, it was Rs. 11,500 crore.

Therefore, the given amount suggests that even in nominal

terms we will not see any increase in budgets for the scheme over the next four years. This is very disappointing given the fact that the mid-day meal scheme has been suffering from stagnant budgets over the last few years. Economist Jean Drèze estimates that taking inflation into account, the allocation for the mid-day meal scheme has been reduced by 32.3 per cent between the years 2014 and 2021."[20] But then, we also need to question if the mid-day meal remains the top draw of sending kids to schools now that governments (both state and central) already provide enough ration to poorest of the poor households? In the mid-nineties, one of the authors has worked extensively in tribal areas of Jhabua-Ratlam as producer on DECU project of ISRO, and has personally witnessed the mid-day meal being the only reason the Bhil tribals used to send their kids to schools. Hunger, not education used to be the main drive. Today, the priorities might have changed. The ration schemes ensured there was no hunger related death in India even in the worst possible times of Covid lockdowns. The matrix has changed, and the politicians might be reading it better than the economists. Earlier, it used to be the economists planning and the politicians implementing the programmes. Now the two-handed economists are relegated to post-event analysts for analysing what worked and what didn't. Ironically, what doesn't work for economists these days, works rather well for the politicians working on re-election strategy.

What's Ahead?

Even those who are not very optimistic or bullish about the future economic prospects of India accept one thing: declining population growth will ensure that per capita incomes in the country grow at about 4 per cent a year even in a poorly managed economy for the next 10 to 15 years. They also accept the fact that extreme poverty will decline further and reach below 5 per cent in the same time period from about 13 per cent now if you calculate incomes. They also accept that sanitation, drinking water, cooking gas, pucca houses will be the norm by then which means vastly improved human development indicators.

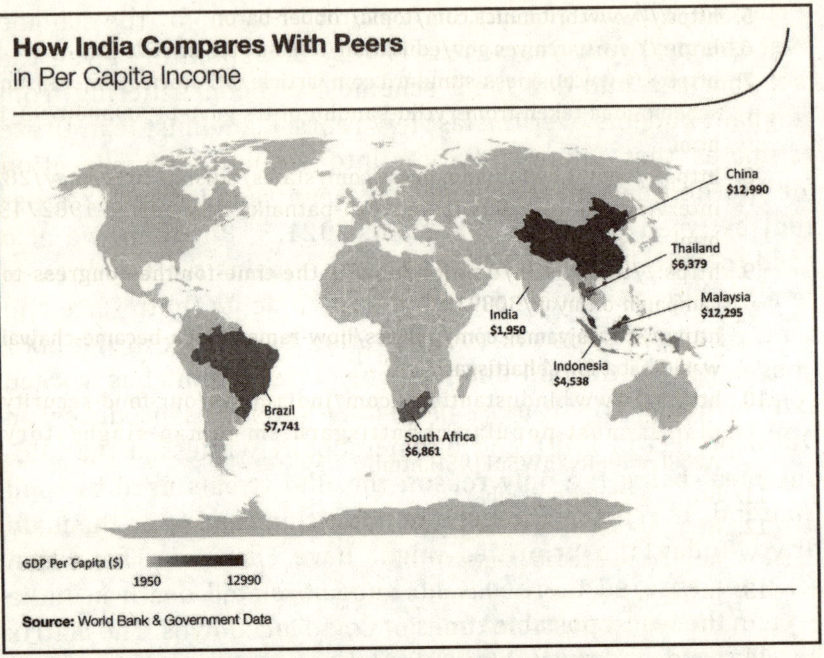

The question that would worry ambitious politicians who want to keep getting re-elected is this: if all the basic necessities of life like health, education, sanitation, drinking water, electricity, roads and highways are fulfilled, what welfare measures will they adopt to keep luring voters? You can accuse politicians of being many things. But you can't accuse them of not being adaptive, pro-active and innovative. The next generation of pro-incumbency stars will innovate new welfare schemes and measures. Have no doubts about that. We don't!

References

1. https://www.news18.com/news/politics/kejriwal-campaign-begins-4-515064.html
2. https://www.ndtv.com/india-news/lok-sabha-elections-2019-manmohan-singh-narendra-modi-government-left-economy-in-dire-straits-2033290
3. https://www.hindustantimes.com/india-news/cm-shivraj-singh-chouhan-banks-on-schemes-to-better-tally-in-madhya-pradesh-but-faces-risk-of-fatigue/story-65MVSeZNR1pWxvAYrPxYDO.html

4. https://www.merriam-webster.com/dictionary/welfare
5. https://www.britannica.com/topic/robber-baron
6. https://www.archives.gov/education/lessons/fdr-fireside
7. https://www.business-standard.com/article/pti-stories/pm-s-kisan-scheme-idea-taken-from-rythu-bandhu-of-trs-govt-119033000793_1.html
8. https://www.newindianexpress.com/states/odisha/2019/may/28/interview--more-kalias-for-naveen-patnaiks-new-odisha-1982743.html
9. https://theprint.in/opinion/now-is-the-time-for-the-congress-to-campaign-on-nyay/308910/
https://swarajyamag.com/politics/how-raman-singh-became-chawal-waale-baba-for-chhattisgarh
10. https://www.hindustantimes.com/india-news/our-food-security-plan-is-most-popular-chhattisgarh-cm-raman-singh/story-iWqFLofEPhRxXhW5uFUi5H.html
11. https://rchiips.org/nfhs/
12. https://asiahouse.org/news-and-views/amartya-sen-indias-healthcare-education-mess/
13. https://www.deccanherald.com/content/74309/cycling-success-bihar-girl-inspires.html
14. https://www.newindianexpress.com/thesundaystandard/2021/nov/28/madhya-pradeshs-ladli-laxmi-yojana-nurturing-dreams-of-the-daughters-2388981.html
15. https://scroll.in/article/993899/cash-transfers-votes-from-women-and-muslims-7-reasons-why-mamata-banerjee-crushed-bjp-in-bengal
16. https://www.cnbctv18.com/politics/clean-sweep-for-bjp-in-2019-polls-here-are-key-flagship-schemes-which-helped-narendra-modi-win-3440541.htm
17. https://rss.onlinelibrary.wiley.com/doi/pdf/10.1111/j.1740-9713.2019.01271.x
18. https://archive.indianexpress.com/news/the-tragedy-of-prohibition/490493/0
19. https://www.news18.com/news/india/assam-govt-to-shut-down-all-state-run-madrasas-sanskrit-tols-says-himanta-biswa-sarma-2948509.html
20. https://thewire.in/government/pm-poshan-mid-day-meal-scheme-renaming-poor-budget-allocation.

□

4

YOUR WEAKNESS IS MY STRENGTH

There is no doubt that charisma, popularity and even a personality cult are important ingredients to ensure pro-incumbency. As is at least some honesty of purpose in helping the underprivileged voters through innovative welfare schemes. Even a clean and decisive image can play a decisive role. But an oft-ignored factor is the how the persistent weakness of the opposition helps incumbents keep coming back to power. When chief ministers are personally popular, re-election becomes a stroll in the park. And if they are not, winning a re-election is not a cakewalk; but the incumbent struggles and manages to hold on to office. This chapter will analyse both types of weaknesses and strengths.

1998 has been a historic year for the Bharatiya Janata Party. In March that year, a seemingly ragtag coalition called the National Democratic Alliance led by Atal Bihari Vajpayee won a narrow victory in the Lok Sabha elections. Vajpayee was duly sworn is as Prime Minister and it looked as if his government would last longer than the 13 days it had in 1996. The world sat up and took notice when he announced the formal acquisition of nuclear weapons, followed closely by a similar announcement from Pakistan. Vajpayee appeared to be headed for greatness the way Jawaharlal Nehru had predicted many decades ago inside the parliament during a debate.

Amidst all this, hardly anybody except party strategists in the Congress and a section of media professionals who seem to gloat when there is bad news for the BJP noticed the trouble brewing in the Delhi unit of the 'saffron' party. The big bosses were too busy ironing out the nitty-gritty of NDA coalition politics. Back in 1993, the BJP had won a comfortable majority in the first assembly elections after Delhi was made a state (albeit without control over the police as in other full-fledged states). Delhi was considered to be a bastion of the BJP. No one knows if it was a panic driven fire-fighting move or a strategic one when Sushma Swaraj was made the chief minister just a few months before assembly elections were due.

The BJP lost to the Congress; the likeable Sheila Dikshit was made the chief minister and the BJP has NEVER won assembly elections to Delhi after that. That is indeed embarrassing for a party that claims to be the largest in the world and once considered the 'state' of Delhi a backyard bastion. It lost three successive times to a Sheila Dikshit-led Congress between 1998 and 2013 and 'effectively' lost three successive times to Arvind Kejriwal-led Aam Aadmi Party between 2013 and now. Sure, it was the largest party after the 2013 assembly elections. But it was a Congress backed Kejriwal who became the chief minister. He has remained chief minister since then except a brief period of Central rule. Delhi under Sheila Dikshit gave Congress 6 out of 7 seats in the much talked about 2004 elections in which Congress just about managed to become single largest party. If you simply put the six odd Delhi seats in BJP tally, the dynamics would have changed as BJP would have become the single largest party and back-channel talks with DMK, which was part of NDA for six long years till 2004 elections, would have turned the tables. We need to relook at importance of being Sheila Dikshit in the 10 years long revival of Congress between 1998 to 2008. She delivered 7/7 Lok Sabha seats in 2009 with more than 57 per cent vote share. Arvind Kejriwal, even in his back-to-back unbelievable landslides, has not been able to breach the vote share that Sheila Dikshit got for Congress in 2009 elections. She never got her due, but in absence of a good opposition in Delhi, she successfully delivered what no other contemporary CM could ever do. Forget about vacuum of leadership in opposition, even if you talk about popularity of leaderships within the same party, you just need to watch the recording of 2010 Commonwealth Games opening ceremony.

While each Congress politician present in the glittering ceremony was humiliatingly booed by the public sitting in the stadium, the only person cheered by them was their Chief Minister. If even Sheila Dikshit could not overcome the negativity propagated by UPA-2 in 2013 Assembly elections, the verdict of 2014 was damn easy to read.

Just imagine this: here is a political party BJP, that has grown to be so formidably large that it has completely replaced the once mighty Congress as the fulcrum of Indian politics. It has breached the south fortress by winning Karnataka and is fast emerging as a serious contender in Telangana in last few years. The fact that separate statehood for Telangana was originally a BJP-led issue which they dumped under pressure of Chandrababu Naidu under coalition dharma (or rather drama, to be precise) and gave away that movement on a platter to KCR, has a lot to do with the impeding rise of BJP in the state. Meanwhile, It has won Assam twice; where under similar coalition drama it allowed AGP to delay an almost certain arrival of BJP by almost 15 years. The coalition dharma to rule at centre did put the BJP growth plan in different state in a long hibernation, particularly in many states which were considered smaller and more inconsequential than even a minor regional party. It has silenced the sniggers of critics by winning Haryana twice. It has more than 300 Lok Sabha seats, winning 7 out of 7 in Delhi, both in 2014 and 2019. It has a towering and arguably the most popular ever prime minister of India in the form of Narendra Modi. All three municipal corporations of Delhi have been ruled by the BJP for ages. And yet, when it comes to the assembly elections, it has failed, and failed again and again since 1993.

No Strong Regional Leaders or Narratives

This seemingly inexplicable weakness of an opposition party or alliance is also a key factor behind the pro-incumbency phenomenon in Indian politics witnessed in this century. We will see later in slightly more detail how the once seemingly but by now clearly terminal decline of the Congress and its myriad weaknesses of the party helped fuel the pro incumbency 'waves'.

But the 'weak' party in Delhi assembly elections is the BJP. As the chart shows, the BJP has managed to consistently win around 35 per cent of the vote share in the state since 1993. Except that one year, Sheila Dikshit ensured that the Congress vote share remained above the BJP till 2013. After that, Arvind Kejriwal has simply gobbled up the traditional Congress vote (leaving it with zero seats in 2015 and 2020) and added some of his own, leading to two successive historic mandates, leaving the BJP embarrassed, red-faced and humiliated.

Before the assembly elections of 2020 happened, journalists Roshan Kishore and Vishan Mohammed Kawoosa wrote an insightful piece for the *Hindustan Times*: "Delhi, compared to other Hindi belt states, does not have a significant number of people who live in abject poverty. According to the 2015-16 National Family and Health Survey (NFHS), the share of households belonging to the lowest wealth quintile—lowest 20 per cent of the population of India—is much less in Delhi than in other states, just 0.2 per cent.

This also means that the share of people who would have benefitted from the flagship welfare programmes launched by the Modi government is much lower in Delhi....The AAP, on the other hand, is banking on gains from its own popular welfare model. The schemes include zero water bill up to 20,000 litres of monthly consumption, zero electricity bill up to 200 units of monthly consumption; and subsidies for those who consume up to 400 units; improvements in government schools and hospitals and opening of Mohalla clinics, free travel in DTC buses for women, caps on fee hike in private schools, etc. ...If the AAP retains power in a comprehensive manner, it will mean that a governance-driven, ideologically agonistic brand of politics can hope to counter the BJP."[1] Their analysis proved to be eerily prescient.

Can demographic changes in the city state explain this persistent weakness of an otherwise powerful party like the BJP? Once upon a time, Delhi was dominated by Punjabis and other Hindus who were Partition refugees. They found comfort in the 'pro-Hindu' rhetoric of the Jan Sangh which became the BJP in 1980. No wonder, the Delhi BJP was dominated by Punjabi leaders till recently. But demographics have changed and a major share of the voters belong to 'Purvanchal', mostly Bihar and Uttar Pradesh. And herein lies the dilemma. In Lok Sabha elections, the same 'Purvanchalis' vote overwhelmingly for the BJP, giving it a 57 per cent vote share and 7 out of 7 seats. The Purvanchalis also overwhelmingly prefer the BJP in their own states during Lok Sabha elections and to a lesser extent in assembly elections. And yet, when it comes to assembly elections in Delhi, it is Arvind Kejriwal for them. The BJP now has prominent 'Purvanchali' faces in Delhi with Lok Sabha MP and popular Bhojpuri star Manoj Tiwari leading the campaign. It resulted in nothing except more humiliation by Kejriwal. The message and the lesson is clear: you may be a formidable national party with a Lok Sabha majority. But you also need vote catching, popular and mass leaders at the state level to win assembly elections. Simply relying on the charisma of one man, Narendra Modi, will not help.

As assembly elections since 2018 have shown, the BJP has lost elections in Chhattisgarh, Rajasthan, Madhya Pradesh and failed to win a majority in Karnataka. In 2019, it lost Jharkhand and Odisha, just about scraped through in Haryana and was hoodwinked by the Shiv Sena in Maharashtra. In 2020, it lost Delhi and its alliance barely eked out a narrow win in Bihar. If the Congress had not asked for more than what it could chew, and contested only about 35 seats rather than 70 seats where it struggled even to find proper candidates, we would have easily seen Tejashwi Yadav as CM of Bihar in that election. In 2021, it was humbled by Mamata Banerjee in West Bengal, won in Assam again and formed an alliance government in Puducherry. It is not a relevant factor in Tamil Nadu and Kerala which also went to polls in 2021. This is almost like the 1980s where the Congress was dominant in national politics but kept losing assembly elections. In November, 2020, journalist Nistula Hebbar quoted analyst Rahul Verma after herself pointing out how the BJP in state politics was a lamb compared to the lion tithe party was in Lok Sabha elections: "According to political analyst Rahul Verma, co-author of the well-regarded book *Ideology and Identity*, the BJP going into polls without Prime Minister Modi's strong presence is a problem for the party. "Prime Minister Modi is the most charismatic face that the BJP has and has a proven record of affecting the vote, but when it comes to faces at the state level, the Opposition has an advantage, which is going to be the case in the upcoming elections too," he said.[2] Both were accurate in their assessment when the same reasons led to Mamata Banerjee sweeping aside the seemingly formidable BJP challenge in the 2021 West Bengal assembly polls.

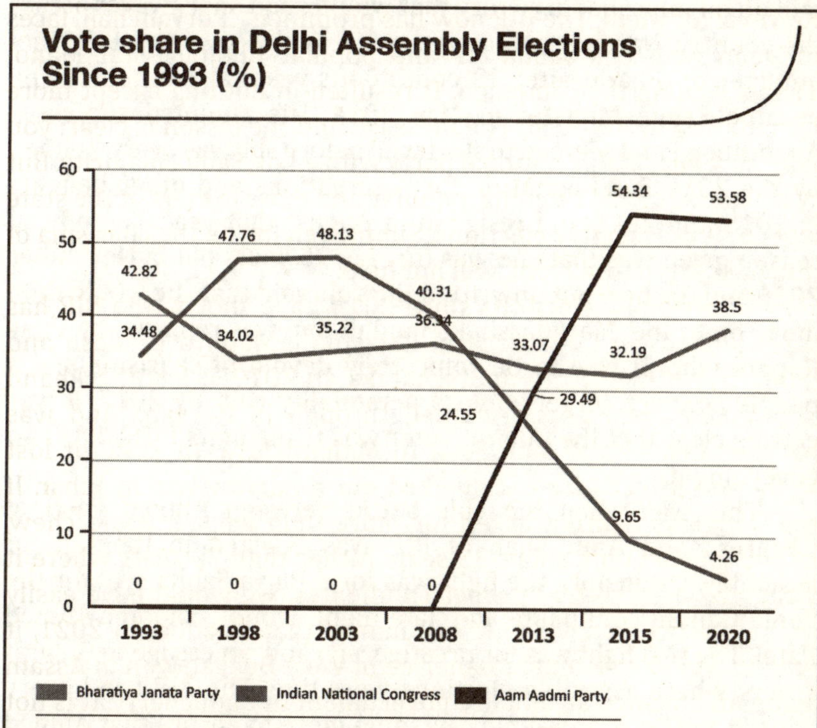

Note: AAP was formed in 2012 and contested its first election in 2013

Source: Election Commission of India

The Gujarat Agony for Congress

As Delhi shows, you can be a virtually permanent 'weak' opposition despite a respectable vote share of 35 per cent. The agony of the Congress in Gujarat is even more acute. It has not been able to defeat the BJP in assembly elections since 1995.

Remember, this was the party that won a massive 149 out 182 seats in 1985 by stitching up an unassailable alliance of Patels, Muslims, Kshatriyas and Dalits. Even today, the party wins around 40 per cent of the vote share in assembly elections. Parties in states like Maharashtra, Bihar, Uttar Pradesh, Tamil Nadu, Kerala and many others would die or kill for a 40 per cent vote share. But even that doesn't help the Congress in Gujarat.

For a while in 2017, it looked as if the Congress could finally pull off an improbable victory that would send shockwaves across the country. Narendra Modi was gone as the towering BJP chief minister of Gujarat after 13 continuous years at the helm as he became Prime Minister in May 2014. His anointed successor Anandiben Patel seemed to start well before she was overwhelmed by the 2016 Patel agitation for reservations and other benefits in 2015 and 2016 and resigned in August that year. The official reason given was that she was turning 75 years old in November 2016 and the new but unwritten BJP rule said that she would then move on to the 'Margdarshak Mandal'. She was replaced by Vijay Rupani who proved to be completely devoid of charisma and a people connect, forget about a personality cult. By 2017, it was getting clear that the Gujarat voter was tiring of its BJP MLAs and government.

This was when the epic battle between Ahmed Patel of Congress and Amit Shah of BJP was enacted in the Gujarat assembly. Ostensibly, the fight was for a Rajya Sabha seat for the Sonia Gandhi confidante and 'late night' trouble-shooter Ahmed Patel. The real fight was for prestige, ego and a message to Gujarat voters where assembly elections were due. The BJP tried every trick in the book and some say, some more to ensure that Ahmed Patel lost. The Congress was not sitting twitching thumbs. Its government in Karnataka offered five-star resorts to the Congress MLAs in the state and kept them in gilded luxury to prevent any defections. There was high drama on the day of the voting and the matter went to the Election Commission of India which ruled in favour of Patel after hours of late night hearings and arguments. This was not just an ego boost for Patel but a shot in the arm for the Congress. Youthful leaders like Hardik Patel, Alpesh Thakore and Jignesh Mevani representing various castes allied with the Congress. Vijay Rupani remained as lacklustre as ever. It was only an impassioned and hectic last week of emotional campaigning by Narendra Modi that saved the BJP's bacon. On the day when results were being declared, there were occasions when the Congress led in more seats than the BJP. Pundits on live TV started talking about a monumental upset. That was not to be. Though the BJP failed to touch 100 out of 182 seats in ages, it retained power. The Congress tally improved remarkably to 77; still short of a majority. It won 40 per cent of the votes and it was practically a matter of 10 odd seats which in case flipped, would have resulted in BJP losing the majority. In many states, that 40 per cent vote share would have ensured a comfortable victory for Congress. But not in Gujarat where the BJP vote share touched 50 per cent in the assembly elections. For three decades now, the Congress has failed to bridge this vote share divide as the chart indicates. Wracked now by internal squabbles and a rudderless leadership at the top in Delhi and with Ahmed Patel gone (he passed away in 2021), the odds again look stacked against the Congress in assembly elections due by the end of 2022 though anti-incumbency against the state BJP government remains high. One would like to have a keen eye on the votes polled by AAP in Gujarat and its impact on Congress fortunes, as these will inevitably have an impact on the BJP tally by default.

In a column for the *Hindustan Times*, journalist Rajdeep Sardesai explains why the Congress failed to breach the BJP fortress in 2017: "Almost all of Gujarat's cities have a large aspirational middle class that seeks affluence and rapid growth: Narendra Modi described it as the 'neo-middle class' in the 2012 elections. For this class, the Modi persona symbolises hope of 'achche din', as represented in physical terms by the gleaming flyovers and new townships across these cities. For this class, the Sabarmati River front in Ahmedabad, for example, is held up as an example of 'vikas' as are Surat and Vadodara's multi-storey malls. It is for this class that the image of Modi campaigning in a sea-plane is so attractive: it only strengthens his image as a Superman-like hero.... the Congress's appeal of change resonated in many parts of rural

Gujarat because the Modi model offered no solution to genuine agrarian distress and the prime minister's shrill rhetoric was unappealing. It didn't work in an urban milieu that still sees the prime minister as an agent of an aspirational new order and the Congress as part of a discredited ancient regime."[3] In that column, Sardesai goes on to write that with 43 per cent of its population being urban, the state offers a big advantage to the Congress which is still very strong in rural Gujarat. But as subsequent paragraphs will show, that is not the only problem that the Congress faces as it withers away in state after state.

Congress Versus BJP in Gujarat Assembly Elections Since 1995: Seats Won

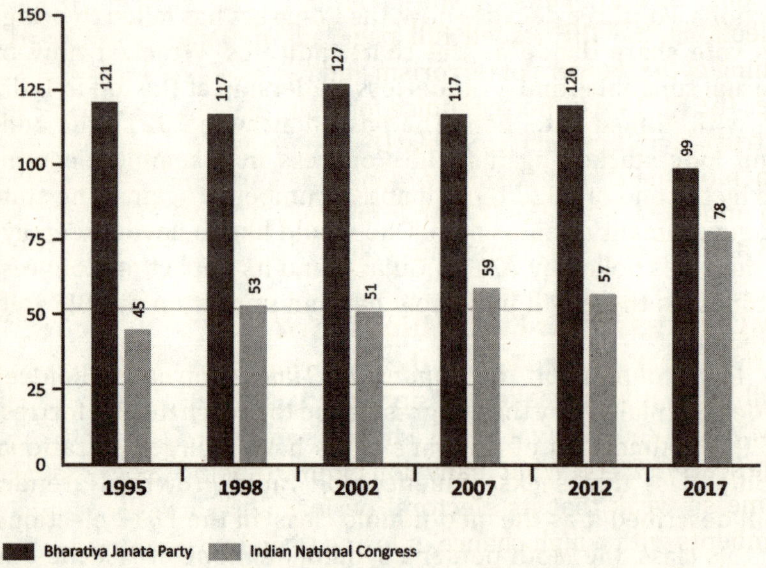

Source: Election Commission of India

When we talk of a 'weak' opposition helping incumbents stay in power, we have seen how even a powerful party like the BJP that rides roughshod over others becomes a meek and weak church mouse when it comes to state assembly elections in Delhi. But then, Arvind Kejriwal is the undisputed choice as chief minister of Delhi even for voters who swear by Narendra Modi as the prime minister. In a C-Voter survey conducted in Delhi on the eve of the 2019 Lok Sabha elections, 65 per cent of respondents said they wanted Modi as the PM. About 60 per cent of the same respondents wanted Kejriwal as the CM of Delhi (see chart). Why Kejriwal scoring over Modi in Delhi, BJP supporters seek consolation from the fact that even the late Sheila Dikshit scored over the then prime minister Atal Bihari Vajpayee in 2003 when the later was at the peak of his popularity. In fact, she was so enormously popular and enjoyed so much goodwill amongst citizens of Delhi that she won three consecutive elections. Even in 2008, when 26/11 happened just before the Delhi assembly elections, the public anger, rather rage was so widespread amongst Indians that it looked as if the Congress and Sheila Dikshit could be in trouble. On the day of elections, the BJP issued full page ads in Delhi newspapers warning of the dangers of terrorism and not so subtly hinting that it (i.e., the BJP) was a better choice for Delhi. No dice. Delhi voters still trusted and preferred Sheila Dikshit. It was only scams, the Anna movement, the Nirbhaya gangrape-cum-murder and the deep unpopularity of the UPA that finally felled her electorally in 2013 after 15 years of continuous rule.

How Congress Pulls Even Allies Down

Her defeat in a symbolised the end of an era for the Congress. We all know it was weakening since the late 1980s as a national party. We all know how it fell to a historic and humiliating 44 Lok Sabha seats in 2014. What many don't know that the Congress has become so weak that its electoral performance actually helped incumbents with a high chance of losing to end up winning again. Gujarat has been described in detail. But elections and results in two more states are telling examples of this fatal weakness. Let's start with the now forgotten 2016 assembly elections of Tamil Nadu. The incumbent chief minister J. Jayalalithaa was facing anti-incumbency. She had won the 2011 assembly elections by leading an alliance where her party was allotted 165 out of the total 234 seats in the assembly. Many wondered how the imperious and aloof 'Amma' with a personality cult of her own would actually run an alliance with an assorted list of parties. In the end, the election results indicated that her Amma image was very much intact and that she might have won without depending on allies. After all, the AIADMK won 150 of the 165 seats given to it; a landslide by any yardstick. It soon became bye bye time for her allies, many of whom rushed into the arms of the rival DMK.

Despite many political; setbacks over the decades and despite the visible ageing of the patriarch M. Karunanidhi, the DMK remained a formidable regional party with a strong grassroots base of cadres that remained steadfastly loyal even during the worst of times; like during the Emergency when many cadres including current chief minister and son of Karunanidhi M.K. Stalin were jailed; or like 2001 when soon after her assembly election victory, Jayalalithaa seemed to have ordered the Tamil Nadu police to not only arrest the former CM Karunanidhi at midnight, but also drag him out his bedroom and his house in front of TV cameras. Anyways, both are now dead and gone and not directly related to the fatal weakness of the Congress.

The 'state' of Indian politics may be driven by pro-incumbency, but it is not as if anti-incumbency has disappeared. By 2015, there were visible cracks in the personality cult of J. Jayalalithaa. Her legions of loyal followers continued to literally idolise and worship her. But the 'non believers' started having doubts. The ongoing trial in corruption charges had once again resurrected the possibly mythical image of J. Jayalalithaa as an empress who had thousands of shoes and sarees. It was around this time that Stalin, who had become the de facto boss of the DMK, sensed an opportunity to stitch a rainbow alliance and oust an increasingly unpopular and even medically ailing Jayalalithaa. Corruption was hardly an issue as like the voters of Lalu Prasad Yadav in Bihar, the Jayalalithaa cult transcended 'small' things like corruption. A powerful alliance against Jayalalithaa was duly formed to fight the 2016 assembly elections.

It was here that the DMK perhaps made the fatal mistake of underestimating the fatal weakness of the Congress party. Sure, the Congress, like all weak negotiators, argued in loud and shrill voices about being given a 'respectably high number' of seats that befitted a more than 100-year-old legacy party; never mind the present reality. In a fit of inexplicable generosity, the DMK allotted 41 seats to contest in the 2016 assembly polls out of 234 seats and kept 180 seats for itself, the balance going to smaller allies. It was a unique election, also from the perspective that Jayalalithaa forced all her alliance partners to contest on her party's symbol of 'two leaves'. She asserted, and won against all odds.

How Congress Spoilt The DMK Chances in 2016 Tamil Nadu Assembly Elections

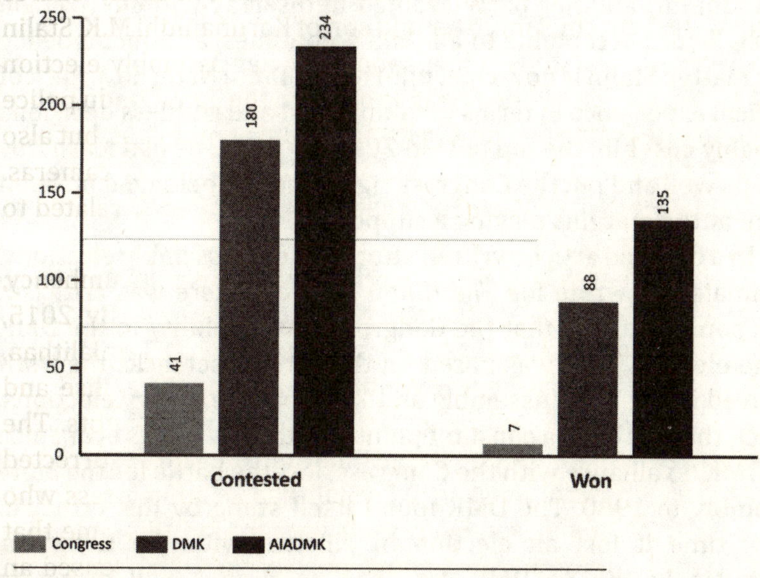

Source: Election Commission of India

In the end, all credit to her for bucking anti-incumbency, fighting like a wounded, ailing and still fierce lioness and winning 135 out of 234 seats: 17 more than the simple majority mark of 118. Most would call it a comfortable majority. But it was a close call and the late Jayalalithaa still owes a note of thanks to Rahul Gandhi for her last hurray before she passed away. The DMK won 88 out of the 180 seats it contested, getting virtually no help from the dilapidated Congress machinery. That works out to a strike rate of almost 49 per cent. The once mighty and now fatally weak Congress managed to win 7 out of the 41 seats it contested; a pathetic strike rate of 17 per cent. What if the Congress had matched the DMK strike rate of 49 per cent? It would have won 20 seats (see chart). The AIADMK tally would have come down to 122, a very narrow majority. It's all hypothetical and germane now, but what if Stalin had put his foot down in 2016 and refused to give so many seats to a decrepit Congress? He did precisely that in 2021 and after creating the usual thunder, the Congress meekly accepted the crumbs offered to it. Jayalalithaa was gone (so was Karunanidhi) and her party seemed in disarray without a single visible leader acceptable to all. And sometimes, anti-incumbency does matter. Stalin is now chief minister of Tamil Nadu now. Lack of political experience in terms of taking hard and ruthless decisions probably cost him the top post in 2016. By 2021, he had learnt his lessons well and put the Congress right where it belonged in Tamil Nadu: at the margins playing a support role.

In a detailed article written after the 2016 assembly elections, P. Ramajayam wrote for *The Hindu Centre*: "There was criticism from some quarters that the Congress was a liability to the DMK in the election. This was based on the serious setbacks the DMK received in the 2011 Assembly and 2014 parliamentary elections. In fact, this has been a constant point of attack by critics ever since the DMK, in alliance with the Congress, lost the battle for the State Assembly in 1980. The DMK found itself stung by this criticism every time it lost an election in alliance with the Congress. Interestingly, the AIADMK, too, had suffered a poll defeat in alliance with the Congress in 1996."[4]

A Bitter Lesson for Young Tejashwi Yadav

If M.K. Stalin was relatively inexperienced in 2016 when he was already 62 years old, the then 30-year-old Tejashwi Yadav was even more so in 2020 when Bihar went for assembly elections. Survey after survey was showing that Nitish Kumar was one of the most unpopular chief ministers. In the C-Voter daily tracker poll, an abysmally low number of respondents were happy with his performance through 2019 and 2020. If there was a clearly visible example of anti-incumbency working against a three-term chief minister. Shivraj Singh Chouhan remained popular even after three terms as chief minister even though he lost narrowly in Madhya Pradesh. If a still popular Chouhan could lose, what chance did an unpopular Nitish Kumar have? Opinion polls all showed a very close fight; with some predicting Nitish Kumar would scrape through while others predicted Tejashwi Yadav could become one of youngest ever chief ministers of a major state. He could feel, smell and sense victory in the response crowds gave him during yatras and rallies.

But then Tejashwi Yadav not only repeated the fatal mistake made by M.K. Stalin in 2016, he compounded and magnified it. The Bihar assembly has 243 seats. As usual, the Congress started making loud and some would say, extraordinary, demands over the number of seats it wanted to contest. That's all part of the game when seat distribution negotiations start. Lalu Prasad Yadav was still in jail (or a guest house if you must) or in hospital and anyway not allowed to campaign. He dispensed long distance advice to Tejashwi though there were rumours that the two did meet facilitated by the UPA government in Jharkhand. But that is immaterial. What matters is that Lalu Yadav is known to have a soft corner for Sonia Gandhi and 'her' Congress. Nobody besides the two will never know what prompted them; but the Congress was given 70 seats to contest. The RJD kept 144 for itself, the balance going to other smaller alliance partners. When the results were announced, it turned out that the NDA led by Nitish Kumar had eked out the narrowest of victories with 125 seats, just three more than the majority mark. The UPA or the MGB (Mahagathbandhan) was not too far behind with 110 seats.

Once again, the Congress proved its mettle by winning a miserable 19 out of 70 seats; a strike rate of 27 per cent while the RJD won 75 out of the 144 seats it contested; a strike rate of 52 per cent. Another alliance partner the CPI (Marxist-Leninist) won 12 out of the 19 seats it contested; a strike rate of 63 per cent. Forget the CPI (ML), if the Congress had managed a strike rate of even 50 per cent given the widespread unpopularity of Nitish Kumar and serious allegations of corruption, poor governance and lawlessness, it would have won 35 seats. That would have meant 126 seats for the Tejashwi Yadav-led alliance and 109 seats for the Nitish Kumar-led alliance. Guess who would have been chief minister of Bihar? Even with a much more modest 40 per cent strike rate for the Congress, the MGB would have won 119 seats to 116 by the NDA. Guess whom the five AIMIM elected members would have eventually supported in the name of secularism.

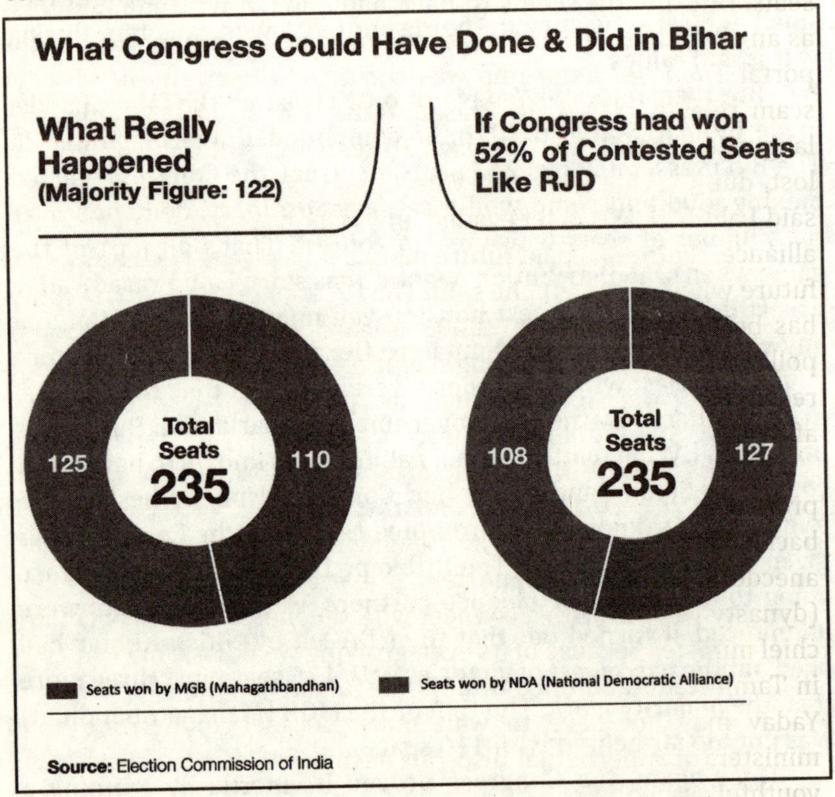

Journalist C.G. Manoj wrote for *The Indian Express* even as the final results were being declared and singled out the Congress for its miserable performance. He pointed out how it lost badly in direct contests with the BJP and fared poorly even in the Muslim-dominated Seemanchal region. He quoted CPI(ML)

general secretary Dipankar Bhattacharya who said. "I think if we could have formed an alliance earlier and the seat allocation was more rational...For example...I think at least 50 seats for the Left and 50 seats for the Congress would have probably been a more reasonable, fair distribution of seats. That could have possibly affected the results better."[5]

One year after that, the RJD refused to share any of the two seats that went to by polls for the state assembly. Both the seats had been won in 2020 by the JD(U) and it successfully retained both seats. But the RJD seems to have had enough with the Congress as an ally that is proving more of a burden. In an interview to the portal *The Print* before he was convicted in yet another fodder scam related case, Lalu Prasad Yadav had used his trademark language to proclaim: "We gave 70 seats to the Congress but they lost, due to which we lost. Vote Congress ke paas hai hi nahi..." said Lalu. The RJD chief evaded any response on the future of the alliance, "Future ka baat future mein dekha jayega (will talk about future when it comes)," he said. The RJD-Congress alliance, which has been in place since 2000—except for the 2009 Lok Sabha polls when the Congress fought alone—is already teetering, if two recent party decisions are any indication."[6] It finally ended a year after the assembly election disaster.

At least the BJP has not taken down anyone else with its prolonged misery in Delhi. But the Congress, one could argue backed by electoral data and evidence, apart from apocryphal anecdotal tales from reporters did prevent two mass leaders (dynasty yes, but with a connect with the masses) from becoming chief minister because of its ever-growing weakness; once in 2016 in Tamil Nadu and once in 2020 in Bihar. Who knows, Tejashwi Yadav may not have to wait more decades to become chief minister; or a perpetual also-ran despite his dynastic, caste and youthful credentials.

There are other states in which the seemingly terminal decline of the Congress has not played spoilsport for other parties who happen to be allies. But is has definitely helped an incumbent winning with bigger and bigger margins in every election as even its core base of voters starts deserting the Congress. A classic example is Odisha, where the terminal decline of the Congress is not the primary reason for Naveen Patnaik winning five consecutive terms and looking good for a sixth when elections are due in two years. But it has made the task of repeatedly winning elections easier for him. In the 2019 assembly elections, the vote share of the Congress party slipped below 10 per cent; a sure sign that it is heading for complete irrelevance in Odisha, like it already is irrelevant in Tamil Nadu, Andhra Pradesh, Bihar, Uttar Pradesh and West Bengal amongst others.

The Odisha Files

There are two things about Odisha. The first is that it was one of the states that gave clear warning signals to the Congress in 1967 that it could not take voter support for granted. But for two unusual elections in the 1980s that delivered a thumping majority to the party in 1980 and 1985, it has been a classic case of a slow, gradual and painful march towards extinction. The second is that the most towering political personality of the state is not Naveen Patnaik, but his father Biju Patnaik even two and a half decades after his death. Biju Patnaik was a real-life legend. A trained and experienced pilot, he himself flew soldiers to Srinagar in 1947-48 when 'tribals' from the then newly created Pakistan invaded Jammu & Kashmir. He flew a dramatic rescue mission to Indonesia to spirit away the then President Sukarno, his pregnant wife and others when a military coup had overthrown the popularly elected leader. It was during this rescue flight that the former President of Indonesia Meghawati Sukarnoputri was born and named by Biju Patnaik; a fact still acknowledged by the lady herself. Meghawati, because she was literally born and rescued in the Megha (the clouds) and Sukarnoputri because she was daughter of Sukarno. He was a true maverick who became a successful industrialist and then lost interest. He encouraged his two sons and a daughter to develop a taste for reading and all things eclectic. His daughter is Gita Mehta, a successful author married to one of the most powerful men globally in the publishing industry; Sonny Mehta of Alfred Knopf. Truly, they rarely make men like Biju Patnaik any more, forget politicians.

Coming back to Congress and Odisha, after the 1967 warning, most of the 1970s was spent in short-lived Congress and Janata Party governments, apart from President's rule and the Emergency. The dismal failure of the Janata Party experiment led to a spectacular comeback for Indira Gandhi as Prime Minister and the Congress in the driving seat in most states, including Odisha. The chief minister of Odisha then, J.B. Patnaik could hardly be called charismatic or even a leader with a mass appeal and a direct connect with the voters. But by then, Indira Gandhi had no need for politically tall and popular leaders. By 1984, it was evident that he and his government were not very popular or rated highly; though these are subjective and possibly opinionated reports that came in the media. Biju Patnaik had started thundering again. But on October 30, 1984, Indira Gandhi addressed a public rally in Odisha and flew back to Delhi.

The next day, on October 31, 1984, she was assassinated by her bodyguards. This book offers a homage both to her and to the thousands of Sikhs butchered in Delhi and other cities as an act of 'retribution'. But then it moves on. There was special sympathy for Indira Gandhi in Odisha because her last public meeting was organised there. Suddenly, there was a massive sympathy wave in the national and most of the state assembly elections that followed. The Congress, despite the seeming unpopularity of the chief minister won an even bigger mandate. The Congress actually won about 51 per cent of the popular vote share in the assembly elections, an unprecedented feat in the state (see chart). But that was soon squandered away as the chief minister J.B. Patnaik seemed to become even more unpopular with voters in Odisha. Whether media professionals are doing their work of reporting honestly and objectively without masquerading their personal prejudices as the opinion of the masses usually represented by 'taxi drivers', is ultimately decided when election results are out. In the 1990 assembly elections, the Congress vote share plummeted from 51 per cent to less than 30 per cent and the number of seats won crashed from 117 out of a total of 147 to just 10.

How The Congress Collapsed

The popular 'Bull of Odisha' as he was popularly known, the ace pilot-cum-lapsed-industrialist-cum-maverick politician was back at the helm. But ever energetic as he was, age was catching up with Biju Patnaik. He was already 74 years old when he took oath as chief minister of Odisha in 1990. Though he remained extremely popular with the people of Odisha, they were not terribly fond of the way his government was being run. A visibly ageing and tiring Biju Patnaik conducted the last major campaign of his life when assembly elections became due in 1995.

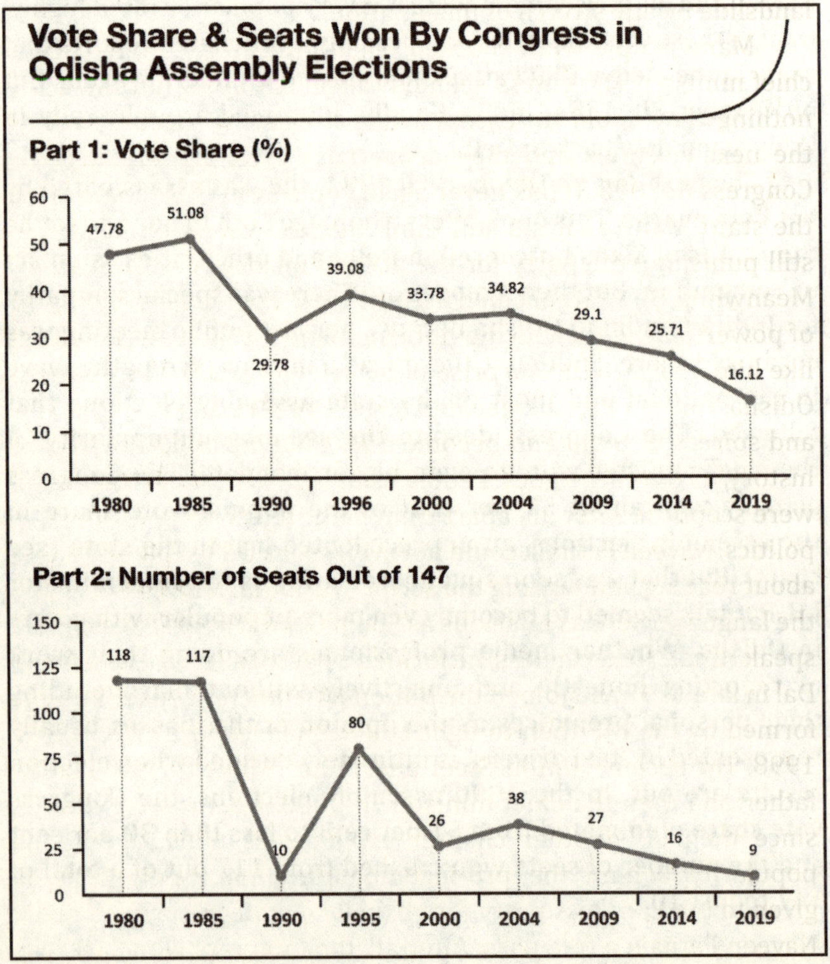

Do remember, his son Naveen Patnaik was then what could be described as an erudite socialite based in Delhi, miles away from anything remotely political. The Congress was an alternative to the government run by Biju Patnaik who was already 79 years old. But voters were wary of seeing the unpopular J.B. Patnaik come back as the chief minister. The electorate was 'promised' by the party that another leader other than J.B. Patnaik would be chief minister if the Congress was voted back to power. The voters swallowed the bait; though not very enthusiastically as the party won 80 seats, a comfortable majority in an assembly with 147 seats; but not a landslide by any stretch of imagination.

Many people were shocked when J.B. Patnaik came back as chief minister. The voters seemed to feel betrayed. But there was nothing they could do except when it came to elections. Come the next elections and they delivered a crushing defeat to the Congress in 2000. It has never again come even close to power in the state. Many analysts still think that the voters of Odisha are still punishing the party for the alleged misdeeds of J.B. Patnaik. Meanwhile, Biju Patnaik died in April 1997 and left behind a clutch of powerful leaders who did not command a pan-state popularity like him. Much to the surprise of his friends and to the people of Odisha, Naveen Patnaik decided to give up a life of genteel parties and soirées in Delhi and become a fulltime politician. The rest is history, as the cliché goes. People in Odisha who adored his father were sceptical. After all, apart from being a complete neophyte in politics, Naveen Patnaik could not even speak Odiya fluently, forget about reading and writing the script. His initial attempts to speak the language were as hilarious as Sonia Gandhi's early attempts to speak Hindi! Nevertheless, he formed a party called the Biju Janata Dal in late 1997 and joined the National Democratic Alliance being formed by the BJP then to fight Lok Sabha elections due in early 1998. He became Union Steel and Mines Minister just like his father and then the chief minister in 2000. He has kept winning since then. As another chapter explains his unusual personal popularity behind the pro-incumbency, some credit must be given to the Congress party for virtually disintegrating and giving Naveen Patnaik a free pass. After all, the Congress won 118 seats in 1980. That was the peak. In 2019, it won 9 seats. Perhaps better than the zero in West Bengal last year, but then.

Author Sanjeev Kumar Nayak had forecast the almost complete demise of the party in a January 2019 column for *The Sunday Guardian*, months before the elections were due: "In a pale shade of the party's state of affairs at the national level, the Congress is going through its worst phase in the state too now. Emptying the party ranks like never before, any Congress leader worth his salt is deserting the party for a safer haven these days. Two of its sitting MLAs quit the party and joined the ruling Biju Janata Dal (BJD), while long-time party strongman and former Union minister Srikant Jena as well as ex-MLA and Dalit leader Krushna Chandra Sagaria were expelled last fortnight.

In another bad omen for the party, one of its veterans, Naba Kishore Das—who had managed to hold Congress' fort in western Odisha when the party was facing a rout in other parts of the state—left it last week to join the BJD ranks. Moreover, party's Bijepur by election candidate, Pranay Sahu has also joined the BJD. These developments have certainly delivered a death blow to the age-old party as no pocket in Odisha is left winnable for it anymore."[7]

We started the analysis and examples of 'weak' rivals helping incumbents keep winning elections with the perpetual misery of the BJP in Delhi. Let's end it too with the almost terminal decline of its ally, the regional party Asom Gana Parishad whose youthful leaders once exhilarated Assam by openly defying the mighty Indira Gandhi even after her spectacular comeback as prime minister in 1980. Called the All Assam Students Union (AASU) in its early avatar, it had launched an agitation against 'foreigners' and 'illegal immigrants' in 1979 that paralysed the state and made even the conduct of Lok Sabha elections difficult. Even the 1981 Census could not be conducted in Assam because of the boycott. Against good advice, assembly elections were called for in 1983 that turned out to be a farce and a tragedy. During the election campaign, more than 3,000 Muslims were 'officially' massacred in a place called Nellie. The actual numbers were almost certainly higher. The AASU was adamant about one thing: citizenship or domicile in 1951 or prior to that should be the cut-off year for those wanting to live, work and vote in Assam. Assam was literally burning. Then Rajiv Gandhi became prime minister and won a historic mandate in Lok Sabha elections. Apart from Punjab, he sought peace through talks even in Assam. Thus was born the historic Assam Accord where the domicile cut off was finalised at 1971. This was followed by the birth of another regional party the Asom Gana Parishad led by the former student leaders of AASU.

AGP Sparkles, and then Completely Fizzles Out

Elections were called in 1985 after the Assam accord and an astonishing 92 'independents' won while the Congress was reduced to 25 seats in an assembly of 126. The AGP formed the government. High expectations often lead to disillusionment and that is what happened in the 1990 elections with the Congress winning 66 seats and the AGP crashing to 19. The BJP put up a 'decent' performance by its then standards by winning 10 seats. Remember, that was the era of anti-incumbency and the AGP bounced back again forming a government by winning 59 seats and taking the help of some 'allies'. That was the last time AGP won Assam and has steadily declined over the years; now a very junior partner of the BJP. The Congress made a spectacular comeback in 2001, winning almost 40 per cent of the vote share way above the combined share of allies BJP and AGP. The veteran Congress parliamentarian Tarun Gogoi went back to Assam to become chief minister.

By 2006, the Tarun Gogoi government was not very popular with Assam voters and anti-incumbency should have done its work. The Congress vote share fell almost 10 per cent to just about 31 per cent. But BJP and AGP were no longer allies. The AGP vote share stagnated at around 20 per cent and that of the BJP was rising, but very slowly and marginally. Even with just 53 seats, Tarun Gogoi became chief minister again for the second consecutive time having managed the support of 'allies'. By then, people had started to lose hope in AGP again offering a coherent alternative and the BJP was still struggling to gain more ground. By now, a 'Muslim' party named AUDF led by a perfume baron Badruddin Ajmal was winning a lot of Muslim-dominated seats with his supporters openly batting for immigrants from Bangladesh. Polarisation and the rise of the BJP was just a matter of time. Tarun Gogoi broke an Assam record by becoming the chief minister for the third successive time with the Congress once touching a vote share of 40 per cent and 78 seats. Assam voters rejected the AGP, its vote share falling further to 16.5 per cent. The Congress gained the most as the BJP stagnated even in 2011. The 'Muslim' party which had by then become AIUDF won a bigger vote share than the BJP and many more seats.

Clearly, while Tarun Gogoi was popular, he was not in the league of 'state' superstars like J. Jayalalithaa, Narendra Modi, Mamata Banerjee and to an extent Shivraj Singh Chouhan. It was the virtually terminal, albeit terminal decline of the AGP and the inability of the BJP to grow its support base that played a big role in him winning three successive terms. We have already mentioned how the rise of the 'Muslim' party AIDUF in Assam led to polarisation. The rise of a 'Hindu' party like the BJP became almost inevitable. It happened so swiftly and so massively in the 2016 elections that everyone was stunned and Tarun Gogoi was finally humbled. The BJP vote share jumped from less than 12 per cent in 2011 to almost 30 per cent in 2016 and it formed the government in Assam with 60 seats. The pro-incumbency phenomenon was back in 2021 with the BJP vote share rising further to a tad more than 33 per cent. By the way, the AGP got to contest 29 seats as a junior ally of BJP, managed to almost touch 8 per cent in vote share and won 9 seats. It is perhaps the only major regional party that has ruled a state fading into irrelevance with time. It looks like Mayawati and the Bahujan Samaj Party to join that inglorious group.

In a piece for the portal *The Print*, Karishma Hasnat wrote in March, 2021: "Basanta Deka, educationist and AJP Convenor who had also played a pivotal role in the formation of AGP, believes the party has lost ground because of absence of commitment: "They fundamentally lacked commitments. From the beginning, the AGP leadership has shown lust for power, drifting away from responsibilities, which is now evident in Atul Bora and Keshav

Mahanta's (state minister) leadership. Political activist Shyamkanu Mahanta said, "Without administrative experience, a government cannot run. It was a mistake. They joined and failed. There was no high command to guide them."

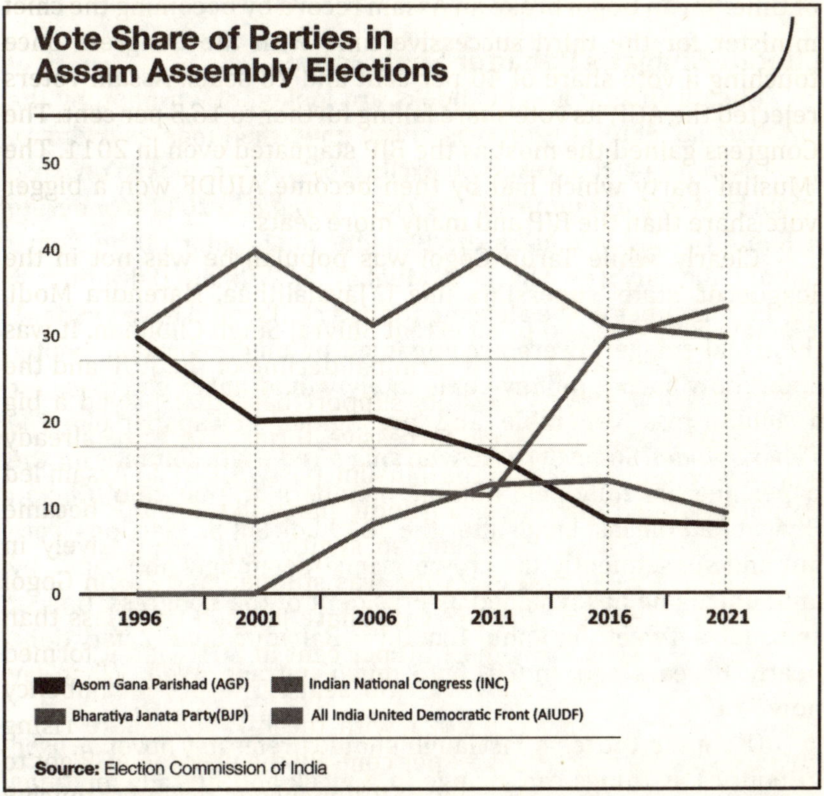

In 1985, the new party inherited a collapsing administration from the Congress. From agitational politics, the leaders had to negotiate the task of governing a state with complex multicultural scenario and limited resources, with deficit in revenue earning. The Assam movement's moral support base was the Assamese middle class. But mis-governance and the failure to address the issue of foreigners soon alienated the middle class. Sarbananda Sonowal, while resigning from the AGP to join the BJP in 2011, had claimed that he was upset because the party was building close relations with All India United Democratic Front (AIUDF) and its chief Badruddin Ajmal while sidelining the illegal immigrants' issue. He had hit out at Mahanta, questioning his growing closeness with Ajmal and for extending tacit support to AIUDF's communal agenda."[8]

Chetan Bhagat's Bahadur Shah Zafar?

Chetan Bhagat and his books are looked down upon by the 'intellectual' elite as examples of the unwashed masses trying to gatecrash into a club reserved exclusively for the chosen ones. So when he wrote a column for *The Times of India* in 2011 wondering if Rahul Gandhi would be the Bahadur Shah Zafar of the Nehru Gandhi dynasty (or The Last Mughal as William Dalrymple, a lifetime member of the aforementioned club would have written), the usual sniggers were accompanied by much nostalgic banter about how such a Johnny-come-lately would never get space for a column in a 'venerable' and 'prestigious' newspaper like *The Times of India*. Some of those who sniggered write columns for the paper and are fully paid lifetime members of 'that club'. Chetan Bhagat had the last laugh after the 2019 Lok Sabha elections were out and subsequently the crown prince 'seemingly abdicated' by announcing he has resigned as President of the Congress. Bhagat sent out a Tweet: 'Is Rahul Gandhi = Bahadur Shah Zafar', done nearly 8 years ago, in 2011, to much outrage. Well. What say now?"[8]

Of course, the term 'last laugh' should preferably never be used in politics as things can change in a week and literally anything is possible. Anything, like Rahul Gandhi becoming the Prime Minister of India in 2024. But the odds of that happening would be like the odds of winning a lottery. It's not as if the Congress cannot boast of pro-incumbency champions in the 21st century. There was Dr. Manmohan Singh whose brave stand in favour of the Indo-US nuclear deal and whose even braver stand of not succumbing to blackmail by the Left parties even if his government fell persuaded millions of urban voters to root for him in the 2009 Lok Sabha elections for a second successive term. Of course, a then booming economy also helped. Then there were Sheila Dikshit and Tarun Gogoi who won three consecutive terms as chief ministers. If you stretch things a bit, Digvijay Singh did win a second consecutive term as chief minister of Madhya Pradesh in 1998. But today; in 2022? The cupboard looks bare unless Bhupesh Baghel in Chhattisgarh and Ashok Gehlot in Rajasthan pull off a near miracle in late 2023. In state after state, the Congress just seems withering away, as we mentioned elsewhere.

Of course, it would be grossly unfair to single out Rahul Gandhi for all the ills that seem to cling on to the Grand Old Party like an army of leeches sucking out its life blood. Some argue that the decline of the Congress began when Rahul was just about born and Indira Gandhi won a thumping victory in the 1971 Lok Sabha elections. It was she who marginalised and emasculated strong state-level Congress leaders after that victory. The effect was: barring a few states, the Congress took about a generation to start ceding ground either to the BJP or to regional parties. For them, Rahul Gandhi is a brave and well-meaning captain trying to salvage a ship that was already hurtling towards an iceberg. Some others are not so charitable. Journalist and author Tavleen Singh has been writing a column called "The Fifth Column" for *The Indian Express* for decades. In the one published in April 2019 after Rahul Gandhi held a press conference to announce the cash transfer scheme called NYAY, she wrote: "The thing I find most repugnant about socialist feudalism in our political parties is the sense of smug entitlement that it breeds in heirs. Nearly all the heirs who inherit political parties and careers (and there are too many) have this unfortunate quality, but none more so than Rahul Gandhi. And, why should he not? He is after all heir to the Dynasty that has ruled India for most of our years as an independent country. And, is today seen by many political pundits as the main challenger to Narendra Modi in the elections that begin this week.

Rahul wears this heavy mantle with arrogance rather than humility. At no time was this more evident than when he released the Congress party's election manifesto last week. As he listed the many, many plans he has to rescue India from the ruin he claims that Modi has wrought in the past five years, I wondered if he knew how arrogant he sounds. Does he know that he sounds more like an entitled prince than the man who wants to lead the world's largest democracy?"[9] Many Indian voters seemed to agree with the strong words used by Singh. For not only did Rahul Gandhi lead the Congress to another rout, he lost the family pocket borough Amethi to Smriti Irani by more than 50,000 votes. The same Smriti Irani about whom Priyanka Gandhi had smiled sniggeringly and said "Smriti Who?" when asked by media persons about the challenger to her brother.

Those were the Days

In his initial years as a politician and an MP, it appeared as if Rahul Gandhi displayed tremendous promise. Political pundits, even those who were not Pavlovian sycophants of the Dynasty, concurred. The Indian and global media was keen to witness the rise of the fifth generation. Journalist Dean Nelson of *The Sunday Times* of London travelled with Rahul Gandhi and Gandhi family loyalist Captain Satish Sharma on a whirlwind tour of Amethi and Raebareli. As visibly adoring crowds waved at the crown prince, he told Nelson: "When he (Rajiv Gandhi) died, he was doing certain things to modernise the country and he was cut short. What he was doing was on the right track. He was bridging the gap between modern India and traditional India. India is rising but I want to see it compete successfully with every other country". As the jubilant crowd cheered and roared on, Sharma made a prediction: "One thousand per cent he will lead the Congress. Manmohan Singh is a great Prime Minister but after that it is Rahul. Look out there. See what is happening. It is destiny. It is beyond anyone's control. He is a free marketeer. He is pro-business. With ten years in the government, he will change the face of India. It is destiny."[10] Among other ones, the prediction about Rahul Gandhi being a pro-business free marketeer sounds a bit odd 16 years down the road.

But there was tantalising hope in 2009 Lok Sabha elections when the Congress surprised even its supporters by jumping from 145 to 206 seats. Analysts and sycophants were quick to hail the young Prince Charming Rahul Gandhi as the party won 22 seats in Uttar Pradesh and swept urban India. Never mind the fact that Congress War Room was not even hopeful for 5 seats in Uttar Pradesh. When C-Voter Tracker predicted 20 plus seats for Congress, one of the authors got calls from so many of the cabinet members in disbelief that one wondered if they actually are confident of a victory in 2009. That is hardly surprising, given the fact that in a personal conversation late Congress stalwart Arjun Singh told the same author right after 2004 drama that it was okay for BJP to be puzzled on why they lost. "Hamare yahan to log ye samajh nahin pa rahey hain ki wo jeetey kyon" (Guys on my side are unable to understand how the hell they actually won) he told the author with his trademark silent smile. He definitely did not believe in plain luck. A rarity among that generation of Congressmen, he always wanted to know the hard reasons for his defeat, and harder reasons for his victory. But it looked as if the prophecy made by Satish Sharma about destiny might come true, after all in 2009. This feeling was reinforced when the self-effacing Dr. Manmohan Singh publicly stated that he would happily step aside and make way for Rahul Gandhi if the later and the party so desired. That was probably the high point and the peak of the political career of Rahul Gandhi. It has been downhill since then. The number of electoral losses suffered by the Congress since Rahul Gandhi became the de facto inheritor in 2009 is probably close to the number of test centuries scored by Sachin Tendulkar. That includes two humiliating and shattering defeats in successive Lok Sabha elections when Rahul Gandhi was prime ministerial candidate. But he, his sister and mother remain the supreme decision makers.

After the BJP lost two successive Lok Sabha elections in 2009, Atal Bihari Vajpayee was old, ailing and no longer active. L.K. Advani was the prime ministerial candidate in 2009 and wanted to be in 2014. The BJP would have none of it. From ground up, there came a clamour for Narendra Modi to be the candidate; a clamour that could not be ignored even by L.K. Advani though he sulked for a long time. Today, the BJP is indisputably led in an authoritarian manner by Modi along with his aide Amit Shah. There is no question of dissent. But do you think BJP workers will still bow down before the duo if they lose two successive Lok Sabha elections? This is anyway not a treatise on intra-party democracy. We only highlighted the decline of Congress as a reason for pro-incumbency becoming the dominant phenomenon. As far as the phenomenon of Modi goes, he, just like what Arjun Singh said, with a twist. He definitely believes spiritually in concept of destiny, but does not believe in anything called plain luck. A rarity among the present generation of BJP leaders, he always wants to know the hardest reasons for his defeat, as he clearly knows the hard reasons for his victory.

But it is worthwhile quoting a few lines from a well-known intellectual who makes no bones about his intense dislike for Narendra Modi and his regime. The Press Trust of India filed a report in January 2020 from Kozhikode where Ramachandra Guha addressed a literature festival crowd: "A 'fifth-generation dynast' Rahul Gandhi has no chance in Indian politics against a 'hard-working and self-made' Narendra Modi, and Kerala did a disastrous thing by electing the Congress leader to Parliament."

Guha said the reduction of the Congress from a 'great party' during the freedom movement to a 'pathetic family firm' now is one of the reasons for the ascendancy of Hindutva and jingoism in India.

"I have nothing against Rahul Gandhi personally. He is a decent fellow, very well-mannered. But young India does not want a fifth-generation dynast. If you Malayalis make the mistake of re-electing Rahul Gandhi in 2024 too, you are merely handing over an advantage to Narendra Modi," said Guha on the second day of the ongoing Kerala Literature Festival (KLF) during his talk, 'Patriotism Vs Jingoism'.

That was in 2020. Perhaps Guha did make an impression on the good folks of Kerala. Because one year later, the voters of God's Own Country did something they had never done in more than 50 years: they gave a second successive and bigger mandate in the assembly elections to the Godless communists led by chief minister Pinarayi Vijayan while the Congress was virtually obliterated despite Rahul Gandhi being a Lok Sabha MP from the state.

Ironically, three powerful chief ministers who symbolise pro-incumbency, Himanta Biswa Sarma, Mamata Banerjee and K.C. Rao were in the Congress once upon a time.

What about Dynasties?

Because of the travails of the Nehru-Gandhi dynasty, there is a perception that dynasty politics doesn't work anymore in India. That's as far from reality as anything you can imagine. The fact is dynasties have been immensely successful in India, literally from Kashmir to Kanyakumari. In Jammu & Kashmir, the abrogation of Article 370 in August 2020 has halted normal political activities like elections. But a new delimitation exercise has been completed and elections will be held soon. When that happens, there are chances that even the third-generation dynast Omar Abdullah might become the chief minister again, like his father and grandfather. In Tamil Nadu where Kanyakumari is based, M.K. Stalin finally realised his almost four-decade old dream of following in the footsteps of his father M. Karunanidhi and becoming the chief minister of the state. In neighbouring Karnataka, H.D. Kumaraswamy, son of former chief minister of Karnataka and prime minister of India H.D. Deve Gowda has become chief minister for a couple of times. We have discussed Naveen Babu at length and Tejashwi Yadav arguably has a great future in Bihar if joins hand with another dynast in form of Chirag Paswan. If not carrying his father's social capital, Akhilesh Yadav would have found it really difficult to win a municipality election, forget about becoming the Chief Minister of Uttar Pradesh. The BJP government in Haryana depends on dynast Dushyant Chautala's support for all practical matters. The Shivraj Chouhan government came back to life after the 2018 cardiac arrest, courtesy the political bypass surgery offered by a certain dynast Jyotiraditya Scindia. In Maharashtra, second-generation dynast Uddhav Thackeray has, unlike his father the late Balasaheb Thackeray, thrown away the 'remote control' and become chief minister of Maharashtra. His son Aditya Thackeray, already a minister in the Maharashtra cabinet is spreading his own wings. Perhaps the only serious danger comes to him is the fact that the English-speaking elitist media seems very fond of him. There is historical evidence to show in the 21st century that such love and affection from the much-talked about Lutyens Media is detrimental to electoral fortunes.

In March, 2019, journalist Azad Ashraf of the portal *Scroll* interviewed Kanchan Chandra, professor of politics, New York University, who edited and wrote the introduction to *Democratic Dynasties: State, Party and Family in Contemporary Indian Politics*. Chandra has a fascinating take on dynasties in contemporary politics: "The Nehru-Gandhi family represents the most prominent political dynasty in India. Its members have occupied the prime ministership and led the Congress party for most of India's post-Independence history. But the more important fact now for understanding contemporary democratic politics in India is the systemic role that a different sort of political dynasty—locally influential but often not nationally famous—has come to play in Indian politics. These dynasties are found in virtually all parties, regions, and social groups. Their founders belong not to an old pre-democratic ruling class—maharajas, rajas and nawabs–but a new elite created through the democratic process. Their members occupy not just top positions such as prime minister, chief minister, or party president but also secondary and tertiary positions burrowed deep within parties and governments, in regional party executives and youth wings, or zila panchayats and block panchayats. And these dynasties taken together are now changing the shape of Indian politics regardless of who becomes prime minister."[12] These words remind one of Chirag Paswan of Lok Janshakti Party and Anupriya Patel of Apna Dal, apart from a clutch of small caste-based parties in Tamil Nadu? In fact, regional parties seem to suffer if they are not driven and ruled by dynasties. Look what has happened with AGP in Assam and AIADMK in Tamil Nadu. Analysts reckon that a somewhat similar fate awaits the JD(U) in Bihar and the BJD in Odisha once Nitish Kumar and Naveen Patnaik are no longer in the picture. The BSP seems to be another example of how the absence of a dynasty can be a fatal disadvantage as the dynastic Samajwadi Party seems to flourish even as the BSP flounders towards irrelevance.

But what about dynasties and pro-incumbency? The only dynast who has a proven track record as a pro-incumbency champion is Naveen Patnaik. But he is a unique case because he was least interested in politics till he was more than 50 and still displays the polite and suave finesse that usually go well with the heat and dust of abrasive, rhetoric driven electoral politics in the country. And yet, this 'non-politician' has proven to be the smartest and arguably the most successful politician of the 21st century, apart from Mamata Banerjee and Narendra Modi. Almost all other political dynasties in India have been successful in passing on the mantle. For example, as we mentioned, Stalin is the chief minister of Tamil Nadu. Y.S. Jagan Reddy, son of Y.S. Rajasekhara Reddy is chief minister of Andhra Pradesh. Uddhav Thackeray is chief minister of Maharashtra. Tejashwi Yadav was deputy chief minister of Bihar for a spell and narrowly missed out on becoming chief minister in 2020. Sukhbir Singh Badal, son of multiple times chief minister Prakash Singh Badal has been deputy chief minister and the de facto chief minister of Punjab between 2012 and 2017 when his 84-year-old father won a surprise second consecutive term in 2012. K.T. Rao is waiting for his chief minister father to pass on the mantle. Akhilesh Yadav did become chief minister once in 2012. But his wait for a repeat stint got longer in 2022.

These dynasties will be tested on the pro-incumbency parameter during the next decade as a new cycle of elections throw up winners and losers. If the likes of Jagan Reddy and M.K. Stalin win their second consecutive terms, one could argue that dynasties add strength to the pro-incumbency phenomenon witnessed so vividly in the 21st century. If they lose, well, there is another day, and perhaps another dynasty in making.

A weak or weakening opposition has clearly been a factor in helping the pro-incumbency phenomenon become stronger in Indian elections. This, as the Bihar example has shown, is often despite the fact that perhaps the incumbents did not really deserve to win, either because of poor performance, or lack of charisma and a personality cult of the chief minister. And the weak link, as we have seen in Delhi, is always the Congress, though it is the 'strongest' weak link! Maharashtra and Assam are two examples of a party or alliance winning two or three successive verdicts when they were not really very popular. But more of that on another chapter on unusual pro-incumbency verdicts in Indian politics, particularly during assembly elections.

References

1. https://www.hindustantimes.com/cities/why-delhi-is-a-difficult-terrain-for-the-bjp/story-aAP6AsgepV8yVPiro6m7NL.html
2. https://www.thehindu.com/news/national/analysis-defeat-of-bjp-in delhi-election-points-to-lack-of-strong-face-and-local-narrative-in-states/article30793568.ece
3. https://www.hindustantimes.com/analysis/gujarat-election-results-2017-why-congress-appeal-for-change-didn-t-work-in-urban-gujarat-rajdeep-sardesai/story-u0aabsXTIGBE3up8tI52HL.html
4. https://www.thehinducentre.com/verdict/commentary/article8866055.ece
5. https://indianexpress.com/elections/bihar-election-results-congress-the-weakest-link-pulling-mgb-down-losing-most-fights-against-bjp-7047029/
6. https://theprint.in/politics/rjd-lost-bihar-in-2020-because-congress-lost-says-lalu-prasad-as-old-allies-ties-get-shakier/826792/
7. https://www.sundayguardianlive.com/news/congress-faces-terminal-decline-odisha
8. @chetan_bhagat. 9.19 A. M, 04/07/19
9. https://indianexpress.com/article/opinion/columns/fifth-column-just-feudal-arrogance-rahul-gandhi-sam-pitroda-5662777/
10. Dean Nelson. 'The next Gandhi. I Will Make India Better Off Than Britain'. The Sunday Times. April, 30, 2006.
11. https://theprint.in/india/dynast-rahul-gandhi-has-no-chance-against-self-made-modi-ramachandra-guha/351416/
12. https://scroll.in/article/917320/interview-the-wide-appeal-of-the-bjp-congress-ends-up-benefiting-upper-caste-dynasties-by-default

□

5
ECONOMICS OR IDENTITY?

The year 2004 can described as the one around which the anti-incumbency phenomenon peaked. In 2003, the fiery and stormy 'poster girl' of Hindutva Uma Bharti was chosen by the oases of BJP to challenge the 10-year rule of Congress led by chief minister Digvijay Singh, the 'devout' Hindu who hates Hindutva. There were multiple and credible media reports of Uma Bharati dancing with joy when the Babri Masjid was demolished while Digvijay Singh was leading in the 'secularism' race by calling the RSS a de facto terror organisation. People of Madhya Pradesh seemed fed up with the unfulfilled promises of development made for 10 years by Singh. Besides, there was an emerging consensus that Prime Minister Atal Bihari Vajpayee was becoming as popular as Jawaharlal Nehru and Indira Gandhi in their heydays. The election results appeared almost pre-destined. The BJP won 42.5 per cent of the vote share and 176 out of the 230 seats, reducing the Congress to 31.7 per cent of the vote share and 38 seats. This is as resounding a slap as anti-incumbency slaps go. Some people joke that Digvijay Singh has never really recovered from that shock humiliation. Five years back he had defied all our tracking polls which were showing all signs of anti-incumbency. The odd thing was, in the 1998 assembly elections all our predictions of anti-incumbent verdict came true, barring Madhya Pradesh. One of the authors, who was the lead researchers of that round of elections, was completely stumped, when the BJP *prabhari* (in-charge) of MP elections told him that "your surveys on public anger are correct but eventually your prediction will go wrong, simply because Digvijay Singh will win again". Coming from a BJP leader, this was weird. The author tried to understand from him what exactly was wrong in his surveys. "Well, your surveys in all other states will be correct, but not in MP. Because Diggi has managed it well." After the elections results were our, the author called that BJP *prabhari* to understand what exactly he knew that our surveys failed to pick up from the ground. It was the same team, same methodology, same algorithms that gave perfect results in all other states, but not in MP.

"Just watch out for invalid votes in the final results, you will know" said the BJP leader in-charge.

But off course Digvijay Singh 'managed' the elections well to beat the anti-incumbency sentiment. The authors later wrote a paper on how in big number of seats where the Congress won, the 'invalid votes' were in way more than 'margin of victory'. Diggi Raja indeed managed it well. The 'invalid votes' in paper ballots were his secret sauce. Well, that was the last round of Assembly Elections using paper ballot in Madhya Pradesh. Five years down the lane, the EVM happened, and along with the EVM the idea of managing the 'Invalid Votes' went for a toss, and the anti-incumbent verdict came with such a massive force that Digvijay Singh publicly stated to take a political *sanyaas*. If the ECI ever needs a case study to make a point on why EVMs were a must, they just need to explain the 1998 and 2003 Assembly Elections of Madhya Pradesh.

By the way, that BJP *prabhari* who clearly told the author of his impending failure in Madhya Pradesh surveys so confidently, eventually became PM of India on 16th May, 2014.

Riding the seeming anti-incumbency wave, the BJP thundered past the Congress during the same set of elections in 2003 even in Rajasthan and the newly formed Chhattisgarh. In the desert state, a blue blooded 'Maharani' Vijaya Raje Scindia, sister of top Congress leader Madhav Rao Scindia, did what the princess of Hindutva Uma Bharti did in Madhya Pradesh: she ousted sitting chief minister Ashok Gehlot and won a comfortable victory for her party, bagging 120 of the 200 seats on offer. Even the much-talked about Bhairon Singh Shekhawat could never manage these many seats in Rajasthan. Since its creation in 2000, Chhattisgarh had been ruled by chief minister Ajit Jogi, apparently handpicked by the party boss Sonia Gandhi. While the Congress was a formidable force in the state, Ajit Jogi was unpopular and his government faced serious corruption charges. It appeared to be a very tight election but the BJP won comfortably in the end and Dr. Raman Singh became chief minister.

This was the year preceding 2004. The year after that was definitely the high noon for anti-incumbency. In an era where voters routinely threw out incumbent governments every five years, the state of Bihar led by the rambunctious and boisterous Lalu Prasad Yadav and his clan had proven to be the proverbial outlier. He looked cornered during the 1995 assembly elections when the then Chief Election Commissioner T.N. Seshan vowed to eliminate rigging from Bihar elections. The common refrain was: if the Yadav goons cannot capture booths, how will Lalu win? Win he did, and comfortably despite one of the most stringent security arrangements ever. He later thanks T.N. Seshan when he realised that due to ECI the voters who actually got to vote for the first time in Bihar, were all belonging to the bottom of the pyramid in socio-economic context. And they all were actually his voters. So, for all practical purposes, a clean and transparent election actually helped Lalu Yadav win, simply because his supporters actually got a chance to vote. It was 'Gareeb ka vote' that was looted in Bihar, every time a booth was captured. Lalu became the default gainer of Seshan's electoral reforms. Truth is stranger than fiction, most times.

About halfway into his second successive term, Lalu Yadav had to resign and go to jail on charges of being involved in the fodder scam. A defiant Lalu made his illiterate wife and mother of his nine children the chief minister so that he could rule from hind the scenes. Everybody and their cousin was outraged. This was 'subversive murder' of democracy. Intellectuals were confident that the Bihar voter would teach a lesson to Lalu Yadav in the 2000 assembly elections. The voter taught a lesson to the intellectuals! Lalu, via Rabri Devi won a third consecutive term. This dream run finally ended in 2005 when a JD(U)-BJP alliance won and Nitish Kumar became chief minister.

While teaching the students of journalism, one of the authors used an interesting anecdote to explain Lalu Yadav's successful run in Bihar as 'Hum bhi nangey, tum bhi nangey' phenomenon. Till 1995 happened, the Bihar demographics was explained by Lalu Yadav divided between 'haves' and 'have nots'. So apparently there was a small elite section is Bihar, let's call them 'Babu Saab' who had enough clothes to wear. Then there was majority group, which had literally no clothes. So in 1995 Lalu Yadav told everyone without clothes, if you vote for me, I will give solution to your problem. The overwhelming majority of people without clothes voted for Lalu. After winning, Lalu did not give clothes to the naked or the 'Nangey'. He simply disrobed the clothes from the 'Babu Saab' or the elites, and told the naked: see now everyone is equal. The naked gelt elated and empowered by this new phenomenon of 'Hum bhi nangey, tum bhi nangey' (I am naked and so are you). Social equality was served. To the outside world; it was 'Jungle Raj'. For the bottom of the pyramid, it was social justice. Delivered as raw as it can, and visible as it can.

The C-Voter poll was the only one to tell that Lalu Yadav was winning again in 1995 elections. And again in 2000 when everyone else projected a change. The authors observed the phenomenon of 'Hum bhi Nanegy tum bhi nangey' getting saturated and predicted that this is going to work against all odds till the time the 'have nots' in Bihar get over the sadistic pleasure of the 'haves' becoming 'have nots'. But at some point of time, the new generation of 'have nots' was likely to get over the 'equality in nakedness' phenomenon and ask for a piece of clothes for themselves. That day Lalu Yadav would find it hard to sail through. It didn't take more than 15 years to pass three generations of voters in Bihar politics, and right in 2005, all it took two assembly elections back-to-back, to enable Nitish Kumar along with the BJP sell the concept of 'Sushashan' amid the 'Jungle Raj'. The new generation of Biharis bought it, and since then RJD is out of power. It took the issue of unemployment that made the contest closer between Tejashwi Yadav and Nitish Kumar, but the 2019 sweep of NDA in Bihar was so spectacular that it drew parallels with 1977 or 1989 elections.

Do Voters Count Per Capita GDP?

But what still excites and engages commentators, insta pundits as well as scholars is what happened in 2004. One was the results of the Lok Sabha elections; another was the results of the assembly elections of Andhra Pradesh. Both the results triggered a debate that still rages on: Do Indian voters get influenced by overall economic performance while casting their ballot or are factors like identity still more important to electoral outcomes? There are persuasive arguments on both sides and as it usually happens, there seems no conclusive resolution in sight. Some insist that the Indian voter is coming of age and becoming more rational and mature with every passing election and has started behaving like voters in Western democracies where economic issues dominate elections. We will come to that later; but the authors think the underlying presumption that Indian voters in the past were not mature and rational enough is both condescending and plain wrong. Others insist that identity politics still plays a decisive role in electoral outcomes and will continue to do so no matter how many so called 'experts' talk about GDP and per capita income growth, investments flowing into a state and growth rates in both production and productivity in agriculture which is still the primary source of livelihood in most states.

Our main concern as far as this book is concerned is: like the three reasons specified for the rise and sustainability of the pro-incumbency phenomenon in the 21st century in three separate chapters on personality cults, welfare schemes and opposition weakness, can we add economics as the fourth reason? We are sceptical for reasons that will come evident later. But just one hint along with a question: in the January-March quarter just preceding the Lok Sabha elections, the GDP growth rate had slumped to a 5 year low of 5.83 per cent. For the financial year as a whole, GDP growth rate was 6.1 per cent, down from 6.8 per cent the previous year. The unemployment rate was 5.8 per cent and 6.1 per cent respectively in 2018-19 and 2017-18.[1] By all accounts, India's economic performance was poor and far below the 'Acche Din' promises made by Narendra Modi during the 2014 Lok Sabha campaign. If the Indian voters had cast their ballots purely on 'economic' considerations, Modi should have lost power. And yet, he took the BJP past the 300 mark in the 2019 Lok Sabha elections. How, and why? Nevertheless, the economics versus identity debate is too fascinating and also important to ignore while analysing 21st century politics in India.

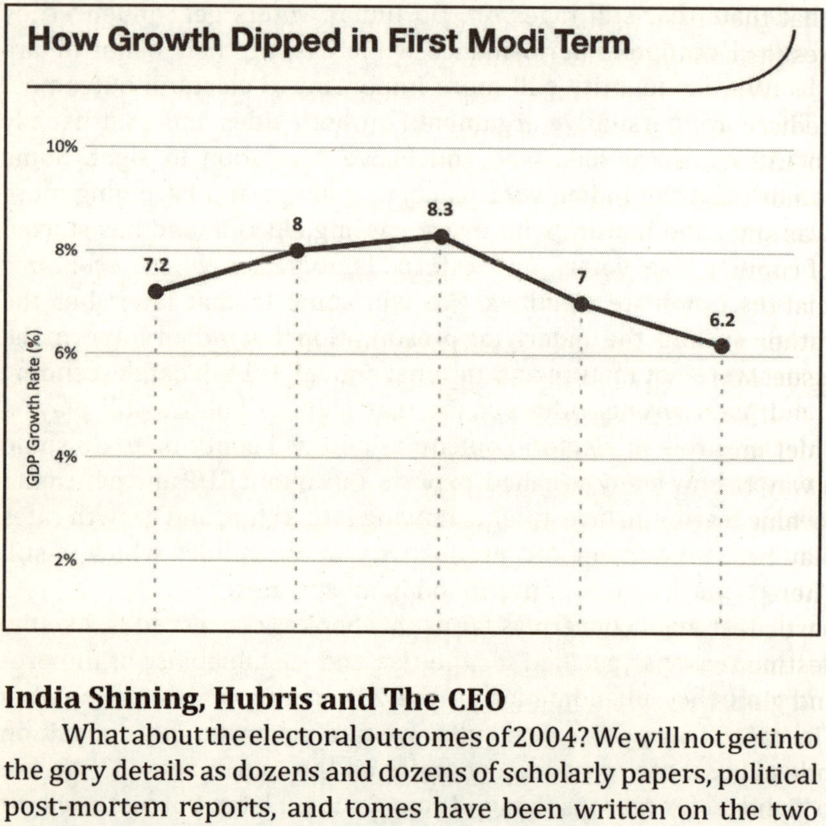

India Shining, Hubris and The CEO

What about the electoral outcomes of 2004? We will not get into the gory details as dozens and dozens of scholarly papers, political post-mortem reports, and tomes have been written on the two electoral outcomes. A brief recap along with accounts of the shock they delivered will be sufficient. Soon after the 2003 assembly elections that saw the BJP win Rajasthan, Madhya Pradesh and Chhattisgarh, the strategic brains trust of the BJP led by the late Pramod Mahajan advised Atal Bihari Vajpayee to take advantage to the pro-BJP 'Hawa' and prepone the Lok Sabha elections. The Congress appeared to be in disarray with president Sonia Gandhi struggling with her language as well as communication skills compared to the masterful oratory of Vajpayee. Some people say a reluctant Vajpayee was 'forced' into the decision. Some say he was more than happy. It really doesn't matter either way because Vajpayee must have seen the multiple opinion polls that gave the NDA a big majority. In fact, even the exit polls barring one after the elections were over gave the BJP led NDA a huge majority in excess of 300 Lok Sabha seats. So confident were some BJP supporters that they didn't even watch TV channels to get a glimpse of live results coming by the minute.

When the results were announced, a stunned India rediscovered the word 'hubris'. The BJP tally dropped from 183 to 138 seats. The Congress tally went up from 113 to 145. There is not much of a difference between 138 and 145. But the blow was still a double whammy. The first was the psychological shock of ruptured overconfidence. The second was the grim realisation that the Left Front with 54 seats and many regional parties would rather go with the Congress citing the 2002 Gujarat riots as the issue. Many regional allies had in any case left the NDA after 2002.

If Vajpayee was lulled and deceived by the 'India Shining', the chief minister of Andhra Pradesh N. Chandrababu Naidu was in a way hoodwinked and taken for a ride by the title of CEO given to him by pundits. In his case, anti-incumbency was already at play because his party had been ruling in the state for 10 years. There is no doubt that he had transformed Andhra Pradesh, and particularly the capital city of Hyderabad into a business-friendly destination. Even his critics admit that. So impressed were Indian and global investors that even the likes of Bill Gates came calling. The capital became a new hub for the rapidly growing IT and ITES industries and its name was unofficially changed from Hyderabad to 'Cyberabad'. It's not as if Naidu completely ignored rural regions of the state. He was the first chief minister to start digitising land records of farmers so that they wouldn't be harassed and extorted by corrupt Tehsildars and other government officials.

But even as he was visibly asking in the glow of praise from Indian as well as global media, Naidu paid little heed to a Congress leader called Y.S. Rajasekhara Reddy who was conducting a long drawn out *padayatra* (yatra on foot) that went on for three months and covered almost 1,500 kilometres crisscrossing crossing

Andhra Pradesh. Not only did Naidu ignore the warning signals that emerged from this yatra, he succumbed to even more hubris as he dumped the BJP as an ally before the elections announcing that he didn't need the help of BJP to win the elections.

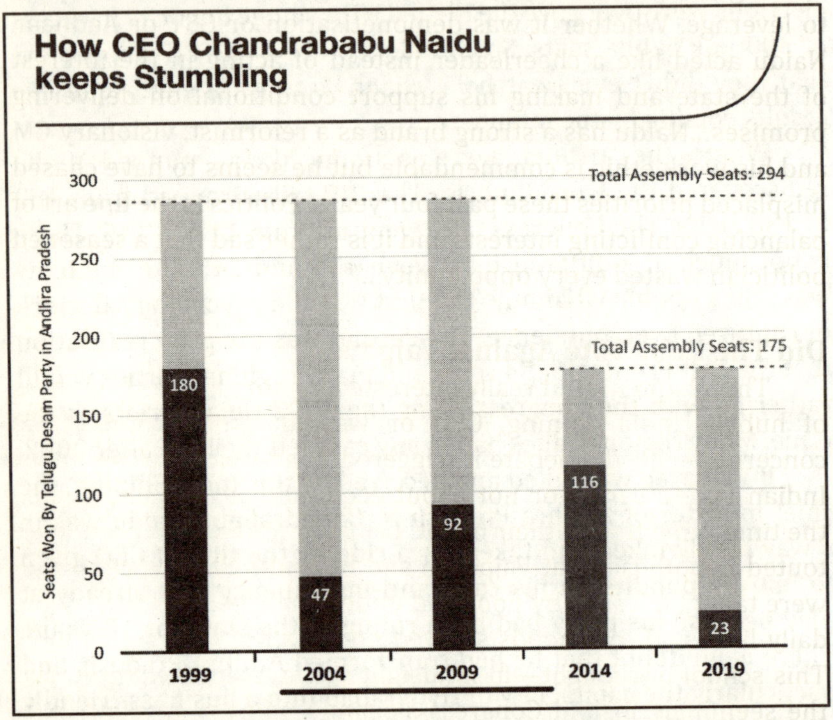

YSR proved to be much smarter and tied up with the newly formed TRS led by K.C. Rao (one of our pro-incumbency stars) and the Left parties while the overconfident Naidu went alone. When results were announced, the Congress had won 38.5 per cent of the vote share, just 1 per cent more than TDP. The difference was made by the 6.3 per cent share won by TRS and the more than 3 per cent share won by the Left. This enabled YSR to sweep the state, leaving the CEO Naidu with just 47 out of 294 seats. Incidentally, Naidu proved history repeats itself by dumping the BJP again before the 2019 elections when he was chief minister. This time, it was YSR Jagan Reddy, the son of late YSR (who died in a chopper crash after winning a second consecutive term in 2009) who humiliated Naidu, reducing the TDP to 33 out of 175 seats.

In March 2018, Srinivas Allapali wrote for the portal *The News Minute* where he virtually forecast the defeat of Naidu in 2019: "As a key player in NDA with a national profile and by offering ministers to BJP, Naidu had significant political capital to leverage. Whether it was demonetisation or GST or Aadhaar, Naidu acted like a cheerleader instead of acting in the interest of the state and making his support conditional on delivering promises...Naidu has a strong brand as a reformist, visionary CM and his work ethic is commendable but he seems to have chased misplaced priorities these past four years. Politics is the fine art of balancing conflicting interests and it is rather sad that a seasoned politician wasted every opportunity..."[3]

Did The Poor Vote Against Vajpayee?

This chapter is not really interested in more in-depth analysis of hubris, India Shining, CEO or wasted opportunities. It is concerned with the debate it triggered in academic circles about Indian voters caring or not about economic performance when the time came to cast their ballot. Let us first deal with the much-touted hypothesis that Vajpayee and his India Shining campaign were taught a lesson by poor and underprivileged Indians whose daily lives and livelihoods showed no evidence of India Shining. This school of thought—in hindsight we must add—argues that the seemingly insipid Congress slogan: 'Congress ka Hath, Aam Aadmi ke Sath' persuaded enough voters to desert Vajpayee and the BJP which was apparently perceived as pro-business and anti-poor. This myth has been spread so repeatedly and so widely that it seems Narendra Modi got frightened when Rahul Gandhi described his government as 'suit-boot ki Sarkar' and devoted the rest of his tenure in proving how pro-poor his regime is. If you go by Modi's rhetoric, you might think this analysis has some value. But it conveniently forgets the fact that virtually all the major pro-poor welfare schemes that helped him win again in 2019 were actually launched in the very first year of his first term. We are talking about toilets through Swachh Bharat, zero balance bank accounts through Jan Dhan Yojana, free gas connections and subsidised gas cylinders through Ujjwala and a massive jump in construction of pucca houses for the poor through the PM Awas Yojana. So there goes the basic premise out of the window. Modi has assiduously cultivated this image from his day one in office.

Vajpayee was different. His government was unapologetically reformist when it came to the Indian economy even though it was a coalition. It is doubtful if Modi with 303 Lok Sabha seats would dare do what Vajpayee did: set up a separate ministry to privatise public sector companies. Sure, he has been courageous enough to privatise Air India which has gone back to its original founders the Tata Group; but to pointedly ignore unrelenting criticism both from the implacable Left and more criticism from Luddite sections of the Sangh Parivar was typically Vajpayee. His regime's policy decisions to allow mobile phone companies to share revenues instead of paying a high and fixed license fee actually led to the telecom revolution. The decision to impose a Rs. 1 per litre cess on petrol and diesel to invest massively in highway construction has left a lasting impact. The 'controversial' policy allowing foreign investment in the insurance sector has actually created tens of thousands of new jobs (without the state-owned LIC and others losing a single one) and decent livelihood opportunities for hundreds of thousands of agents. Vajpayee without doubt was a true reformer when it came to economics. Soon after his death in 2018, the news agency IANS spoke to industry bodies and wrote a story carried by most media outlets including NDTV. "The second generation of economic reforms introduced under his visionary leadership contributed greatly to a facilitative investment climate which in turn promoted India's rapid growth," CII President Rakesh Bharti Mittal said...FICCI mourns the loss of former PM Atal Bihari Vajpayee. It is a very sad day for India. He was one of the most dynamic leaders who ushered in an era of reforms, progress and took the country forward," FICCI President Rashesh Shah said. Mr. Vajpayee is remembered for various policy actions that led to rapid growth in telecom, power, financial sector, insurance, agriculture, education and national highways that contributed hugely to unlocking the nation's economic potential."[4]

Take just one example: mobile telephones. Though mobile phone services were officially launched in 1995, it virtually remained a dream for ordinary middleclass Indians with a reasonable monthly income. It was a bit like an AC for a Zomato or Flipkart delivery executive. She can buy an AC for sure opting for the myriad EMI options available today. But from where will she get the money to pay her huge electricity bills if she uses the AC regularly? Something similar happened with mobile phone services till the late 1990s. How many could afford to pay Rs. 24 per minute for making a local call and Rs. 16 per minute for receiving a call? The culprit was the fixed and very high annual license fee that companies had to pay the government. The Vajpayee government changed the policy in 1999 and whereby operators could pay a share of their revenue every year instead of the license fee. That allowed operators to reduce call rates drastically and competition for subscribers grew rapidly. According to a write up in *The Indian Express*: "The next few days will see yet another milestone in telephony in India. By May-end or early June 2006, the mobile phone population will cross the historic one hundred million mark. The mobile phone population was 96.92 million by April 2006 (with 3.88 million additions in April). And the landline population was 49.75 million by March 2006 (with 0.3 million additions in April). This exciting moment is special on many counts.

The mobile phone started ringing in Kolkata on August 23, 1995. It crossed one million in 1998, three million in 2000, five million in 2001, 10 million in 2002 and finally 100 million in 2006! The mobile phone population, at 44 million, exceeded the landline population on October 18, 2004, and early next month, mobile phones will be double that of landlines! As per a Press Information Bureau release, the total phone population crossed 100 million on January 14, 2005."[5]

Mythically Myopic Voters

Some of the biggest beneficiaries were not the super-rich but the real ordinary Indians. Thanks to very cheap call charges, plumbers, carpenters, electricians, barbers and other professional service providers suddenly discovered new and hitherto unimaginable avenues to increase their earnings. Were these ordinary voters not farsighted enough to visualise these changes when they voted Vajpayee out in 2004? Or as some experts are prone to pontificate, the Indian voter was not mature or rational enough to take the right decisions? In December, 2012, Vivek Kaul interviewed Vivek Dehejia and Rupa Subramanya who had co-authored a book *Indianomix*: *Making Sense of Modern India* for the portal *Firstpost*. They explained why it was wrong to presume the BJP lost 2004 because of pro-market policies: "We think it is one of the interesting contributions of the book. I would agree with you that it is a controversial hypothesis because we have this received narrative of the 2004 election—which is that the poor voter had punished the BJP/NDA for the triumphalist India Shining campaign. Even the BJP bought into this interpretation. This has had far-reaching consequences. If you look at the political history of India since 2004, what was the lesson that was drawn? The lesson that everyone drew from the so-called disaster of the India Shining campaign was that you cannot win an election based on economic reform, economic policy and economic success. Our argument here is that if you look at the numbers, if you look not just at the seats won but at the vote shares as well, you get a different story. Yes, there was a swing away from the NDA, but the actual vote share difference between the NDA and the UPA was just over 2 per cent. The NDA won 33.3 per cent of the vote and the UPA won 35.4 per cent of the vote. For us that 2 per cent difference in vote share can equally be attributed to a number of other explanations, such as bad luck, as it is to anything else. Or let me put in another way; if you look at those results, basically it came down to a coin toss. A third of the voters voted for the NDA, another third voted for the UPA and a third voted for somebody else. As we see it, the role of luck and randomness in an outcome should not be underestimated."[6]

You could argue that the duo are unabashed free market advocates who don't understand the rhythm and pulse of the real India, which largely rural and poor. Sure enough, journalist Manini Chatterjee provided the other ideological viewpoint in a piece for the journal Seminar in 2004: "Over the last five years, the Vajpayee government's aggressive championing of pro-market and neoliberal economic policies increased its acceptability among the rich and upper middle class but alienated it from the rural and urban poor as well as middle and lower middle classes. Of the 135 municipal corporation areas that comprise urban India, the BJP lost in 120—indicating the extent of erosion in its middleclass base. The irony is that in its efforts to be 'moderate' (i.e., dilute the Hindutva-oriented rightwing image), the Vajpayee government acquired a pro-rich rightwing image that proved equally harmful to its dream of replacing Congress as India's natural party of governance."[7] Chatterjee argues that since the BJP lost in 120 out of 135 municipal corporation areas that comprise urban India, it proves her point about people rejecting the 'neo-liberal' policies championed by Vajpayee.

Real Numbers Don't Lie, Or Mislead

Its selective use of data to suit a predetermined agenda is an original sin that both the Right & Left are guilty of. What does the real data of the 2004 elections say? It is not rocket science if you take the trouble of closely looking at the data provided by the Election Commission of India. Even Chatterjee and her fellow travellers will agree that the really poor, underprivileged and marginalised voters of India are found predominantly in Odisha, Jharkhand, Bihar, Chhattisgarh, Madhya Pradesh and Rajasthan. Whichever parameter you adopt, these are the poorest states in India. How did they vote in 2004? Did they decisively and roundly reject the 'neo-liberal' policies of Vajpayee as they should have?

Among the big states where the BJP and the NDA did badly was UP where it won just 10 out of 80 seats. But the losing streak had started in 1999 itself when its winning tally halved from 58 in 1998 to 29. Besides, in 2004, the formidable former backward class chief minister of the state Kalyan Singh (under whose watch the Babri Masjid was demolished) quit the party. Even when not in power, the poor voters of UP gave just 10 seats to the BJP in 2009. Nothing to do with pro-market, neoliberal policies. The next is state where the NDA fared poorly was Bihar, where it won 11 out of 40 seats. That was the high noon for Lalu Yadav whose RJD scored its highest ever vote share of 30.67 per cent. The UPA adding up Ram Vilas Paswan's Lok Janshakti Party and the Congress won 29 seats. In Jharkhand too, the NDA won just 1 out of 14 seats despite winning more than 12 per cent vote share than the main rival Congress. The UPA 'alliance' did the trick. In Chhattisgarh, largely poor, tribal and also newly created like Jharkhand, the NDA won 10 out of 11 seats. In Odisha, the NDA won 18 out of 21 seats. In Madhya Pradesh, the BJP won 25 out of 29 seats and in Rajasthan, it won 21 out of 25 seats. If you add it all up, the NDA won almost half the total seats in the really poor and rural states. That's not a debacle or a revolt of the proletariat against the capitalists! If you exclude UP which had its own unique political and electoral dynamics since 1998, the NDA performance in the other states becomes 85 out of 120. We can therefore quote this data to 'prove' that the desperately poor Indian voter living in villages wholeheartedly endorsed the pro-market and unapologetically 'reformist' policies of Vajpayee. We will do no such thing as anyone with some knowledge of numbers and some brains can play around with data to 'prove' anything. But let's

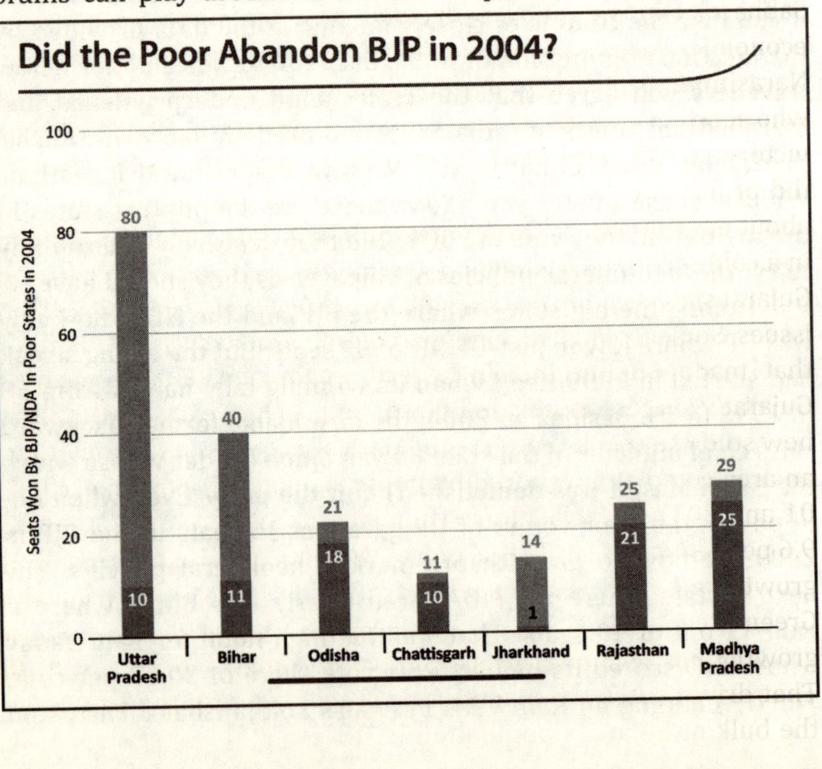

at least be honest enough to agree that the 2004 verdict was not on India Shining. For the first time in five decades, BJP won a majority of the rural seats in India which used to be backbone of Congress and other opposition parties. The BJP sweep in rural India only explain that 'India Shining' was an aspirational phenomenon which got traction in Rural India, but somehow failed in Urban India which witnessed a drop in turnout across the country. The poor and rural population voted in bigger turnout and their mandate went for BJP. However, the BJP, which is still analysed by majority of Western 'experts' on India as 'urban, middle class, upper caste, Brahminical party', actually lost all its urban stronghold. Whether it was due to over-confidence or due to complacency factor, that jury is still out even after two decades of that historic election.

The debate raged on in academic circles while political commentary, barring a notable few, subsided till the 2009 Lok Sabha elections as it was 'decided' that economic reforms and economics do not win votes in India. The argument was persuasive: Narasimha Rao ushered in reforms and lost followed by Vajpayee who accelerated 'second generation' reforms and also lost. But the victory of Narendra Modi for a second successive term in 2007 did provoke at least some analysts to start thinking and talking about economists. Swaminathan Anklesaria Aiyar wrote about it in a column in *The Economic Times* in 2009: "When Modi won the Gujarat state election in 2007, the media focused on Hindu-Muslim issues. Some journalists highlighted rapid industrial development that made Gujarat India's fastest growing state. I mentioned Gujarat's successful port led development. However, an excellent new study suggests the secret of Modi's success lay in agriculture, an area completely ignored by political analysts...Between 2000-01 and 2007-08, agriculture value added grew at a phenomenal 9.6 per cent per year. This is more than double India's agricultural growth rate and much faster than Punjab's farm growth in the Green Revolution's heyday. Indeed 9.6 per cent agricultural growth rates is among the fastest recorded anywhere in the world. That drives home the magnitude of Gujarat's performance. Since the bulk of Gujarat's population Is still rural, this mega boom in agriculture must have created millions of satisfied voters. Yet, I did not see a single media analyst mention it."[8]

If Modi could leverage the resources available to a heavily industrialised and reasonably well-off Indian state with high tax revenues to bring about a near miracle in agriculture in Gujarat, what Shivraj Singh Chouhan has done in Madhya Pradesh then goes beyond the realm of miracles. If you want to find a true agriculture success story in India at a time when everyone is talking about the depth and intensity of farm distress in India, it has to be Madhya Pradesh. Ironically, the political and electoral gods are so fickle that it was agrarian protests in Madhya Pradesh in 2017 that became the main reason for the extremely narrow loss of BJP in the 2018 assembly elections despite getting a higher vote share than the Congress. Perhaps anticipating this, Harish Damodaran wrote for *The Indian Express* just before the elections were concluded in 2018: "Whether or not Shivraj Singh Chouhan returns as Madhya Pradesh's Chief Minister after Wednesday's vote, he will probably go down as someone who has steered through an agricultural and rural transformation of his state no less remarkable than what Partap Singh Kairon accomplished in post-Independence Punjab. And ironically, much of Chouhan's achievements came during the period when the Congress-led UPA, and not his own BJP, was in power at the Centre. Till the 2006-07 crop year, procurement of wheat in MP rarely crossed 5 lakh tonnes (lt). By 2011-12, that had reached 85 lt and MP soon overtook Haryana as the largest contributor to the central pool after Punjab... Assured government procurement at MSP plus bonus led to MP's wheat output more than doubling from 62 lt in 2005-06 (when Chouhan first became CM) to over 145 lt in 2011-12."[9]

Damodaran then cites reputed agriculture economists like Ashok Gulati who apparently thought that the government was fudging the production figures in the later years of Shivraj rule because there seemed to be no commensurate rise in procurement. So Damodaran is not sure if the government estimate of wheat production of 20 million tons (the second largest in India after Uttar Pradesh) is accurate or not because government estimates showed procurement had stagnated at about 7 million tons by the same year. Perhaps the MP government didn't have enough money to buy all wheat being produced. We don't know as we are no experts on these matters. But Damodaran cites another telling piece of data in his analytical piece. Before he became CM, tractor sales in MP were falling and sales were at 12,487 units in 2006-07. By 2017-18, they had zoomed to 72,858 units. Surely Shivraj Singh Chouhan could not have fudged tractor sales figures as they are released by an industry body called Society of Indian Automobile manufacturers (SIAM) over which he had no control or influence whatsoever? In 2021, his persistence in chasing an agriculture miracle finally satisfied even sceptics like Gulati when it became clear that the state had procured a record 13 million tons of wheat the previous year and now is neck and neck with Punjab for the number crown in procurement. This is truly remarkable and explains why Shivraj lost so narrowly in 2018 while his counterpart and party colleague Dr. Raman Singh lost badly in Chhattisgarh. So yes, economics does affect electoral outcomes in the slightly longer term.

Even as Aiyer wrote about the importance of the largely ignored 'academic' report, political commentators were busy doing a post-mortem of what caused the UPA to come back to power. One set argued that the pro-poor and pro-rural policies pushed by the Sonia Gandhi led National Advisory Council and adopted by the Manmohan Singh regime like farm loan waivers and the rural job guarantee scheme that offered 100 days of paid work a year to anyone in rural India who wanted it, were the ponies that did the trick. Another set argued that the unprecedented growth rates of GDP and a massive rise in the 'consumer economy' driven by an aspirational middle class were responsible for the UPA retaining power with an improved mandate. Both sniped at each other. The irony is that both were right; in their own ways.

The five years of the first UPA term were indeed unprecedented for the Indian economy. It had never grown so fast since 1947 and it hasn't grown so fast since then for an extended period of five years. In August 2018, *The Indian Express* carried a story that pretty much says all about GDP growth between 2004 and 2018: "The average economic growth rate, or Gross Domestic Product at factor cost, was 8.87 per cent during the first term (2004-05 to 2008-09) of the UPA government, which fell to 7.39 per cent during its second term (2009-10 to 2013-14). In contrast, the average growth rate in first four years of the NDA government was recorded at 7.35 per cent (2014-15 to 2017-18).

This data was presented in a report of the Committee on Real Sector Statistics, which was submitted to the National Statistical Commission recently. The data shows that the only year India grew in double digits was 2006-07 when growth touched 10.08 per cent. Growth fell to 7.16 per cent in 2008-09, as the global financial crisis of 2008 affected financial markets and economies across the world. In last two years of UPA government, the growth rate fell to 5.42 per cent and 6.05 per cent, respectively, in 2012-13 and 2013-14.[9] An 8.87 per cent average annual growth rate over five years means a phenomenal average growth rate of almost 7 per cent a year in per capita income. No wonder urban India was cock-a-hoop. But the UPA also offered a promise and hope to rural India through the farm loan waivers and job guarantee schemes. This was more messaging than concrete growth because both were implemented towards the end of the first UPA term. But it worked. To that extent, one can safely conclude that the 2009 Lok Sabha verdict was perhaps the first big election in India where economics not only played a major role, but also trumped over important issues like identity to deliver a pro-incumbency verdict. So, can we conclude that economics started playing as important a role as identity during elections and in delivering pro-incumbency verdicts?

The Bihar Paradox

The example of Bihar indicates how such conclusions can lead you to quicksand of contradictions. According to official data, the average annual growth rate of GDP in Bihar between 2005-06 and 2015-16 was 10.5 per cent; a spectacular rate of growth even if one accounts for the low GDP base of a poor state like Bihar. The chief minister of the state Nitish Kumar won a fabulous second consecutive term in 2010 and an incredible third successive term in 2015. What role did the annual growth rate of 10.5 per cent?

A surface analysis would lead any commentator or scholar to say that there is a significant statistical correlation between high GDP growth rates in Bihar and the re-elections of chief minister Nitish. The next step towards the quicksand is easy: economics triumphed over identity in Bihar, a state known for caste cleavages, apart from religious polarisation.

To some extent, one can say that the 2010 verdict was a positive one where good governance and better economic outcomes led to genuine pro-incumbency. The NDA alliance of JD(U) and the junior partner BJP had won a mandate in 2005 to govern well and remove '15 years of jungle raj' witnessed under the Lalu Prasad Yadav dispensation between 1990 and 2005. Chief minister Nitish Kumar did deliver on governance, law and order and basic infrastructure. He did launch innovative welfare schemes (More about welfare vs economics in this chapter) and the average GDP growth rate was jaw dropping. This resulted in caste considerations being temporarily swept aside as the NDA completely swept the state winning 206 out of 243 seats. The RJD, despite the formidable Muslim-Yadav combination backing it up managed to win just 22 seats and its vote share dropped by about 4.6 per cent to 18.84 per cent, which is less than the combined share of the Yadav-Muslim vote in the state. One can safely conclude that in 2010 at least, identity took a back seat.

But not so in 2015 when Nitish Kumar won a third consecutive term as chief minister. In 2015, identity dominated, and like how. When Narendra Modi was announced as the formal prime ministerial candidate of the BJP in September, 2013, the 'secular' Nitish Kumar could not digest the decision that appeared so blatantly 'communal'. The JD(U) left the NDA and contested the 2014 Lok Sabha elections alone to be humiliated and reduced to 2 out of 40 seats when the Modi 'wave' swept Bihar and Uttar Pradesh. By the time the 2015 assembly elections were announced, it was time for Nitish Kumar to plot revenge against Modi. The first thing he did was to form a formal pre-poll alliance with the RJD and the Congress. In a way, the sheer arithmetic of this alliance had sealed the election verdict with Yadavs, Muslims, other OBCs and Maha Dalits backing it up. The BJP hope that the Narendra

Modi chemistry might work again proved to be a hopeless one. Nitish Kumar pounced on a remark made by Modi about the 'DNA of Bihari people' and made it an election issue. The RSS chief Mohan Bhagwat gave further ammunition to the Mahagatbandhan by making a controversial remark just weeks before the election about the need for a social review of the reservations policy. This was anathema in the cradle of Mandal politics. The 'secular' alliance won 178 of the 243 seats on offer. Just forget about the impact of 10.5 per cent GDP growth on the electoral outcomes this time. The RJD was out of power since 2005 and won 22 out of the 168 seats it had contested in 2010. Did economic performance result in a phenomenal turnaround when it won 80 out of 101 seats contested and became the largest party in the state? You thus see the pitfalls of analysing even pro-incumbency outcomes in a complex country like India where identity might take a back seat on some occasions, but never leave the bus. So, treat economics very gingerly as a factor in electoral outcomes or pro incumbency verdicts, no matter what political commentators and scholars say.

It's the Economy, Stupid

Even in the so-called democracies of the developed West, the entry of economics as a serious and decisive factor is a relatively new phenomenon. It was christened the "It's the Economy, Stupid" factor in the last decade of the 20th century. In 1990, Iraq invaded Kuwait and created a global crisis (one that led to virtual bankruptcy and economic reforms of 1991 in India). The United States of America led an alliance of democracies to bring Iraq to heel and teach a lesson to dictator Saddam Hussein to respect the sovereignty of other nations. In the first war that was televised live across the world through satellite TV, America soundly defeated the Iraqi army and threw it out of Kuwait completely by early 1991. The American president George Bush Senior was hailed and feted across the country. It appeared that a second successive term for him during elections in 1992 were a slam dunk, as the Americans would say. George Bush was a Republican and the rival Democratic Party seemed unable to find a suitable challenger to the sitting president Bush.

An obscure Governor named Bill Clinton from an obscure state Arkansas was nominated as the Democratic candidate and challenger. How Clinton overcame all the seeming odds and turned the elections around in his favour is the stuff of legends. He kept hammering on one point: the American economy was doing badly under Bush and Clinton would do a better job. So persistent and so convincing was Clinton that American voters made Bush a one-term president by voting him out; a rare occurrence in the country. And possibly unheard of for a president who had won a war, even if it was against a tinpot dictator like Saddam Hussein. Since the 1992, the role of economics in political outcomes in the West has become a hot topic of discussion in academics as well as mainstream media.

An editorial in the *Aitken Journal* in 2020 summed up the phenomenon and its relevance even in contemporary times quite well: "It's the economy, stupid". That famous phrase comes to mind as we publish today the fourth installment of our series on the upcoming presidential election. Reporter Colin Demarest takes a look at the economy, which has suffered greatly because of the coronavirus pandemic, and what it means when voters head to the polls.

"The economy, stupid" phrase can be traced back to James Carville, who was a strategist for Bill Clinton's successful 1992 presidential bid. The story goes that Carville posted a sign around campaign headquarters with three phrases, and the economy one was the most memorable. It soon became the rallying cry for the Clinton campaign and later entered pop culture lore.

Carville was right, though: Most Americans of voting age care deeply about their finances. The global factors of the economy have a broad impact on so many facets of our lives, including our wages, our employment status and our savings/retirement accounts."[10]

Since then, economics has featured prominently as a factor whenever elections happen in large western, developed democracies like the United States or tiny ones like New Zealand. One of the reasons ascribed to the enduring popularity and staying power of Angela Merkel as the Chancellor of Germany, apart from her sober, commonsense approach to issues, was her success in ensuring that the German economic juggernaut never badly faltered or slowed down, not even after the developed economies of the west were battered and bruised by shocking 2008 global financial crisis. The 'unaffiliated independent' Emanuele Macron who did not really belong to any traditional political party was given the Presidency of France by voters because they seemed convinced, he was serious and determined to revive the economic fortunes of the country, a feat that both the socialists and conservatives had failed to perform. Even in England in 2019, voters trusted the maverick conservative Boris Johnson to deliver better economic outcomes in a post-Brexit Britain than the Labour Party that seemed stuck in a time warp of 'outdated' economic policies.

Forget the developed democracies of the West. Economics has mattered and has been a factor in Indian elections for ages despite the caste, ethnic, religious and other identity-based 'politics'. For people familiar with past elections, the high price of a simple staple toppling governments is actually a metaphor that Indian voters do not tolerate persistently high inflation. And economics has played a role since long; the only point of dispute being to what extent compared to identity. If you back 55 years, 1967 was the first elections during which the Congress lost its complete and overwhelming monopoly over power. It won the Lok Sabha with a narrow majority and lost 10 state assemblies. Scholars and pundits have since long debated this so called 'landmark' election in India. Reasons ascribed have been regional aspirations, linguistic pride or chauvinism, the steady, if slow rise of an economic right wing and simple voter fatigue-cum-anti-incumbency. The second factor was very much at play, but due to economic reasons. Twenty years after Independence, the hopes and aspirations of ordinary Indians of a better and brighter economic future lay virtually shattered. The catch is: there wasn't even enough food to eat; forget about other things. An estimated 2,00,000 Indians died during the famine of 1965-67, the last famine that India faced. The death toll would have been in millions if countries like America had not shipped free food during that period. There was bound to be some impact on elections and there was.

Indira and Economics

If the then Prime Minister Indira Gandhi received a warning on the economic front in 1967, she got a resounding endorsement because of primarily economic reasons. The Congress had split in 1969 and Indira Gandhi went ballistic with her socialistic policies starting with nationalisation of banks. By the time the 1971 elections came, arrayed against her was the might of the old Congress guard along with the unabashedly pro-market Swatantra Party that had surprised many by winning 47 seats in the 1967 elections. Indira Gandhi kept repeating that her socialistic policies would economically transform India while her rivals were serving the interests of rich capitalists and industrialists. Her 'Garibi Hatao' slogan was full of an economic promise. The Indian voter trusted her economic promise and gave her a resounding re-election mandate. But within a few years, the economic situation had worsened even further with persistent food shortages, shortages of almost everything, serpentine queues in front of ration shops, high inflation and a new phenomenon that reverberates even today: chronic unemployment, particularly among the educated youth. And then came the oil shock of 1973 when prices more than doubled leading to a deepening of the crisis.

Some out-of-the-box thinkers contend that the Emergency was more due to economic rather than political reasons like the "Sampoorna Kranti" (Total Revolution) declared against Indira by the Gandhian Jai Prakash Narain. Prabash Kumar Dutta wrote a thought provoking and interesting analysis for *India Today* on June 26, 2018, 43 years after the 'authoritarian' Indira Gandhi imposed Emergency. The headline was self-explanatory and reveals what many historians and pundits fail to point out while arguing the reasons and factors that led Indira to impose Emergency. The headline was: "Did Indira Gandhi Impose Emergency to Escape Economic Crisis?"

"But an analysis of the prevailing economic conditions suggests that Indira Gandhi might have used the political agitations against her to escape the economic crisis that her government had failed to manage....". The rain gods also did not help out Indira Gandhi. Monsoon failed in succession in 1972 and 1973. Most parts of the country faced droughts. Massive shortage of food grains was reported from all regions pushing the prices up. India was still importing food grains for sustenance. The 1971 war had eaten up a large chunk of foreign exchange reserve, which depleted further with rising cost of food grain import.

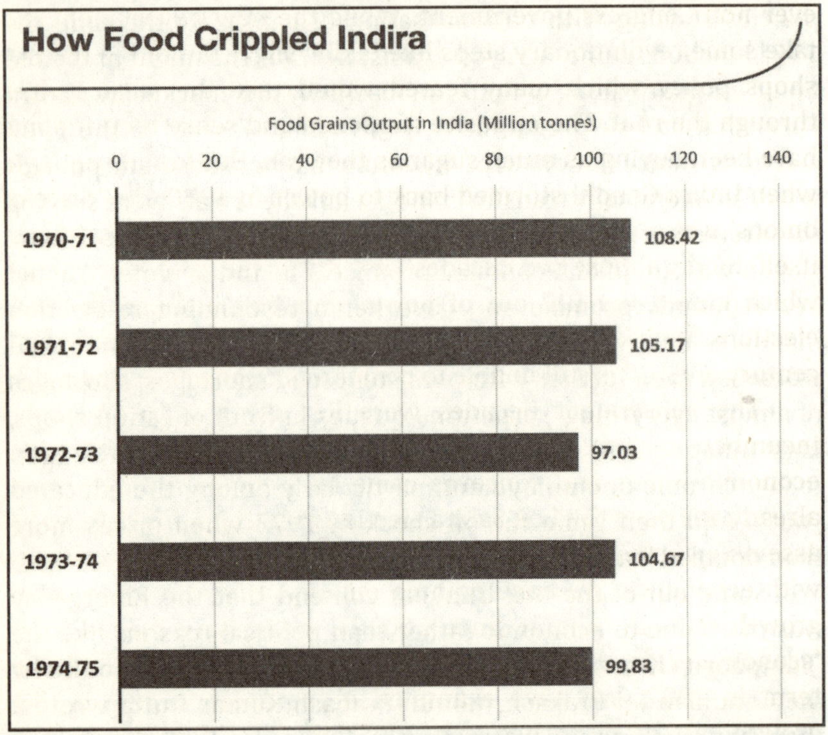

The failed monsoon and fall in agriculture production also led to drop in power generation and very low demand for manufactured goods. Industrial production went down. Lay-offs were too frequent and too many in all industrial centres. This led to sharp spike in unemployment....

International developments too damaged India's economy in pre-Emergency days. West Asia was in turmoil and 1973 oil shock drained foreign exchange reserves of India further as the crude oil prices jumped four times from USD 3 per barrel to USD 12 per barrel within days. Though petrol and diesel prices were under government control, the prices of petroleum products and fertilisers increased sharply. Rising prices were bogging Indira Gandhi government down in public eyes. Inflation was 22 per cent in 1972-73, over 20 per cent in 1974 and over 25 per cent in 1975". A perfect recipe for economic disaster. Emergency followed and so did the post-emergency 1977 elections which gave India its first ever non-Congress government. While the new government did take some revolutionary steps like taking sugar out of the control shops policy which many feared would take the sugar prices through the roof. The opposite happened and sense then Indians have been buying as much sugar as they can. But funnily enough, when Indira Gandhi stormed back to power in 1980, the 'price of onions' was a major electoral issue. And as if on 'history repeats itself' mode, almost two decades later it was the 'prices of onions' which kicked the BJP out of power equation in Delhi in 1998 elections. Such strong was the kick that it has been almost quarter century and BJP is still unable to come back to power in Delhi.

The subsequent decades were lost to identity and anti-incumbency. It was only in the 21st century that economics and economic issues and concerns came back to the fore. We have already analysed the Lok Sabha elections and the Andhra Pradesh assembly elections and examined what relations they had, if any with economics. We have pointed out how the near miraculous growth rates in Gujarat since 2000-01 could have played a big 'economic' role in Narendra Modi winning a second successive term in 2007. We have examined if the average annual GDP growth rate of Bihar between 2005 and 2015 had any role in the pro-incumbency verdicts in favour of Nitish Kumar. We have concluded that while economics did play a decisive role in some electoral outcomes where identity took a back seat; but never really went away as a factor. This debate resumed with furious vengeance when Narendra Modi was anointed as the BJP prime ministerial candidate. By then, scams, policy paralysis and poor governance had left the Indian economy in a mess.

Back to the Future

Modi offered the Gujarat model of government as an alternative that would work wonders for the Indian economy, just as it had for the Gujarat economy. Fans of Modi of course, believed him wholeheartedly. Many independent observers, who were fed up with the UPA regime also believed that Modi sounded credible when he talked about economic reforms and growth the only way for India to emerge as a moderately prosperous country in the future. The series of 'Vibrant Gujarat' events made headlines across India. It was a big contrast to the national economy, as well as the economic situation in different states. Many of them were eventually disappointed as the reforms they were hoping for never happened, the growth rate of GDP became relatively anaemic and religious polarisation struck deeper roots in society. Habitual critics of Modi gloated and fired off "I told you so" missives at independent commentators even as they simultaneously lamented the demise of their idea of a pluralist and inclusive India. According to this group of critics, Modi was a shameful symbol of crony capitalism who had sold his soul and mortgaged the future of the Indian economy to a few favoured tycoons 'who got richer while the poor got poorer'. There is simply no data or evidence to back up these rhetorical claims. But like politics, even commentary and journalism nowadays is largely about rhetoric to suit your pre-set agenda.

Let others judge and decide if Modi is a failure or success. One thing he did succeed in is highlighting the seeming conflict between economics and identity during his 2013-14 election campaign. Let's go back to what one of his most trenchant and relentless critics told a 'Left' oriented audience in Kerala in 2013. In the words of Teesta Setalvad: "Well before the era of Narendra Modi, Gujarat had been set for communalism and its rural anti-minority and anti-constitutional policies. It is a fact that Narendra Modi took it to the ultimate extent. There was no resistance from trade unions, civil society, professional organisations and business bodies. This was planned in such a way that rapacious globalisation policies could be implemented. The PR exercise being carried out for the makeover of Narendra Modi is backed by the neo-liberal corporates which have amassed a significant number of shares in television channels. This disruptive nexus is a threat to the country, democracy and free speech."[12] All we can say is: Phew!

Some other critics of Modi are thankfully more sober, measured and with respect for data. No one in her right senses will say that Milan Vaishnav of Carnegie Foundation is a Modi fan. But around the time Ms. Setalvad was fuming and fulminating, Vaishnav co-authored a small piece (by academic standards) in 2013 where he pointed out some exciting research that was going on about economic performance and electoral outcomes in India. While admitting that a comprehensive data driven analysis between 1980 and 2012 had shown no significant or substantive direct link, he did feel that the Indian voter had changed in the 21st century: "Detecting a shift in Indian voter behaviour is one thing, but understanding why this shift occurred is a more complex enterprise. The increasing electoral rewards for good economic performance could be indicative of a gradual maturation of India's democracy, which involves a number of reinforcing components.

The heady growth years of the 2000s may have fundamentally altered the behaviour of the Indian voter, triggering what's been called a 'revolution in rising expectations'. As one noted economist put it, "People at all levels, especially the poor, had discovered that unlike during the first four decades of independence, rapid improvement in the economic fortune was possible." In other words, the so-called *aam aadmi* (common man) tasted the fruits of rapid growth and has begun to demand that governments deliver more of the same.

During the same period, of course, India witnessed an explosion in the degree of political competition. This increase in competition may have also contributed to a tighter link between vote choice and economic outcomes. With robust competition and a clearer picture of the menu of available options, voters today have a greater number of credible 'exit' options if the incumbent underwhelms."[13]

Identity Comes Back

Going by this logic, the 2014 Lok Sabha elections was about economics. The voters punished the UPA for its perceived miserable economic performance in the last few years of its second term.

The voters also believed that the competitor Modi leading the NDA would deliver the vastly improved economic outcomes they had personally experienced in the previous decade of record growth rates. In case you forgot or missed, we have quoted Vaishnav even in the introductory chapter where he and other academicians had started paying serious attention to pro-incumbency and if economics and pro-incumbency were directly linked.

But in Indian civilisation, even the gods are fallible. So, to expect a hypothesis to deliver what you want is like expecting Hindu gods to be like their Abrahamic counterparts. The fact is: identity politics never went away. Even as Modi was creating history for the BJP in 2014, state elections in erstwhile Andhra Pradesh saw identity politics at its peak. Back in the 1980s, voters in Andhra had punished the Congress for hurting Telugu pride by voting film star N.T. Rama Rao to a landslide victory. They felt hurt and betrayed again in 2014 and gave zero seats to Congress. They gave zero even in 2019. Meanwhile, K.C. Rao rode the wave of Telangana pride to humble the Congress which wanted to take credit for creating a separate state.

Soon after the 2014 Lok Sabha polls, assembly elections were held in some states. Haryana stands out. Not just because it gave a majority to the BJP for the first time, but also because the party consolidated the non-Jat voters in its favour. Literally overnight, the BJP transformed from being a fringe player in Haryana to the ruling party. We have already discussed the 2015 Bihar elections. The Assam assembly elections of 2016 reflected the power of identity politics. Like Haryana, the voters gave a majority to the BJP for 'protecting' Assamese and Hindu culture from being gobbled up by a rapidly changing demographic profile. The peak of identity politics came in Uttar Pradesh in 2017 a few months after demonetisation had severely disrupted the livelihoods of poor people. But so strong was the 'Shamshan versus Kabristan' narrative that the NDA won 325 out of 403 seats in the assembly. Economics had been pushed to an obscure corner in that election. Or maybe it was repackaged in form of identity politics post demonetisation. The sheer scale of sadistic pleasure that 'have-nots' derived from the surprise move of demonetisation requires another book altogether. What we can say in retrospect for sure is that demonetisation was a grand failure in whatever task it was supposed to achieve. It did deliver a weird side effect though. The majority of the bottom of the pyramid did suffer, but their suffering was minuscule in comparison to the wealthy top of the pyramids. And that top of the pyramid was there to see in every village and mohalla of Uttar Pradesh. Just ask anyone around if you happen to be from UP and you will be entertained with juicy stories on which wealthy person in which mohalla or village had to suffer more in recycling their ill-gotten cash at a steep loss. Our Demonetisation Tracker month after month and year after year gave only one directional output of Public Perception: it was a right thing to do. Yes, you read it right. People suffered but all they said it could have been implemented in better way. But even today a huge majority at bottom of the pyramid still find happiness, or rather sadistic pleasure, in the fact that the mohalla level Ambani-Adani suffered. That explains the 325 seats that BJP managed to win in Uttar Pradesh.

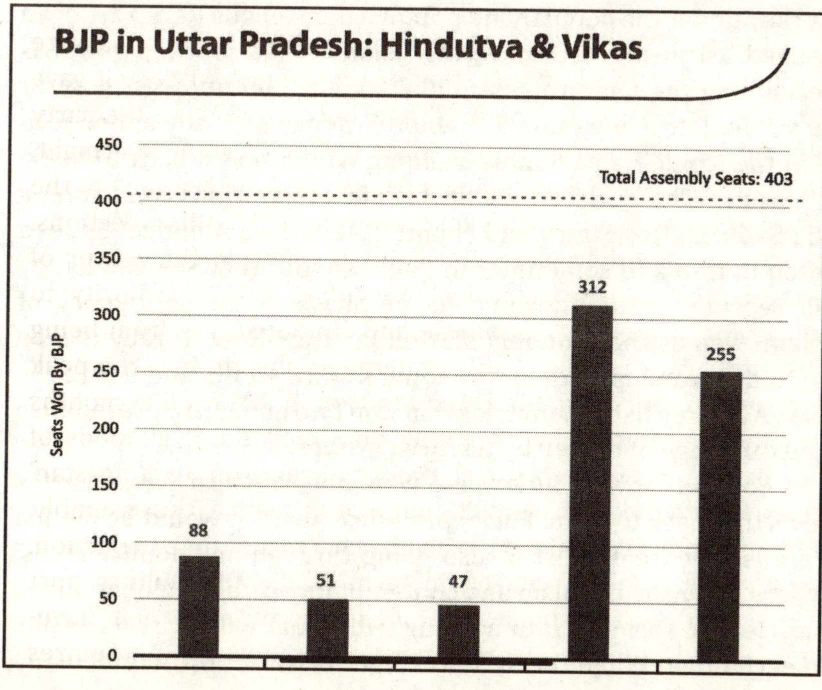

Its Global, and Visceral

For decades, some genuinely concerned and some subtly, or even blatantly racist, commentators from the liberal media in the West wondered how the Indian electorate was stubbornly clinging onto identities based on caste, ethnicity and religion when it came to voting. While the racist lot gloated about backward, feudal and even medieval instincts of Indians, the genuinely concerned ones looked for both explanations and for changes in voting behaviour in the largest democracy in the world. There was both relief and a little bit of celebration in this century as scholars first started noticing how Indian voters were becoming more 'mature' as they started taking economics as an important factor while making voting decisions. Many didn't realise that even as they were expressing genuine concern or gloating, the so-called 'mature' democracies of the West were beginning to fall back upon identity politics. Perhaps the first to do so was Turkey that straddles both the West and the 'Orient'. A resolutely 'secular' country for decades where all public manifestations of faith were virtually prohibited, Turkey under the popular and populist demagogue Rayep Erdogan started earnestly rediscovering Islam. That journey towards reclaiming the nation's essentially Islamic identity was more or less complete a few years ago when Erdogan officially announced that the iconic Hagia Sophia building would revert back to being a mosque. The Turks don't take out demonstrations condemning the Satan United States and chanting "Death to America" as seen often in Iran and sometimes in Pakistan. But they seemed happy till recently with Erdogan who emphasised the supremacy of Islam even as the economy started tanking. Now, Turkey is a de facto dictatorship with an economy in dire straits and a place in the FATF Grey list of countries that don't do enough to prevent use and exchange of money by terrorist groups.

You can dismiss Turkey as a wannabe 'Western' power that is reverting back to form. Racial prejudice apart, it would be foolish because the 'real' West is also going through an 'identity crisis' where nativism, jingoism and contempt for so-called global values has cleaved societies into warring tribes that will give no quarter to each other. When the Syrian refugee crisis hit the world, many

European countries either willingly or reluctantly offered shelter and refuge. But countries like Poland and Hungary flatly refused claiming they wanted to preserve the Christian values and "safe streets where women would not be raped by criminals". This was identity politics of the worst kind. Soon, Austria turned right and put restrictions on Islamic practices and mosques that preached hatred towards the Christian West. Even the cradle of liberalism in Europe, France, banned the hijab. The liberal poster boy Macron managed to win the Presidential elections again in 2022, defeating the far-right Marie Le Pen, only after turning himself right in terms of identity politics. What Macron has done in terms of 'dealing with Islam' will make Indian right-wing politicians look like kids. One of the authors has covered the French elections personally over these years and twenty years back he witnessed that weird election when father of Marie Le Pen, the original Jean Le Pen made a surprise entry to the run-off. The entire Left and liberal class was aghast and made a beeline behind centrist Jacques Chirac which resulted in one of the most one sided elections in French history. Jean Le Pen managed less than 18 per cent votes in the run off. Compare that to results in 2022 when his daughter managed to win more than 40 per cent, that too in a campaign where Macron actually did many things while 'dealing with Islam' that might have made Jean Le Pen proud. For all practical matters, France today is voting on identity politics, with just two options of right or far-right on the table.

But the real shock came in 2016 for globalised 'liberals' when British citizens participated in the so-called Brexit referendum and voted to leave the European Union. Those who voted for Brexit said they wanted to preserve the unique British identity and would be damned if some bureaucrat sitting somewhere in Europe could tell them what to eat and drink and where to buy from. Brexit was considered a watershed moment for the simmering identity war between the globalists and the nativists. The massive failure of the polling industry in estimating and predicting the Brexit sentiment was bound to happen considering the inherent confirmation bias in majority of the liberal class reading 'glass half full' while the situation was 'glass half empty'. The fact was, in almost all the polls on Brexit in UK the gap between 'yes' camp and the 'no' camp was touch and go and very much within the margin of error for such surveys. But the confirmation biased of liberal analyst stop them short of reading what was clearly written on the wall.

But that was child's play compared to what was happening across the Atlantic in the United States. The confirmation bias of the liberal media was in full display again. The C-Voter tracker happened to be among the only two media trackers in US which continuously mentioned a 'probable' Trump victory in electoral college, even though Hillary Clinton was leading in the national vote share. There was no 'secret sauce' here. We simply said it was 'too close to call' when it was too close to call in many swing states, particularly in the rust belt. The 'confirmation bias' did the liberal media in, exactly the way it did in UK across the Atlantic. The much controversial Donald Trump defeated Hillary Clinton to become the President of the United States. The shock was too much to handle and America saw a massive resurgence of culture and identity wars. It is easy to blame Donald Trump for this; but wrong. Sure, he is almost certainly a phoney charlatan. But he merely exploited the already widening cleavages in society; he didn't create them. Surely, he didn't instruct *The New York Times* to sponsor a new look at American history called the 1619 project that asserted that the very formation of America in 1619 was a project conceived and executed to enslave Africans and hold them in slavery? Did he order school boards in some 'liberal' states to club Asian Americans with whites for school admissions as Asians were taking unfair advantage of being minorities and depriving blacks of admissions in good schools? Did he advise Hillary Clinton to describe American citizens who wont vote for her as 'deplorable'? Did he sign a presidential decree that enabled universities to ban the entry of conservative speakers, authors and analysts just because they felt such speakers and authors represented the worst of white racism? The list could go on and on.

In December, 2021, journalist Lionel Barber wrote an anguished column for Nikkei Asia after 'woke progressives' in America forced the removal of a statue of Thomas Jefferson: "Late last month, a work crew entered New York's City Hall and removed a 401-kg, 2.1-meter statue of Thomas Jefferson, author of the Declaration of Independence and one of America's Founding Fathers.

The statue had been in place for the previous 187 years. It was relocated to the New-York Historical Society on a 10-year loan after complaints from black staffers that the slave-owning U.S. president made them uncomfortable. The uprooting of a national icon marks a new frontier in the culture wars increasingly defining U.S. politics and its education system. "It is nothing less than an attempt to destroy any notion of the U.S. as a country built on the ideals of freedom and to forever tarnish the idea that America might stand for anything good," wrote the English historian Andrew Roberts. "If the Founding Fathers of a country were evil, the founding of their country was evil and built upon a lie."

These progressives are known as 'woke warriors,' where 'woke' means being attuned to racial and social injustice. Their army is on the march, with their banners calling for de-funding the police, ending the detention of illegal immigrants along the southern border and passing a multi-billion-dollar Green New Deal. This is more than the cyclical revision of history. Roberts is right: It is an assault on the foundations of the republic."[14]

If identity politics is not going away anywhere in the world, even in the so called 'mature' democracies of the West, don't expect any miracles from India which has a very, very long history of caste, ethnic and religious differences, if not cleavages. Do remember: even before the first whites set forth on their journeys to 'discover' what they thought was India and reached the shores of America, India was going through religious conflict. And don't forget, even before the Magna Carta was signed about a 1,000 years ago, caste oppression was perhaps the norm in Indian society. With such long historical memories hard wired into our psyches either in writing or through oral traditions, expecting the Indian voter to abandon identity while exercising her right to vote is like asking an elephant in Africa to welcome a rifle-toting hunter out for a trophy.

So, economics will occasionally affect electoral outcomes, but voters could anyway switch back to identity politics.

Growth or Welfare?

In the chapter on the impact welfare schemes have on the pro incumbency phenomenon, we have discussed how welfare schemes led to often vast improvement in physical as well as material well-being of beneficiaries who have been termed 'Labharthis' in this Modi era. We saw the dramatic impact of the 'Rythu Bandhu' scheme launched by Telangana chief minister K.C. Rao on his re-election chances. The scheme offered Rs. 8,000 a year in direct cash transfer to a farmer for acre of land owned. The average per capita income of a small farmer owning three acres would not be more than Rs. 100,000 a year. For him, an additional Rs. 24,000 a year was like manna from heaven. The question is: where does that money come from? The obvious answer is: taxes. So, the argument is that higher rates of economic growth lead to a rise in tax revenues that would enable a smart politician to provide more welfare schemes to benefit the poor and then win more elections. But politicians often don't have the luxury of thinking that far ahead into the long term. As for the beneficiary, she would rather have the cash right here and now than wait for high GDP growth rates that may or may not materialise. So a new debate on growth versus welfare has been ignited, especially in the aftermath of the Covid pandemic that cruelly exposed inequalities in societies across the world, including India.

In an essay for the Observer Research Foundation in October, 2020, Sangeet Jain writes: 'The dichotomisation of welfare and growth—treating welfare as a temporary means to keep people afloat while prioritising growth—was never really fit for use but feels especially dated today. It is certainly not fit for a future in which work is likely to be both structurally underpaid and scarce. We require an architecture that can support workers in making the transition to a greener economy and a world of less work.[30] Social security can no longer be a luxury or an avoidable cost, it has to be seen as an investment in building a more equitable, just society. [31] It is time for India to revisit its old welfare versus growth debate. Social security must complement quality employment and needs to be designed as such."[15]

Economics is no doubt too important a long-term factor to

ignore for any country that aspires to increased prosperity. But so is identity and so is welfare for people who live on the edges of absolute poverty. There would be a handful of statesmen like pro incumbency politicians who will chase not just re-election votes, but also a legacy and a place in history books. But by and large, they will leave the task of raising growth rates to professionals while they dream of new welfare schemes to get more votes. That's why, despite its enormous importance, we have not included economic performance as a key reason behind the pro incumbency phenomenon.

But mistaking the voter preference for immediate welfare over faster long-term growth is pure myopia. The woman in a household gets no immediate benefit when schemes enable and encourage her daughter to pursue an education in schools and colleges so that she can become a financially independent adult. To that extent, even a bicycle provided to her daughter for easing her daily trip to school is a turning point. A laptop given by government to her kids: that's truly long-term. A toilet built in her house with government support is not a matter of hygiene, which a majority of armchair analysts understand. It is a matter of the physical security of her daughter, simply because the mother personally knows the pain of being sexually abused, or the fear of being sexually assaulted while going to the field in darkness of early morning hours or late evening past dusk. And the woman votes for it. That too in historic large turnouts, not just in terms of filling up the decades' old turnout gap, but actually surpassing the males in terms of electoral participation. While the male counterparts are still looking at emotive issues using their hearts, she is voting on the real hard issues of her daily life using her head. To that extent, she is also voting for long term economic growth. She may not understand the jargon; but has enough common sense to know the long-term economic impact of a decent education.

References

1. Central Statistical Organisation & Periodic Labour Force Survey, National Statistical Organisation
2. https://www.indiatoday.in/magazine/cover-story/story/20050103-

india-in-2004-return-of-congress-fall-of-bjp-dictatorship-of-left-788521-2005-01-03
3. https://www.thenewsminute.com/article/wasted-leverage-flip-flop-four-mistakes-andhra-cm-naidu-made-78577
4. https://www.ndtv.com/india-news/atal-bihari-vajpayee-piloted-2nd-generation-economic-reforms-india-inc-1901720
5. https://archive.indianexpress.com/news/mobiles-racing-past-the-hundred-million-mark/168736/
6. https://www.firstpost.com/india/its-luck-explaining-sonias-rise-bjps-2004-loss-and-cricket-debuts-562632.html
7. https://www.india-seminar.com/2004/539/539 per cent20manini per cent20chatterjee.htm
8. https://m.economictimes.com/swaminathan-s-a-aiyar/agriculture-secret-of-modis-success/articleshow/4805278.cms
9. https://indianexpress.com/article/explained/simply-put madhya-pradesh-assembly-election-cm-shivraj-singh-chouhan-agriculture-transformation-a-farm-story-5467975/
10. https://indianexpress.com/article/business/economy/as-per-new-gdp-measure-upa-decade-growth-revised-up-to-8-12-hit-10-in-2006-07-nda-panel-5312686/
11. https://www.postandcourier.com/aikenstandard/opinion/column-its-the-economy-stupid-as-true-today-as-in-1992/article_68d78e91-94c6-5f4a-860c-c97684f5e8c6.html
12. https://www.indiatoday.in/india/story/did-indira-gandhi-impose-emergency-to-escape-economic-crisis-1269992-2018-06-26
13. https://www.newindianexpress.com/states/kerala/2013/may/15/Rectify-anti-people-policies-UDF-government-told-477410.html
14. https://carnegieendowment.org/2013/12/19/does-good-economics-mean-good-politics-in-india-pub-53988
15. https://asia.nikkei.com/Opinion/America-s-woke-warriors-are-on-the-march
16. https://www.orfonline.org/expert-speak/reimagining-work-welfare-indian-economy/

6

OF SPOILERS AND UPSETS

We have seen the factors, social, political, economic and even personal that have been responsible for the 'wave' of pro-incumbency verdicts witnessed during elections in the 21st century. More often than not, it is the personality cult, the personal popularity of the leader with a unique connect with the masses and the increasingly 'presidential' style and nature of elections. Somehow Indian psyche seems to be more attuned to the presidential form than the parliamentary form of electoral democracy. Our historical and cultural context of 'Raja' and 'Praja' might have everything to do with this. We do vote in a Westminster model of Parliamentary democracy borrowed from the British, but while voting our instincts on decision making is more like presidential form of electoral democracy. Everyone talks about the Narendra Modi phenomenon while describing how Indian voters are behaving like Americans by choosing a 'President' rather than a Prime Minister. This applies even more tellingly in state elections in contemporary times. The most recent and powerful example is West Bengal. The BJP poured in everything possible to oust the TMC government led by Mamata Banerjee. For a while, it looked as if she might just lose as TMC leaders of various hues abandoned her and made a beeline for the BJP. To twist a cliché, money flowed like milk during Shiv Ratri. Narendra Modi's sarcastic incantation of 'Didi O Didi' and the seemingly rapturous response from the crowds seemed to reaffirm the vulnerability of Mamata Banerjee.

Yet, there was one thing the BJP simply did not have to offer. Who is a BJP leader in the state who is more popular, better known with a proven track record of grassroots 'street Fighting' and politically taller than Didi? There simply was no one who came even close to her. And that proved to be one of the factors behind her third successive term. We have already discussed the power and potency of welfare and women to ensure that pro-incumbency waves do not ebb. It definitely happened with Mamata Didi in 2021 in West Bengal. For the first few terms in office as chief minister, Nitish Kumar epitomised this. Many analysts suggest that his move to impose prohibition in Bihar proved to be a big hit with women voters. Shivraj Singh Chouhan was actually better at delivering welfare and wooing women voters. The more recent Yogi victory in Uttar Pradesh has everything to do with female voters, not just in terms of welfare populism, but more in terms of law and order, that too not via bulldozer that everyone is frantically talking about, but via the toilets that have been made in literally every home classified as bottom of the pyramid. Then we have talked about how weaknesses of the opposition parties and leaders have helped propel pro-incumbency. We have cited the BJP in Delhi and the Congress in Gujarat as just two of the examples that confirm this hypothesis.

But there is another category of pro-incumbency verdicts that is either unexpected or seemingly inexplicable or both. Strange as it may sound, the unexpected and the seemingly inexplicable have actually baffled even pundits, even though they are always ready with seemingly convincing answers, no matter how uncomfortable the questions are. But if you dig deeper, you will find a new cast of characters that have played 'side' roles in the festivals of democracy celebrated in the 21st century. They have been around for ages and will almost certainly be there in the future. They do not have the political capital or support base to win a majority in elections. Yet, they often play a decisive, albeit small role in deciding which way electoral verdicts go. They are called 'spoilers'. Since this book is primarily on pro-incumbency as a 21st century phenomenon, we will focus on 'spoilers' that helped incumbents retain power against seeming odds.

The online resource dictionary.com defines a political spoiler as "a third political party formed to draw votes away from one of the two major parties, thus spoiling its chance of winning an election". And despite their relative irrelevance, researchers seem to have devoted time to them. One such study was authored by Sacha Kapoor and Arvind Magesan in December 2019 that came up with the startling conclusion that 'independents' or spoilers actually tend to make incumbents lose. Since several studies will provide data to show how they have helped incumbents win, we leave it to you to judge, if you have the time and inclination. According to the research study: Independent candidates are often deemed 'frivolous' or 'spoilers' by mainstream political figures and authorities, although there is little to no evidence on their effect on elections. This article finds that independent candidates decrease the chances that a Lok Sabha constituency elects a member of the party or coalition that forms the national government. It suggests that participation by independents has a high price—a lesser role for the constituency in policy making.[1]

Let's first analyse in slight detail two 'family' based spoilers before we move on to the others.

When he first became chief minister in 1970, rock music aficionados were mourning the split announced by the legendary Beatles. Lata Mangeshkar, as ever, mesmerised the nation with haunting songs like 'Babul Pyare' filmed on Hema Malini in *Johny Mera Naam* and 'Hum The Jinke Sahare' filmed on Sharmila Tagore in *Safar*, to name just two. Brazil and Pele had created a new record by winning the Football World Cup for the third time. Sheikh Mujibur Rehman, the founder of Bangladesh had been arrested and jailed by the military dictator Yahya Khan of Pakistan despite winning national elections. And of course, Rahul Gandhi too was born in 1970.

We are talking about Prakash Singh Badal, the 94 year-old Akali Dal leader who has been chief minister of Punjab five times and who is still active in politics, though his son Sukhbir Singh Badal now leads the party. His latest (but probably not the last) election in 2022 Punjab assembly election handed him a rare personal defeat on his own family turf of Lambi. Just in case if he would have won, that would have been a record of sorts at the ripe age of 94 when nobody from his generation is still active in politics. His stint in politics would be more comparable to former chief minister of Tamil Nadu M. Karunanidhi, who passed away at the age of 94 in 2018. But then he was no longer active in politics with his son and current chief minister of the state M.K. Stalin was leading the party. Another leading politician of the country L.K. Advani is within touching distance of the age 95. But he too has not been active in politics for quite a while. Like Advani, Prakash Singh Badal too has seen everything that happened in independent India. They were already adults when the British left in 1947. What a treasure trove of good, bad and ugly stories they would have to share!

In an interview given to the *Hindustan Times* in October, 2021, Prakash Singh Badal did recollect a few significant things: "After 11 stints in the assembly and Parliament, and five terms as chief minister, Badal remembers the initial days of the 1951 polls as 'chaotic'.

"All parties and politicians were trying to consolidate their space," he said.

A young political operative at the time, Badal used to take senior leaders in his Willys jeep to rallies and events, and even drove buses to political events...He remembered the frenetic build-up to the 1951-52 elections due to the steep logistical challenges and the country's first experience with universal adult franchise. "In the first election, ballot papers were used to cast votes, old ghee cans were used a ballot boxes and vote count was written on black boards," he said.[2]

First Cousin Feud

But let's forget nostalgia and come back to politics. The 2012 assembly election verdict in Punjab which reinforced the pro-incumbency phenomenon was actually an unexpected one for many till deeper data dives and analysis revealed some insights. For some pundits, it still remains inexplicable. We have already seen how some states had become used to anti-incumbency verdicts and changes in government every five years since the Congress monopoly had completely collapsed by the 1980s, at least in assembly elections. Older states like Rajasthan, Karnataka and Himachal Pradesh continue to do so (as did Kerala till 2021) along with newer states like Uttarakhand and Jharkhand. Punjab belonged firmly to this category of 'outliers' since the 1980s and remained loyal to the anti-incumbency phenomenon even during the first decade of this century. The Congress and the Akali Dal-BJP alliance kept playing musical chairs with power. The Akalis won in 1985 but didn't last long because terrorism peaked in Punjab after that. When elections were held again in 1992, it was the turn of the Congress to win. The tables turned in 1997 when the Akali-BJP alliance won a famous victory by virtually sweeping the state. The Congress was reduced to just 14 seats in an assembly with 117 members. The BJP perhaps turned in its second-best performance ever in the state winning 18 of the 23 seats it contested. The Akali Dal too created a record of sorts by winning 75 out of the 92 seats it contested. Prakash Singh Badal, then a sprightly young 69 years old, became chief minister for the third time.

Soon after this, the NDA led by Atal Bihari Vajpayee came to power at the centre and you had what is now popularly known as 'double engine' sarkar. But even double engines stall, fail and often go off the tracks as it happened in 2002. The Congress won a simple majority with 62 seats and Captain Amarinder Singh became chief minister. The anti-incumbency virus stuck again in 2007. There was no wave and no sweep; just good old fashioned anti-incumbency. The Akali-BJP alliance won 67 seats and the Congress managed a respectable 44 seats. The rising star this time was Manpreet Badal, the bright cousin of Sukhbir Singh Badal who was made the finance minister and did remarkably well by all standards. Then the Akali Dal was stuck by a common disease in Indian politics called the dynasty preference syndrome. It has happened across India. To name just a few, it happened in Assam with the Congress when Himanta Biswa Sarma realised that chief minister Tarun Gogoi was determined to promote his son Gaurav Gogoi as the future leader. It happened with the once trusted lieutenant of Mamata Banerjee Suvendu Adhikari who realised he would have to take orders in the future from her nephew Abhishek Banerjee. And it happened with the Shiv Sena in Maharashtra when the charismatic Raj Thackeray revolted when party Supremo Balasaheb Thackeray decided that his own son and cousin of Raj, Uddhav Thackeray would be the future leader. What happened with the Akali Dal in Punjab is similar to what happened with the Shiv Sena in Maharashtra.

Soon after the alliance took over the reins of the government in Punjab, differences between the cousins Sukhbir and Manpreet started cropping up. Ostensibly, the differences were over managing finances of the state and the economic policies followed by the alliance. In reality, it was a war of egos and a bigger war over who would take over after Prakash Singh Badal. The father inevitably chose the son and a stage was soon reached by 2010 when Manpreet made his dislike and criticism of Sukhbir public. Manpreet was 'sacked' from the Akali Dal in October 2010 and soon formed his own party called the People's Party of Punjab. By then, serious allegations of corruption had emerged against Sukhbir Singh Badal and his allegedly lifestyle. It seemed the voters of Punjab too were unhappy, if not angry with the alliance government.

By the time the 2012 assembly were round the corner, there was near unanimity amongst political commentators and pundits that the anti-incumbency musical chairs game would resume in the state. As the elections came closer, a plethora of opinion polls suggested that the Congress was coming back to power with Captain Amarinder Singh as chief minister. People shrugged knowingly. The votes were cast after a high-decibel campaign and then came the exit polls. Almost all of them said voters had opted for the Congress to rule Punjab. And then everyone was shocked when the results were announced. The Akali Dal-BJP alliance had beaten all odds and created a kind of history in Punjab by winning a second successive term with a combined total of 68 seats. The Congress had to be satisfied with 46 seats and wait another five years before the 'Udta Punjab' level of anger amongst voters swept the alliance out of power. Many pundits gave various reasons for this unexpected verdict; most centre around the growing unpopularity of the Congress led UPA regime at the centre. The most influential Punjab-based English newspaper commented soon after the results in a piece by Naveen S. Garewal: "The SAD—BJP emerged victorious due to several reasons. It announced populist manifesto that promised continuing subsidies through schemes like atta-dal, pensions, free electricity and water, etc. In contrast, the PPP that was opposed to withdrawal of subsidies was completely voted out....Punjab, like Haryana, has an important lesson for the region. Alternating government every five years is now a thing of the past, reasonable governance with welfare measure for the people can ensure a repeat mandate. It has happened in Gujarat, Bihar and now people have started evaluating performance."[4] Perhaps written in a hurry, the piece forgot Sheila Dikshit, Shivraj Singh Chouhan, Dr. Raman Singh and Naveen Patnaik.

But the smarter ones, at least those who understand numbers figured it out. At 42 per cent, the alliance had a 2 per cent higher vote share than the Congress. But it was Manpreet Badal whose revolt against his cousin Sukhbir that ironically cost the Congress the election. His party won approximately 6 per cent votes that were predominantly anti-alliance without winning any seats. *The Tribune* piece quoted above does mention: "The PPP got six per cent votes that damaged the Congress more than it could harm the Akali Dal." Without Manpreet, the Congress could have romped home. The pro-incumbency verdict was unexpected, but not inexplicable.

More First Cousin Feud

Almost exactly the same thing happened in Maharashtra in 2009 during the assembly elections. The founder and patriarch of the Shiv Sena Balasaheb Thackeray too had to anoint an inheritor of his controversial, albeit potent legacy. On one side the unassuming and almost self-effacing son Uddhav Thackeray who did not outwardly appear to be that keen on the hard grind of politics. But appearances, as later events have proven, can be very deceptive. Uddhav Thackeray clearly lacked the charisma and the flair for biting words and provocative remarks that his father Balasaheb Thackeray displayed all too often. Even hard-core Shiv Sena supporters liked Uddhav; but that was that. He didn't seem to inspire them with fiery rhetoric to take to streets and attack sundry shops, movie theatres and offices.

In contrast, the nephew Raj Thackeray seemed not just a natural born politician of the Shiv Sena kind, but also a natural inheritor of the Balasaheb legacy. He gave fiery and provocative speeches; his interviews to the media were full of combative repartee; he led from the front and even had Balasaheb often sending out cryptic signals that Raj Thackeray would one day lead the Shiv Sena once he was gone from the scene. There was a kind of consensus among political commentators that Raj Thackeray, and not Uddhav was the future of the Shiv Sena with the later playing an advisory role from behind the scenes. The family would stay united and work together with the then junior partner BJP to regain power they had lost in the 1999 assembly elections.

But tensions were brewing not just in the Thackeray family, but also in the Shiv Sena. Its alliance with the BJP had lost the second successive assembly elections in 2004 to the Congress-NCP alliance. The former Shiv Sena chief minister personally anointed by Balasaheb, Narayan Rane had already revolted and bolted. There was a bye-election necessary in 2005 in the Mavlan assembly constituency where Narayan Rane announced he would contest as a rebel Shiv Sena candidate. A furious Balasaheb Thackeray, according to both political gossip and reports, wanted to teach a personal lesson to Rane. By then, his son had startlingly started taking a lot of interest in politics. His direct access to the patriarch as a son was an advantage enjoyed by Uddhav that Raj didn't have. Movie-style friction and tension was brewing between the two cousins and it was becoming increasingly clear that Balasaheb had to make a choice sooner or later.

He made his move by asking the son Uddhav to personally take charge of the Mavlan assembly bye election campaign to 'teach that ungrateful upstart Rane' a lesson. Readers who are more imaginative can already hear thundering background music as Raj came know of the news and realised he would never be the inheritor. The father had chosen the son and that was that. Publicly, he soldiered on nevertheless, though the fissures, the recriminations and the bitterness was becoming increasingly apparent. Then the Mavlan assembly seat voters delivered a hammer blow. The rebel Narayan Rane, who currently happens to be a Union Minister in the Narendra Modi cabinet, not only won the bye election handsomely, but also ensured that the official Shiv Sena candidate lost his deposit.

Political gossip and the kind of media stories that follow suggested that Mavlan proved to be the final straw for Raj Thackeray. Not only did he realise that he would lead the party in the future, he saw no future for the party under a 'weak' leader like his cousin Uddhav. He too became a rebel and organised a public meeting towards the end of 2005 where he announced he was quitting the Shiv Sena and blamed Uddhav Thackeray for his exit. He told his supporters that for him, Balasaheb was a god, is a god and would remain a god. At the same time, Raj said that it would be impossible for him to work with Uddhav as they differ fundamentally in thinking. After a tour of the state, Raj Thackeray formed the Maharashtra Navnirman Sena, a new regional political party that would protect and promote Marathi pride and aspirations even better than the Shiv Sena. The parting was mutually bitter. It was almost seven years later at the funeral of Balasaheb that the two cousins publicly shared their sorrow together in front of live TV cameras. The grief and loss was palpable, but cynical political observers called it a re-run of a Bollywood movie or an Ekta Kapoor serial.

There were many efforts made by well wishes, it seems. But they failed. In a piece for the magazine *Open* in 2012, Haima Deshpande writes: "Ego and ambition seem to be the big stumbling blocks between the cousins that make it hard for them to join forces. Unlike the late Sena chief who believed in remote-controlling his men, Uddhav and Raj are both keen on wielding direct power. Both see themselves as Maharashtra CM and neither is willing to play second fiddle to the other...Ambitious wives on both sides are said to be working to ensure that the cousins do not patch up. Uddhav's wife Rashmi and Raj's wife Sharmila, it is said, will never allow a merger as they see larger independent roles for themselves in the state's power structure."[4] Who said Indian politics cannot resemble Bollywood style drama once in a while?

You might well ask: what has all this to do with the fact that the Shiv Sena-BJP alliance lost the Maharashtra assembly elections for the third successive time? Well, Raj Thackeray did exactly what Manpreet Badal later on did in Punjab in 2012. But while the Manpreet revolt ended up harming the Congress, the Raj revolt harmed the Shiv Sena and the alliance. His party won 5.75 per cent votes that could have gone to the Shiv Sena alliance and helped the Congress-NCP government which was very unpopular then, manage to win a third successive term.

After 2009, the rise of the BJP in the state was unmistakable. Having failed to agree on a seat sharing arrangement, the two fought the 2014 assembly elections separately. The BJP became by far the largest party with 122 seats, almost double than the 63 seats managed by Shiv Sena. BJP polled 28 per cent votes on standalone basis which was almost 10 per cent more than what Shiv Sena managed to get. Even in Shiv Sena home turf of Mumbai region, BJP managed to win 15 in comparison to 14 odd seats won by Shiv Sena. The MNS of Raj Thackeray polled more than 3 per cent at state level, but was definitely much bigger spoiler in Mumbai-Thane-Konkan belt and played his own role in humiliating Uddhav Thackeray. After some huffing and puffing and hemming and hawing, Uddhav Thackeray swallowed his pride and accepted Devendra Fadnavis of the BJP as chief minister and the Shiv Sena was now very much the junior partner in the alliance. The two rode the pro-incumbency phenomenon in the 2019 assembly elections and won a comfortable majority with Devendra Fadnavis as the CM face. But in a totally unexpected move, Uddhav abandoned the BJP and joined hands with the Congress and NCP to form a government with him as the chief minister. Who could have thought the unassuming and reluctant Uddhav Thackeray of the Vajpayee era would pull off a political stunt like this? Commentators say Uddhav finally has had the last laugh; but in politics, last laughs don't last very long.

Exit First Cousins, Enter Real Brothers and Grandsons Feud

Haryana, where else? The state which has the original 'Kurukshetra' has all the rights to re-narrate tales involving brothers, cousins and even grandsons fighting for the power equation. A lot has been discussed on how the BJP under Modi-Shah managed to win Haryana by weaving the non-Jat umbrella in a state where entire politics was defined as Jat equation for almost seven decades. So, what happens when a party in power manages to increase its vote share by 3 per cent from previous elections, leads by almost 10 per cent votes over the runner up party, and still the end result is a hung assembly with the leading party falling short by 6 seats. It is fine that the leading party forms the government again, but had to take support from a newly formed regional party which won 10 off seats in first ever attempt. The party in question is JJP, led by a young dynast Dushyant Chautala.

The political history of Chautala's deserve a book on its own. But to sum up, the political capital and legacy of Chaudhary Devi Lal was abused to the hilt by his son Om Prakash Chautala. All through the 80s and 90s and till 2014, the BJP played the role of side kick to the Chautala's, just the way it did in many other states under coalition dharma of Atal-Advani era. The two sons of Om Prakash Chautala: Abhay and Ajay fought over this political capital but this didn't spill over on the streets. Ajay Chautala's son Dushyant won his first Lok Sabha election as INLD candidate in 2014 by a slender margin of 30k votes. He formed his own party JJP in 2018 after his uncle Abhay Chautala expelled him, fearing he was out sizing his own popularity. As a JJP candidate Dushyant lost by a huge margin of more than 3 lakh votes to BJP candidate in 2019 Lok Sabha election. In the 2019 Lok Sabha, his party managed to win only about 5 per cent votes in entire state.

Fast forward to 2019 and find his 5 per cent swell to 15 per cent votes, all at the expense of the BJP, which lost almost 20 per cent votes when compared to its historic all time high vote share of 58 per cent in Lok Sabha elections just a year back. The C-Voter tracker had been consistently pointing out the anger against the BJP CM Manohar Lal Khattar all these years. That Mr. Khattar has been consistently rated among India's most 'unpopular' CM in the India Today's Annual Report Card in Mood of The Nation polls carried by C-Voter, hardly makes his position enviable. While in the Lok Sabha elections the popularity of PM Modi superseded everything else, the ratings of unpopular CM was bound to result in a downswing in the assembly elections.

However, the fact that majority of this downswing went to JJP, not the Congress puts up a weird angle to the spoiler theory. Arguably, the votes swinging between BJP and erstwhile INLD, and now the JJP, were all anti-Congress votes. In the Lok Sabha elections, they concentrated behind BJP but in Vidhan Sabha elections they split between BJP and JJP. So was the JJP playing a spoiler for the BJP or the Congress? Many analysts thought he spoiled the chances of Congress, as the Jat voters at the state level would have voted against the BJP and supported the Congress under ex-CM and still popular leader Bhupinder Singh Hooda. This sounds like a legit argument, but if they actually considered BJP to be so much anti-Jat, why did they rally behind the party just a year back in Lok Sabha election? The answer is in 'split-vote'. But the only difference being, now the split vote is swinging between BJP and a BJP-alliance partner. And for all practical matters, the role of JJP was of a spoiler against the BJP. Simply because there is no other instance in Indian electoral history where a leading party with almost 10 per cent vote gap over the runner-up party, falls short of majority and the final result is a hung assembly. And yet, the bottom line ends up in a pro-incumbent verdict with the help of the same party which played the spoiler. Politics is definitely stranger than fiction.

In Manipur, Everyone Expected the Unexpected but not Like this

The most unexpected pro-incumbent verdict came in Manipur in 2022 Assembly elections. Not because Manipur is alien to pro-incumbent verdict. In fact, Manipur must be one of state showing longest streaks of pro-incumbent verdicts even when the Congress was in power. The 2017 elections in Manipur didn't really give a clear anti-incumbency verdict. The Congress was still the single largest party in the 60-member house with 28 odd seats, falling short just by 2 seats for another term. The BJP won only 21 seats, but with other smaller parties managed to form the government for the first time in Manipur. In short, the Congress was caught napping and the BJP did a repeat of Goa in Manipur by proactively forming the government.

Five years down the line, the N. Biren Singh-led BJP government had its own fair share of problems that come along with any minority government. Ideally, the Congress should have been the default gainer from the routine anti-incumbency. But what the state of Manipur witnessed was nothing short of a miracle. While the BJP managed an upswing of just about 3 per cent votes, it resulted in a full majority with 32 seats. This is not something that normally happens after a shaky minority government completes five years in power; it is the main opposition party that goes for a complete meltdown. The Congress lost more than half of the 35 per cent votes it polled in 2017 elections and its vote share came crashing down to less than 17 per cent votes resulting in just about 5 odd seats.

What is even more weird about the Congress meltdown in Manipur is the upswing of NPP founded by the North East stalwart P.A. Sangma, and hold your breath, the JD(U) founded by the Bihar stalwart Nitish Kumar. Does that even make any sense to you? While NPP is ruling in neighbouring Meghalaya with P.A. Sangma's son Conrad Sangma as CM, it is known to have a decent traction in other NE states. So, the jump of NPP votes from 5 per cent in 2017 to 17 per cent in 2022 made it the biggest opposition party with 7 seats, eclipsing the Congress is still palatable. What's not, is the fact that Nitish Kumar's JD(U) polled about 11 per cent votes won 6 seats, one more than the royal tally of 5 managed by the Congress. This added insult to the injury for the Congress. And as if to rub in salt to those insulted injuries, the Naga Peoples Front, which contests only in the peripheral 9 odd seats where Naga voters are concentrated, won 5 out of those 9 seats with an impressive 8 per cent vote share.

As we are writing, on the floor of Manipur house, Congress in not the main opposition party. It is not even the second largest opposition party. Hell, it's not even the third largest opposition party as that honour is shared with NPF which is a fringe player in power equation. Now all these three parties with impressive numbers: the NPP, the JD(U) and the NPF also happen to be BJP allies. While NPP and NPF are part of BJP-led NEDA (North East Democratic Alliance), the JD(U) in Manipur is nothing short of a miracle. Never mind the fact that it was part of the BJP strategy to provide enough resources and plant JD(U) as an optional landing pad for all winnable candidates that the party was unable to field for various reasons. The strategy was to stop them going over to the Congress and keep them in buffer. A clinical masterstroke played by NEDA convener and BJP mastermind in North East region—Himanta Biswa Sarma. He ensured that the Congress meltdown is so complete that it can't even be counted as a spoiler anymore in Manipur politics, forget about blaming NPP, JD(U) or NPF playing the spoiler.

From BJP as a Spoiler to Congress as a Spoiler in Telangana

We have discussed the back-to-back TRS victories in Telangana. While the various aspects of pro-incumbency worked well in Telangana, the spoiler impact is evolving and swinging in different ways as the politics of the newly founded state is maturing. The first election of Telangana assembly happened as a part of unified Andhra Pradesh along with 2014 Lok Sabha elections. Right after the election the two state assemblies were carved out with TDP winning a majority in Andhra Pradesh and TRS winning 63 out of total 119 seats with 34 per cent vote share. Remember, the elections happened in unified Andhra, and even the parties like TDP and YSRCP contested on seats falling under the new Telangana state. While the Congress was completely wiped out and Andhra as the contest primarily got bipolar between TDP and YSRCP; the contest in Telangana went multi-cornered with the Congress emerging as the main opposition party polling 25 per cent votes and 21 seats.

The spoilers in Telangana polled rather well. The TDP polled almost 14.5 per cent votes and managed to win 15 odd seats while the YSRCP polled only 3.5 per cent votes and managed just 3 odd seats. Together these two 'Andhra' parties polled 18 per cent votes and exactly 18 assembly seats. Basically, the Congress could claim that these two parties played spoiler and denied the GOP a pro-incumbent verdict. Please remember the Congress was in power in the outgoing unified Andhra assembly. We will discuss the role of the BJP and AIMIM in a while.

Fast forward to five years later and we see TRS holding on to power with impressive 47 per cent votes winning them 88 seats in Assembly. Congress did manage to increase its vote share by 3 per cent but its seats tally came down to 19 seats. The erstwhile 'Andhra' parties TDP and YSRCP were completely wiped out in the realistic political polarisation of Telangana. So where did the votes of spoiler 'Andhra' parties go? It's easy to decode that. That 18 per cent odd vote bank got neatly transferred to TRS, which witnessed an upswing of 13 per cent votes and Congress with an upswing of 3 per cent votes.

It is important to observe here that the other two 'spoilers', BJP and AIMIM remained literally static. The BJP remain static at 7 per cent votes and its tally of 5 MLA came crashing down to just 1 seat. The AIMIM polled around 3 per cent and its tally of 7 MLAs remained the same, all coming from the Muslim dominated seats of Hyderabad region. So, the meltdown of TDP and YSRCP did not help BJP or AIMIM. It did not even help the Congress. It just went lock, stock and barrel to TRS. In other words, they were not really 'spoilers'. They were essentially anti-Congress votes and once the Telangana equations were rebooted, they swung to the most dominant anti-Congress party: TRS. Slam dunk.

Now fast forward by just a year to 2019 Lok Sabha elections. Surprise, surprise; the BJP swings from 7 per cent to almost 20 per cent votes while the Congress doesn't come down. It actually takes its vote share up by 1 per cent to get 29 per cent votes. AIMIM remains static at 3 per cent votes. But the TRS vote share comes down to 41 per cent, which please remember, is still more than 34 per cent that it polled in 2014 assembly elections. So, the BJP upswing of about 13 per cent votes, primarily comes from anti-Congress votes that had gone to TRS just a year back, and all other non-TRS, non-Congress, non-AIMIM votes in Telangana. The BJP led in 21 assembly segments, almost at par with the Congress leads during the 2019 Lok Sabha elections. This shows the emergence of a split vote phenomenon that we are witnessing across India. The anti-Congress votes swing to BJP in Lok Sabha elections and counter-swing to non-BJP regional option in Vidhan Sabha elections. The prime example being the massive swings of anti-Congress votes between AAP and BJP in Delhi. In fact, in Delhi the anti-BJP votes also swing between AAP and Congress in similar fashion. The only difference being, in Telangana, the only known anti-BJP votes remain static with AIMIM.

So, is there any spoiler here? Unfortunately, not. But the upward journey of BJP in Telangana continues as evident from various bye-elections that have happened post the 2019 Lok Sabha elections. In majority of such elections the BJP has emerged as principal opposition to TRS. Those who don't remember the politics of 90s, there is a kind reminder that between the much talked about 1996 Lok Sabha and 1999 Lok Sabha elections, there was also the nearly forgotten 1998 Lok Sabha elections. In that critical election the BJP had polled almost 20 per cent votes in unified Andhra Pradesh, which forced the smart Chandra Babu Naidu to join the NDA before the 1999 Lok Sabha elections. The BJP under Atal-Advani duo was way too eager to grow beyond the Vindhyas and it just offered that 20 per cent groundswell on a platter to TDP.

Another important tit-bit is that in Telangana region of unified Andhra, in the much-forgotten 1998 Lok Sabha election the BJP had polled almost 27 per cent votes on the issue of separate statehood for Telangana. This was the time when BJP did not have a pan-India appeal, and no face to depend on in Andhra/Telangana. This was also the time when Karnataka happened to be the only southern state where BJP had polled more than 20 per cent votes. Many readers might find it surprising that much before TRS happened, at the national political circus, it was the BJP which always highlighted the demand of a separate Telangana state.

In 2006, one of the authors interviewed L.K. Advani for his signature program on Zee News during his Bharat Suraksha Yatra. In the yatra leg of Hyderabad to Nagpur, there was a stoppage at Adilabad and the author was surprised to see the huge number of people wearing pink turbans (signature dress of TRS) coming out to greet LKA. Asking them why they were attending a BJP programme when they belong to TRS, almost everyone said they used to be BJP *karyakartas* (workers), but as they BJP dumped the Telangana statehood demand, they were forced to join TRS. When the author asked Advani regarding the same, he simply said it was done keeping in mind the coalition dharma of that time.

Actually, it was under acute pressure of TDP chief Naidu. Post the 1999 alliance with TDP, the BJP dropped the demand altogether as part of coalition dharma, and thus handed over the entire 'thali' to an equally smart associate of Chandra Babu Naidu named K. Chandrashekhar Rao aka KCR. It's an open secret that KCR wanted a much bigger role, and he got a readymade issue and groundswell the moment BJP dumped the demand for separate Telangana statehood. The rest is history. It remains to be seen if the pro-Congress votes in Telangana remain with the Congress in coming years, or they get transformed into anti-TSR vote at some point of time. That will define the future course of pro-incumbency politics in Telangana.

Who Sabotaged Tejashwi in Bihar?

Not all spoilers emerge from dynastic family feuds. In contemporary times, the man most accused of being a 'spoiler' is Asaduddin Owaisi, the boss of the AIMIM, a predominantly 'Muslim' party with roots in Hyderabad that nevertheless claims to represent all underprivileged sections of India, including Dalits and extremely backward castes. It is difficult to figure out whose leaders spout more religiously provocative and incendiary rhetoric: the AIMIM or those of the VHP and Bajrang Dal. But let that be. The extremely narrow victory of the NDA in the Bihar assembly elections in 2020 is (apart from the miserable performance of the Congress) is ascribed to Owaisi and his party AIMIM. The party contested 20 seats, won five and apparently damaged the prospects of the RJD-led alliance in the rest of the seats. Senior RJD and Congress leaders accused him of being the B Team of the BJP, a charge he tauntingly throws back at them while insisting it is time so called 'secular' parties stopped treating Muslims and Dalits like dirt and then taking their votes for granted.

As he has started expanding the national footprint of AIMIM (it is already a force to reckon with in pockets of Maharashtra), the charges will continue to fly thick and fast. But electoral data analysed by Aditya Menon of the portal *The Quint* seems to suggest that it is actually Chirag Paswan who almost pulled off the heist of being a spoiler in Bihar, not Owaisi. He writes: "For instance, LJP chief Chirag Paswan openly said that his aim was to defeat the JD(U). In 33 seats, it was found that the LJP polled more votes than the JD(U)'s margin of defeat. Since the LJP fielded a number of candidates with a BJP background, this was considered a way of preventing the transfer of BJP votes to its alliance partner, the JD(U). Chirag Paswan campaigned saying Modi was his god and he was merely playing role of Hanuman to Narendra Modi. The C-Voter trackers continuously said that the role of Hanuman was getting way too uncomfortable for the ruling alliance. One of the authors also said on live TV that the Hanumanji is certainly flaring up fire all around with his proverbial tail, only problem is that he is torching up the building in Ayodhya now, not in Lanka. And if he continues to do so, it would end up torching the tally of JDU and eventually making it touch and go for the NDA forming the government again.

So has the AIMIM done the same to the Mahagathbandhan? Now the seats won by the Mahagathbandhan or the AIMIM itself are constituencies where NDA was defeated, so there is no question of the AIMIM helping NDA win here.

Our focus therefore, should be on the six seats that the NDA won. Let us look at the NDA's margin of victory and the votes polled by AIMIM...Therefore, we can see that only in one seat did the AIMIM poll more votes than the NDA's margin of victory—Raniganj in Araria district."[5]

But the real spoiler in Bihar assembly elections were not really AIMIM or LJP. It was the Congress. Just like the 'hit-wicket' in cricket analogy, the Congress as part of RJD alliance actually became a liability. While the LJP was damaging the JDU, it was the Congress which was throwing away all the anti-incumbency dividends in the dustbin. The Congress played the spoiler not by cutting votes, but by simply gifting away the votes. It forced the less-experienced Tejashwi Yadav to concede 70 odd seats to Congress, when clearly they were not even in a position to find 35 off proper winnable candidates across the state. They simply gifted away 51 out of these 70 seats to the NDA. Had the RJD contested 35 more seats from the seats dumped by Congress, we might have been looking at Tejashwi Yadav as the CM of Bihar right now. Compare the performance of Congress with another RJD alliance partner, the CPIML. The ultra-Left party won as many as 12 out of the 19 seats it contested. It was the pathetic strike rate of the Congress that resulted in a pro-incumbent verdict. It was a classic play of hit wicket when an alliance partner of the main challenger in momentum helped a pro-incumbent verdict for people facing anti-incumbency anger.

Some pro-incumbency verdicts that were unexpected this century were not caused by any spoilers. They were genuinely unexpected by many and were caused by a combination of the three factors we have already analysed in depth in three separate chapters. They are: personality cult, welfare schemes and weak opposition. Odisha in 2009 and Kerala could be considered two prime examples of this.

Stalin Learns from Tejashwi what Tejashwi didn't Learn from Stalin's Failure

We have talked about the historic pro-incumbent verdict won by Jayalalithaa in 2016 Assembly elections in Tamil Nadu. The spoiler in that particular election was the same culprit which played the exactly the same role of spoiler with Tejashwi Yadav in Bihar four years down the line. We have explained what Amma did as a leader of her party and alliance, was complete centralisation when she forced all alliance partner to contest on her symbol of 'two leaves'. The DMK under Stalin committed the mistake of budging down under pressure from alliance partner, particularly the Congress. The Congress snatched as many as 41 seats to contest within the DMK alliance, winning only 8 seats with the worst possible strike rate polling just above 6 per cent votes. In short, Congress spoiled all the chances of Stalin becoming the CM.

Probably Stalin wouldn't have accepted this mistake if Tejashwi Yadav would not have repeated it in Bihar. By the time world acknowledged that Congress is the biggest liability within the UPA ledger, it was too late for Tejashwi. What happened in Tamil Nadu was a hypothesis. A repeat of that in Bihar converted that into a theorem. A learned Stalin did in 2021 what he should have done in 2016: cut down the Congress to size. He offered only 25 seats to the Congress in 2021 Assembly elections, which the Congress was forced to accept after much drama. How prudent was that step? Well, the Congress buyout by Stalin's popularity managed to win 18 out of those 25 allocated seats while polling just 4 per cent votes. The Congress seats jumped from 8 to 18 while contesting only about half of the seats it contested five years back. Stalin became the Chief Minister by mitigating the biggest liability on his balance sheet. Something that Tejashwi Yadav seems to have learnt as well, but only after letting go the golden opportunity in 2020.

Mayawati Almost Spoils the Party

By the time assembly elections became due in early 2012 in five states, Mayawati was the chief minister of the most important one, Uttar Pradesh. More importantly, her soaring prime ministerial ambitions had not yet been smashed to smithereens by the hard knocks that persistent electoral setbacks deliver. Her expansion plans at that moment hinged on Punjab and Uttarakhand. Punjab was always a priority state for the BSP as it had a Dalit vote base of well above 30 per cent. But all she could do in Punjab was add to the cup of woes of the Congress along with Badal family rebel Manpreet by winning 4.2 per cent of the vote share without winning a single seat. It goes without saying that Dalit voters in Punjab usually voted for Congress as Jat-Sikhs were home with Akalis in socially polarised equations at grass roots. Hardly a surprise that her role was more aimed at restricting the Congress rather than winning anything on her own. Since then, as the fortunes of Mayawati seem to have faded, both electorally as well as otherwise, contesting Punjab elections are just a formality for her, like in 2022, when even in an alliance with SAD it failed to get more than 2 per cent votes and managed to win only one single seat.

But if she played a small but probably significant role in ensuring a pro-incumbency verdict for the Akali-BJP alliance and denying the Congress a victory it was sure of, Mayawati almost pulled off another pro-incumbency spoiler role the same year in Uttarakhand. Since the state neighbours Uttar Pradesh where she was chief minister, her party could devote considerable manpower and resources to Uttarakhand, even though even her supporters knew that she had no chance of winning a majority in the abode of Gods, the Devbhoomi. In the chapter on personality cults, we have already discussed how the BJP in Uttarakhand, the ruling party, seemed to be in disarray despite the 'last minute' reinstatement of General B.C. Khanduri as the chief minister. The Congress almost looked certain to win. But Mayawati pulled off the role of a spoiler almost helping the BJP retain power. The BSP won almost 13.5 per cent of the vote share. The Congress was just 0.5 per cent ahead of the BJP and actually fell 4 short of the majority mark by winning 32 seats while the BJP won 31. The Congress did manage to form a government there; but it is doubtful if the BJP of today led by Modi and Shah would have let that happen. Post-2014, they did what they were supposed to do and 'rebels' ensured to bring down the unstable Congress government.

The history repeated itself five years later in 2022 assembly elections, when even after changing 3 CMs within a year before the polls, and even after the sitting CM losing his own seat, the BJP managed to win a back-to-back second mandate in Uttarakhand. A state knows for a routine pendulum swing on anti-incumbency every five years, defied the historic trend and resulted in a pro-incumbent verdict. In C-Voter tracker, it showed all signs of anger in public perception, particularly against the CM and sitting MLAs, yet the popularity of PM swept everything aside. The public of Uttarakhand did manage to drive home the point that they were upset by defeating the sitting CM, but they also ensured defeat of the main challenger Harish Rawat.

But the real spoiler was again the BSP polling almost 5 per cent and added by another spoiler AAP polling 3 per cent of the votes, which would have easily gone to the Congress in a routine election. Add these 8 per cent votes and you can see the arithmetic helping the BJP in a pro-incumbent verdict. Much of this has to be blamed at the Congress central leadership, which did the unthinkable task of keeping Harish Rawat busy in Punjab all the way till the elections actually came knocking down on the doors. How on earth can you keep away your most popular leader in an election bound state and use him as a 'prabhari' in another state? As the results came in, one of the authors summed it up on live national networks comparing to a spectacular 'baraat' (bridegroom's procession), where everyone is dancing on the street in full regalia, but the 'dulha' (groom) is pulled down from the 'ghodi' (mare) and sent away to dance in someone else's baraat in another state. So the *baraat* lands without any *dulha* and the bride decides to run away with the standby groom standing right there all the time.

Now do everything, but don't blame the bride. In all fairness, the bride in all her frustration did punch hard and knocked out even the standby groom blue and black, but eventually settled for the proverbial fact that 'ladkey ka khandaan achha hai' (the boy's family seems to be alright). How could she marry the hero who was dumped by his own family?

Back in 2017, the BJP swept Uttarakhand and Uttar Pradesh. But in Goa in the same round of elections, the ruling party BJP won 13 seats while the Congress won 17. Even the sitting CM of BJP lost his own seat. The majority mark was 21. 'Miraculously', as the senior Congress leader Digvijay Singh dispatched from Delhi was discussing who would be the Congress chief minister, the BJP had already formed the government in Goa! Now repeat the same 'baraat' narrative explained in case of Uttarakhand and you will understand what happened in Goa five years back. Now imagine the sitting BJP CM lost. The mandate was given to the Congress as the single largest party. The bride was waiting, but the forget the 'dulha', even the entire 'baraat' forgot to arrive on the set date and time. The 'samadhiji' (parent-in-law) just slept in his hotel, while the 'muhurt' (auspicious moment for the ceremony) went by, and the bride went along with the standby. Five years down the lane, it was pro-incumbency part-2, fully supported by spoilers line MGP+TMC polling almost 13 per cent votes and AAP cutting away another 7 per cent from the anti-incumbent universe. This time around, a new spoiler, RGP, polled almost 10 per cent of the angry voters while winning just one single seat. The Congress trailed by 7 per cent votes behind BJP and all these spoilers polled almost 30 per cent votes together. All the 'baraatis' dancing in five different directions and fighting each other while the bride eventually settles for the dependable standby. Why blame the bride?

Now expect the AAP do the same damage to Congress prospects in other states, resulting in more pro-incumbent verdicts even in states where routine pendulum verdicts based on anti-incumbency have been a historical norm.

Naveen Finally 'Comes of Age'

Another unexpected, so to speak, pro-incumbency electoral victory came about in the 2009 assembly elections in Odisha. We are talking about Naveen Patnaik and his party the BJD. For two consecutive terms, he had partnered with the BJP to win elections and become chief minister. The conventional wisdom was: while the BJD might find it difficult to defeat the still formidable Congress on its own, an alliance with the 'rising' BJP virtually guaranteed victory. It did for two successive terms. Then the horrible Hindu-Christian riots took place in tribal pockets of the poor and backward district sometime after a revered Hindu spiritual leader Swami Lakshanananda Saraswati was brutally gunned down along with his followers inside his Ashram allegedly by Maoists. Hindu right-wing groups with the tacit support of the BJP blamed the Christian missionaries active in the area. Sporadic cases of violence led to massive riots where thousands of Christian houses were burnt. Mercifully, the death toll was not very high in comparison to other such riots in recent past.

Naveen Patnaik used this opportunity to sever all ties between his party and the BJP and announced the end of the alliance. Analysts were shocked. The refrain seemed to be: why is Naveen Patnaik determined to commit political hara-kiri and destroy the legacy of his legendary father Biju Patnaik? After all, the Congress had won 34.82 per cent of the vote share while the BJD had won 27.6 per cent of the votes. It was the 17.11 per cent share won by the BJP that gave the alliance a combined 44.7 per cent vote share, enough to win a second successive term. Was Naveen Babu (as he was known by then) thinking he alone with his poor Odiya travel across dusty villages of Odisha and convince voters that he alone is a better bet than the BJP and the Congress? With the BJP claiming to become stronger by the day, how would the BJD close the vote share lead enjoyed by the Congress?

But the 2009 elections gave him an unexpected third term. As explained in the chapter on personality cults of the pro-incumbency stars, in many ways it was gamble that could have backfired. But Naveen the Delhi-based socialite-turned-reluctant politician finally got his own personality cult and became a consummate hero of the masses for voters of Odisha after the 2009 elections. But how did he achieve the unexpected. Well, the BJP turned out to be a paper tiger in the elections, contesting 145 seats, winning 6 and forfeiting deposits in 93 seats whilst vote share dropped about 3 per cent to 15 per cent. But the real surprise package was the 5.6 per cent drop in the Congress vote share to 29.1 per cent. Even during the Biju Patnaik wave in the 1990 assembly elections, the Congress had a bigger vote share. But then, we have already analysed and explained in another chapter how the terminal decline of the Congress has played a supporting role in Naveen Patnaik winning five successive terms. The interesting thing is: Naveen Patnaik took away the traditional voters of both the Congress and the BJP in 2009. That is an extremely rare occurrence in Indian elections, both at the state and the national level.

In February, 2009, Biswamoy Pati, a historian at Venkateswara College, Delhi wrote a commentary for the journal *Economic and Political Weekly* where he advised Naveen Patnaik to sever all ties with the BJP (it had already been done) and called even the BJD anti-poor: "It is in this context that the BJD needs to think about its political future. If anything, it has to rethink seriously about continuing its bankrupt economic policies that have caused immense damage to its image...In fact, the government policies have caused immense suffering to the tribals and Dalits of Orissa, and are antithetical to the dreams of the founder of the BJD—the late Biju Patnaik (also known as 'Biju' Patnaik)."[6] Naveen proved both the right and the left wrong. Frankly, no one knows exactly why both Congress and BJP supporters plumped for Naveen Babu in 2009, despite all the heady and heavy-duty analysis offered by pundits. Personality cult? Yes. But Vasundhara Raje Scindia had lost a few months before that despite her own personality cult? Welfare schemes? At that point in time, other state chief ministers were ahead of Naveen Babu in this game. Opposition weakness? Yes. But exactly what, we will leave it to the scholars to debate over.

The BJP can be Patient

But what about the BJP? Well, it's a bit like the Assam where the regional party the AGP had started its terminal decline in the 21st century but it took a long time for the BJP to beat the Congress in Assam, both in terms of seats and vote share. Results to the 2019 assembly elections in Odisha where Naveen Patnaik won a fifth consecutive term show that the BJP is clambering its way up. While the Congress continued its death throes with a vote share of 16.12 per cent, the BJP managed a formidable 32.49 per cent. But that's still way behind the BJD which won 44.71 per cent of the votes. If the Congress vote share collapses further and moves to the BJP, it is still advantage Naveen Patnaik with elections just about two years away. As virtually all credible surveys show, he is still incredibly popular and the aura around his personality cult has grown brighter. Barring something really strange and unforeseen, Naveen Babu looks set to win a sixth consecutive term in 2024 and break all records by becoming the longest serving chief minister in the country.

But BJP is a patient party. It was first a marginal player and then a junior partner in Haryana. When the regional party INLD started disintegrating, it became the dominant force, bigger than even the Congress. It was the same story in Maharashtra till 2012 when it was the junior partner to the Shiv Sena. That was the year Balasaheb Thackeray died and the BJP is now the dominant force in Maharashtra, albeit outplayed for now by one of the most strange and unlikely alliance between the Shiv Sena, Congress and the NCP (the alliance between the BJP and the PDP in Jammu & Kashmir, some would justifiably argue, was an even stranger one!).

In Bihar, a seemingly fatigued and beleaguered Nitish Kumar has already allowed the BJP to be de facto the senior partner in the alliance. He leaves behind no inheritor. That's the case with the BJD too in Odisha. After Naveen babu who? But we are running ahead of ourselves.

Godless Putsch in God's Own Country

Yet another unexpected and seemingly inexplicable pro-incumbency example is the 2021 assembly election verdict in Kerala. Firstly, Kerala firmly belonged to the half a dozen odd states where anti-incumbency has been the norm for decades. Since the 1970s, the CPI(M)-led alliance (LDF) and the Congress-led alliance (UDF) have been alternatively governing the state after each assembly election. So used had people of Kerala and political commentators become to this regular change in governments that it appeared as normal as rains in Kerala during the monsoon. Added to this was the shock defeat of the LDF in the 2019 Lok Sabha elections. The two sides are so evenly matched that sweeps and landslide victories are extremely rare in the state, both during the state and national elections. But the 2019 Lok Sabha elections proved to be an outlier, a mini version of what the famous author Nassim Nicholas Taleb has described as a Black Swan in his bestselling and captivating book by the same name. Only difference being that the Black Swans are becoming more predicable with C-Voter Trackers. The tracker on national networks projected an unimaginable 17 seats for the UDF on and the UDF performed a near miracle by winning 19 out of the 20 seats on offer. In fact, the only reason the Congress tally in the 2019 Lok Sabha elections went up to 52 from 44 in 2014 is because it gained 15 Lok Sabha seats in Kerala and Tamil Nadu. Imagine its plight otherwise. Anyways, this result sent shockwaves through political circles in Kerala as the Left had lost even its strongest bastions.

Critics of the Left couldn't stop gloating. For them, this historic defeat was the final nail in the coffin for the Left in India since Kerala was the last for standing. West Bengal looked lost forever, as did Tripura, two states where the Left once dominated.

Some cynics sniggered that the only Leftists left in Nadia would be the gun-toting Maoists who still prayed at the altar of Mao Ze Dong. Dozens of reasons were given for the rout. Perhaps the most persuasive was the backlash by Hindu voters against chief minister Pinarayi Vijayan who seemed determined to implement the Supreme Court verdict of 2018 that allowed menstruating females to enter the Sabarimala Temple. It seems the Hindu voters were also determined to teach him a lesson come elections. They did, and how. But beyond the hype, despair and gloating, there was also some thoughtful analysis. In a column for *India Today* in June, 2019, Jeemon Jacob wrote: "Now, the Left is looking at the 2021 assembly election with dread. The recently concluded Central Committee of the party advised the state leadership to formulate a strategy to win over the traditional Hindu vote bank in the state. Without its core Hindu vote bank, the CPI(M) may not survive another electoral rout."[6]

Opinion is still divided on whether Vijayan heeded the party advice to woo the Hindus back in the Sabarimala issue. What he did was something the Left has always frowned upon; the primacy of the individual over the party. Many people still remember 1996 when the CPI(M) politburo shot down the proposal mooted by many non-Congress and non-BJP leaders to make Jyoti Basu the Prime Minister of India. Party over personality was the motto. Here again the Black Swan was predicted well in advance by the C-Voter Tracker on *ABP* and *Mathrubhumi* networks, purely on the basis of the CM's approval ratings. Our trackers were clearly marking on a daily basis, that the split vote sentiment in Kerala that people might have voted for a better suited Congress for a national election, but at the state level they are still intact with CPM-led UPA. It was a brave call based on public perception data as it defied the historic trend all the way. While the traditional analysts were looking for a routine pendulum verdict based on anti-incumbency and the 19/20 Lok Sabha seats won by UPA just two years back, a confident Pinarayi Vijayan turned it upside down and led a 'presidential' style campaign for the 2021 leaders. There was no usual talk of group leadership. Vijayan projected himself as the undisputed leader and the face of the campaign. And he delivered. The LDF won a second successive term and increased its tally from 91 to 99 in an assembly with 140 members. Perhaps after the late Jyoti Basu, Pinarayi Vijayan will be the next Left CM with a complete sway over the party.

In a piece published in the portal *The Print* soon after the dramatic 2021 verdict, K.P. Sethunath described Vijayan as the Deng Xiaoping of Kerala: "Even as Vijayan and other LDF leaders savour the moment of glory, there is scepticism galore over their commitment to charter a Leftist agenda for governance in the state...This goes well for his supporters, who are eager to project him as Deng Xiaoping of Kerala, championing the cause of private capital for rapid economic development of the state... The personality cult around Vijayan scaled new heights with the sobriquet 'Captain' becoming popular among supporters, causing more discomfort to party veterans. Even the central leadership of the CPM has no option now other than to keep Vijayan in good humour—Kerala remains the only state in India where the Left is in power with a meaningful political clout."[7] So the 2021 Kerala verdict could be termed unexpected, but definitely not inexplicable.

One thing in Indian politics is clear though. The era of 'collective leadership' is dead and buried with charismatic and enigmatic leaders often rising above the party to script their own destinies. The collective leadership may be resurrected when another era dawns in Indian politics. But that promises to be a long wait.

References

1. https://www.ideasforindia.in/topics/governance/are-independent-candidates-unimportant-for-political-representation.html
2. https://www.hindustantimes.com/cities/chandigarh-news/politics-was-simple-but-the-challenges-huge-parkash-singh-badal-on-polls-70-years-ago-101635544431024.html
3. https://www.tribuneindia.com/2012/20120307/main1.html
4. https://openthemagazine.com/features/india/the-takeover-that-wasnt/
5. https://www.thequint.com/news/politics/aimim-asaduddin-owaisi-nda-vote-cutter-muslims-bihar-election-results-2020

https://www.epw.in/journal/2009/09/commentary/biju-janata-dal-signal-change.html

6. https://www.indiatoday.in/india-today-insight/story/the-seven-deadly-political-sins-of-pinarayi-vijayan-1548535-2019-06-14
7. https://theprint.in/opinion/keralas-deng-xiaoping-pinarayi-vijayan-is-showing-bengals-left-how-its-done/651218/

□

7

MODI: MOST POLARISING CHAMPION OF PRO-INCUMBENCY VERDICTS

Well known sociologist and clinical psychologist Ashish Nandy is loved and even revered by a certain section of intelligentsia and the media. His fan base did not seem to diminish one bit even after he pronounced during the 2013 Jaipur Literature Festival that corruption in India was caused almost entirely by OBCs, SCs and STs. Some of his acolytes refused to believe that such an erudite scholar could have made such an outrageously and factually false analysis and offered convoluted explanations about what Nandy meant while making such disparaging, derogatory and downright defamatory remarks against political leaders emerging from other backward castes, scheduled tribes and scheduled castes. But they wholeheartedly endorsed Nandy when he donned the clinical psychologist hat a few decades ago and offered an analysis of the personality of Narendra Modi. In his own wise words:

"More than a decade ago, when Narendra Modi was a nobody, a small-time RSS pracharak trying to make it as a small-time BJP functionary, I had the privilege of interviewing him.... Modi, it gives me no pleasure to tell the readers, met virtually all the criteria that psychiatrists, psycho-analysts and psychologists had set up after years of empirical work on the authoritarian personality. He had the same mix of puritanical rigidity, narrowing of emotional life, massive use of the ego defence of projection, denial and fear of his own passions combined with fantasies of violence—all set within the matrix of clear paranoid and obsessive personality traits. I still remember the cool, measured tone in which he elaborated a theory of cosmic conspiracy against India that painted every Muslim as a suspected traitor and a potential terrorist. I came out of the interview shaken and told Yagnik that, for the first time, I had met a textbook case of a fascist and a prospective killer, perhaps even a future mass murderer."[1]

The Anti-Muslim Image

Almost as if to prove that the venerable Nandy has been right all along in his clinical analysis, many global institutions, media platforms and Think Tanks have competed with each other to use derogatory adjectives for Narendra Modi and his tenure as Prime Minister. While fascism and authoritarianism are two favourite words, perhaps the most widely used is the alleged persecution of minorities, particularly the Muslim community under his watch as the leader of the country. In April 2022, the United States Centre For International Religious Freedom (USCRIF) released its annual report on the state of religious freedom in various countries of the world. According to the report: "religious freedom conditions are taking a drastic turn downwards with the national and various state governments tolerating widespread harassment and violence against religious minorities. The BJP-led government enacted the Citizenship Amendment Act which provides a fast track to Indian citizenship only for non-Muslims from Afghanistan, Bangladesh and Pakistan already residing in India. This potentially exposes millions of Muslims to detention, deportation and stateless news when the government completes its planned nationwide National Register of Citizens."[2a]

The USCRIF is not an activist busybody like Greenpeace or Amnesty International, or even the Human Rights Watch for that matter. It is the official arm of the US State Department. It has now marked India as a country of 'particular concern' along with China, North Korea, Saudi Arabia and Afghanistan. The authors thank the USCRIF for small mercies because it had ranked Afghanistan above India in the previous report when US troops were still there. Now that American troops are gone, Afghanistan is as 'bad' as India in persecuting religious minorities! It has recommended sweeping and stiff sanctions against India. The US government is yet to act on its recommendations. The USCRIF was officially established as a wing of the US State Department under the Bill Clinton administration in 1998 and became a powerful body under George Bush Jr. when his administration launched the global war ('crusade') against terror after 9/11. It is the same body which played a key role in the US State Department announcing in 2005 that Narendra Modi would not be given a visa to enter the United States because of his alleged role in the 2002 Gujarat riots which is often described by global media platforms and activist organisations as a 'genocide of Muslims'.

The *Economist* magazine is not the official arm of the UK government. But the authors are convinced it sometimes forgets that India is no longer a British colony and that its doesn't have to unnecessarily bear the 'White Man's Burden' to teaching manners and civilisation to the country. Before Modi took over as Prime Minister, India was ranked at 27 in its list of democracies. Last year, the rank had crashed to 53 and the Economist had mournfully and officially declared that India is a 'flawed' democracy. The tirade against Modi by the magazine is relentless, perhaps as relentless as the German Air Force bombing London in the early phase of the Second World War. In a 2020 story, the magazine says: "Last month India changed the law to make it easier for adherents of all the subcontinent's religions, except Islam, to acquire citizenship. At the same time, the ruling Bharatiya Janata Party (BJP) wants to compile a register of all India's 1.3 bn citizens, as a means to hunt down illegal immigrants (see Briefing). Those sound like technicalities, but many of the country's 200 million Muslims do not have the papers to prove they are Indian, so they risk being made stateless. Ominously, the government has ordered the building of camps to detain those caught in the net. You might think that the BJP's scheme was a miscalculation. It has sparked widespread and lasting protests. Students, secularists, even the largely fawning media have begun to speak out against Narendra Modi, the prime minister, for his apparent determination to transform India from a tolerant, multi-religious place into a chauvinist Hindu state."[2(b)] The tirade continues even as the authors write this in the backdrop of religious violence, stone pelting and riots triggered during celebrations of the 'Ram Navami' festival.

No matter what Modi and his regime does, the stigma of him being someone who dislikes and persecutes the Muslim community sticks to him like a leech clinging on to a body. This has been so since he was just an ordinary BJP leader without any high office. In the aftermath of the 9/11 terror attacks, the news channel *NDTV* had Modi as guest during a show with celebrity journalist Rajdeep Sardesai as the anchor. One of the authors still recalls the condescending smirk on the face of Rajdeep Sardesai as Modi talked about the growing menace of Islamist terrorism and how the world needs to unite to fight this threat to global peace and security. That day, Sardesai smirked while Modi, who is still not fluent in English, looked tentative and nervous. Sardesai was one of better known and 'credible' names in the media fraternity that covered the Gujarat riots of 2002 that have permanently demonised Modi in a way that the actual genocide of the Sikh community in 1984 never demonised Rajiv Gandhi. Of course, tables do turn. And in 2012, when Modi was campaigning for the Gujarat assembly elections, Sardesai looked visibly nervous and tentative asking questions from the floor of a bus as Modi nonchalantly dismissed his rhetorical questions. In 2014, when Modi became Prime Minister, he was no longer persona non grata for the United States and visited the country with President Obama himself driving him around to see the great monuments of American History around the Capitol Hill and White House. The American establishment bent over backwards to welcome the same person they denied a visa even to enter USA just ten years back. Ironically enough, Sardesai too was in America to cover that visit and etched his name in contemporary social media driven history by engaging in fisticuffs with voluble supporters of Modi in New York.

The Ignorant Rustic Versus the Saviour

Now coming back to sociologist and clinical psychologist Ashish Nandy and his comment on Modi being 'textbook case of a fascist and a prospective killer, perhaps even a future mass murderer', since both the authors do not claim to be either sociologists or clinical psychologists, we refrain from joining this debate. But juxtapose the conclusions about a 'fascist and a prospective killer' with the wise words offered by another famous media personality. When he wrote an open letter to Sonia Gandhi in May, 2009 in his magazine *Tehelka*, Tarun Tejpal was four years away from being accused of rape by a junior colleague. He was controversially acquitted by a Goa court (where the alleged incident occurred) and an appeal by the state of Goa is being heard in the High Court. Like Nandy, Tejpal continues to be openly supported and defended by the sections of intelligentsia and media who revere Nandy. Here are some words from that lengthy and famous letter Tejpal wrote to Sonia Gandhi:

"Your toil has been worthy. Your ragged army of 1996 is a renewed one in 2009. In the process you have so cleverly—and beautifully—played out two key precepts of your extra god. Thou shalt not covet, the last of the ten commandments, so artfully spun as an act of renunciation that it sucked out the wind from the sails of your opponents. And Mathew 5:5, which is also Manmohan Singh 2004: blessed are the meek for they shall inherit the earth. And both have been cleansing of the public in unanticipated ways.

"Yet let me assert it without any ambiguity. Manmohan 2009 needs you as much as Manmohan 2004. He may be the scythe that clears the weeds, but you are still the arm that wields the scythe. To slice cleanly, the arm and scythe must swing in tandem.

"Since I am convinced that your work is far from over, and since I am on Mathew, let me remind you of the exhortation in 10:7. "Heal the sick, cleanse the lepers, raise the dead, cast out devils: freely ye have received, freely give." As one must always do with divine scripture, I could spell out the contemporary burden of every phrase. But that would be fatuous. More than those of us who write of these things, you know best what it is in this calamitous nation to heal the sick and to cast out devils.... No doubt with the help of your extra god, you have done a fine job of bringing up your son. He has humility, decorum, diligence, and he takes the long and inclusive view. We do not like the idea of dynasty, but we abhor the idea of divisiveness more. And yes, as I bid you speed and strength, with the extra god by your side, may I make a final plea. You have given us of yourself, and of your son.

Now will you kindly also give unto us your luminous daughter."[2]

One final revisiting of an analysis of Modi vis-à-vis the Gandhis before we get along with the details of this chapter. Aakar Patel, a former journalist who claims to know Narendra Modi personally has been in the news for some years. When he was head of the India chapter of the 'human rights body' Amnesty International, law enforcement agencies had frozen the assets of the organisation amidst allegations of money laundering and illegal diversion of funds. For those who revere Nandy and admire Tejpal, Patel is the symbolic David fighting against a mighty Goliath which in this case is the regime headed by Prime Minister Narendra Modi. For fans of Modi, he is a Nehru-Gandhi dynasty sycophant and a fraud. We don't know where the truth lies. In 2013, when it was clear that Narendra Modi was the BJP candidate for the post of Prime Minister and a direct challenger of Rahul Gandhi, Aakar Patel wrote the following in his column for the newspaper *Mint*: "For those able to look beyond his superb oratory and humour, the vapidity of Modi's message is striking. It has not been noticed or remarked upon that Modi has never been to a college (his degree is from a correspondence course). His simple views spring from this lack of knowledge. His writing is all in Gujarati. I can claim to know something about this and it is mediocre. He is not well read and has little idea about the world or its history. It will become embarrassing, if he becomes Prime Minister to have him in the same meeting as US President Barrack Obama.[3] In a related column Patel extols the Gandhi's for their 'class' and dismisses Modi as a rustic.

Contemporary media critical of Modi and his policies and actions have an abiding complaint that mainstream media is now so beholden to or terrified of the 'vindictive' Modi regime that have become loudspeakers of the government: 'Godi media' in more popular parlance. Modi fans of course deride such critics as Pidi media. The authors are not concerned with an analysis of these media wars in this book. We have merely used the quotes above to show how Modi dominates discourse. You can detest him or adore him; but he towers like an ever-controversial colossus. Perhaps the only other Indian leader who was so polarising was

Indira Gandhi. One of the authors was 11 years old when Indira imposed the Emergency. He recalls reports and features from the newspaper *Statesman* that he read which either treated her like a goddess or a demon. There is something similar about Modi as he eyes the record set by Jawaharlal Nehru to win three consecutive Lok Sabha elections. He has already been the chief minister and the prime minister continuously for 21 years, a feat even Nehru could not boast of. When you talk of pro-incumbency, you simply cannot find a more potent and powerful symbol of the phenomenon. For all the cringeworthy sycophancy as well as derogatory criticism he faces, Narendra Modi is unique.

Some of his more enthusiastic supporters who ignore historical facts keep tub thumping about how Modi is the only chief minister to ascend the top throne in Delhi. They are plain wrong. Many chief ministers went on to become Prime Minister. Morarji Desai, Charan Singh, V.P. Singh, P.V. Narashima Rao and H.D. Deve Gowda were chief ministers. So there is nothing unique or earthshattering about Modi the chief minister becoming prime minister. What is unique about him are two things: till date, he is the only politician apart from Nehru who has never lost an election, either personally as a candidate or as the candidate for a constitutional post. The only other politician who can flaunt such credentials is Naveen Patnaik, the chief minister of Odisha. Interestingly, both contested their first personal elections after they were 50 years old! The other thing is his ability to polarise; Indira Gandhi being the only other pan Indian politician who could do the same, not in terms on religious or sectarian polarisation, but in terms of getting the population on two extreme poles: one who simply loves you and another who simply hates you.

Modi's Muslim Equation

Ask any Modi hater about the core because of which they hate Modi and almost by default the core issue would be aimed at Godhra, 2002 riots and Islamophobia. The Muslim equation is as intertwisted into Modi-s fate and destiny that it becomes almost impossible to write about his politics and not to touch about the subject. But as political analyst it's also a subject which come in front by default whenever you try to analyse the growth of BJP in India, or the ideological impact of RSS on Indian politics. While there are books galore on the 'new' BJP, the authors fail to understand if there is any change whatsoever in the core ideological beliefs of the 'old' BJP from the 'new' BJP? Or is it that the ongoing momentum of RSS's experiment in politics, which started by loaning a certain Deendayal Upadhyaya to Dr. Syama Prasad Mukherjee way back in 1951. What exactly was the core of the party then? Or for that matter, why exactly the political opponents of the BJP (BJS back then) were so overwhelmingly opposed to what they had to offer in terms of political ideology? Besides, when British India was divided on religious lines, why it was so difficult for majority of secular analysts to understand that a reaction to Muslim Pakistan was absolutely normal human reaction to Hindu-majority India?

The authors firmly believe that it was the overarching umbrella of Congress which carried the 'Garam Dal' of right-wing freedom fighters within the party structure; that delayed the arrival of right-wing politics in India by a decade. The unfortunate assassination of Mahatma Gandhi by a right-wing radical commonly associated with Savarkar-RSS equation; arguably took the Hindu majority nation into a collective guilt and that added ten more years to this process. This is why it took precisely 20 years from 1947 for the BJS to register its first impressive electoral performance in 1967 elections when the Congress was uprooted in huge number of states and managed to win Lok Sabha elections by embarrassingly low majority. The rise of Indian right wing was absolutely inevitable the moment Congress decided to toe the Socialist line of governance under Nehru. It was never a question of 'if' but only a question of 'when'. Remember the much-discussed episode of the Congress committees called by Gandhi in 1946 where 12 out of 15 States Congress Committees had supported Patel and remaining three decided to abstain. Yet Gandhiji ensured Nehru was the person to lead free India as its first Prime Minister. Is it really difficult to understand why the overwhelming majority of Congressmen were in favour of Sardar Patel? From all accounts, it was absolutely undemocratic part of Gandhiji to have put his weight behind Nehru, and being a unquestionable follower of Bapu, the great Sardar accepted his dictatorial decision within a fraction of a second. Well, Patel agreed, but to think his followers just accepted it the way it was would not be a prudent way of understanding Public Perception. Unfortunately, there were no C-Voter Trackers 75 years back, else we would have known the precise number of this overwhelming support for Patel. Still, the fact that 12 out of 15 Congress committees supported him as the 'leader' says a lot about the ground situation at that point of time.

The unfortunate partition of India was the biggest and the only instance in modern history when a huge country, almost ta sub-continent, was being bifurcated, or rather trifurcated on religious demography. To think that the pendulum of Pakistan went in one direction and will remain struck there, without the pendulum of 'remaining' India swinging in to the other direction would be defying the logic and science of simple harmonic motion in terms of human reactions. But Gandhiji's unfortunate assassination was actually used by contemporary narrative builders to keep that swing of pendulum struck in one side of the swing. It was not by default. It was by design. And it was only a matter of time when it would have got released and crashed into the other side of the extreme political swing.

So, rise of right-wing politics was never a question of 'if', but only a question of 'when'. If it would not have been in form of RSS-BJP equation, it would have been some other form. The authors have been looking at the regional politics of India in 50s and 60s for another book project, and were surprised at the number of pro-market right wing options that were popping up in different regions of India. At best, it was a decentralised form of right-wing ideological politics, not necessarily a pro-Hindu politics of that time. The idea of 'inclusive' India was aimed not to be converted into a Hindu Pakistan by our founding fathers. By default, the majority of Hindu population was already moulded into that idea as being inclusive was pretty much culturally part of their identity. The problem was not as though Congress was seen as pro-Muslim party. In India, you can see scores of pro-incumbency champions being pro-Muslim and yet Hindus voting for them all along, ranging from Arvind Kejriwal to Pinarayi Vijayan to Mamata Banerjee to Nitish Kumar and everyone in between. Hindus have no issues voting for any party or politician who is seen as pro-Muslim. The problem for Congress started when the pendulum got released and it hit the public perception that Congress was not just pro-Muslim but actually anti-Hindu. This label of being anti-Hindu has done so much damage to the electoral prospects of Congress that none of the other non-BJP parties, including the religion-agnostic Communist parties, can dare today to be remotely seen as anti-Hindu. So, Arvind Kejriwal runs trains for Ayodhya Darshan, Kamal Nath organises Hanuman Jayanti celebrations on official Congress platforms and Mamata Banerjee chants Chandi-Path on stage just to prove they are not anti-Hindu.

Pro-Hindu or Anti-Hindu?

You may wonder why the authors have taken this weird detour ranging from Patel-Nehru to Mamata-Kejriwal while discussing the pro-incumbency factors in politics of Narendra Modi. This is just to drive home a simple bitter truth: In today's India, as a 'pro-Muslim' politician you can easily win elections after elections after elections as a pro-incumbency champion. But in the same India, it has become almost impossible to win a single election after being tagged as 'anti-Hindu' in public perception. How, why and where exactly did Congress fall into that trap of being tagged as anti-Hindu, is something for the Congress leadership to understand and determine. But the authors are very clear, that this tag has everything to do with the fateful decision that Gandhiji took on 20th April 1946 when he chose Nehru over Patel. If you understand the power of symbolism, then fast forward by 72 years and stop at 31st October 2018, when Prime Minister Narendra Modi dedicated the 'Statue of Unity' to the country. At 182 meters or 597 feet to be precise, this giant statue to Sardar Patel is tallest in the world. With that statue, the appropriation of Congress right wing stalwart freedom fighters by the BJP, whose mother organisation RSS was banned by Patel after Gandhi's-assassination, was complete. Not to forget that among the very first decisions that Modi took as PM in 2014 was to confer Bharat

Ratna to another Congress right-wing stalwart Pt. Madan Mohan Malviya, the founder of the Banaras Hindu University. The fact that Nehru was awarded Bharat Ratna in 1955 when he was serving PM, and Patel was awarded the same in 1991 along with Nehru's grandson Rajiv Gandhi, tells you a lot about the problems and challenges that Congress was bound to face. It was not a question of 'if'. It was only a matter of 'when'.

None of these arguments are to justify the kind of polarised politics that today's BJP is unleashing on India. The authors have zero tolerance for any intolerance whatsoever. But to understand why the public is thinking or behaving the way they are right now; one has to understand the pendulum swing rather than just cursing the mandates. The 'new' BJP under Modi has understood the power of narrative-setting. They know very well that even the 'moderates' like Atal Bihari Vajpayee were equally thrashed and unaccepted by the Indian liberals just on ideological grounds. The narrative-setting Left-liberals would have never allowed Vajpayee to settle in as the right-wing version of Nehru. The 'old' BJP tried hard, but failed. Over a period of time, it took an Advani in a bad cop avatar to pitch Vajpayee as the good cop. Ironically, it took a Modi to make the same Left-liberal ecosystem praise Advani as the old 'moderate'. And now it's taking a certain Amit Shah for the ecosystem to start considering Modi as moderate one. Amit Shah has already a bad cop in name of Yogi Adityanath to clean his slate in comparison, and so on.

The downward spiralling race to this rock bottom is never-ending, but the only saving grace is the Indian public which has ensured that pendulum is still swinging in both ways at state levels. Only difference is the new cardinal rule stating: thou shall be secular and even pro-Muslim, but thou shall never be seen as anti-Hindu. Apart from all other virtues that we have discussed in this book for being a pro-incumbency champion, consider this as the most ironical, yet important virtue. All non-BJP and non-Congress leaders and parties, including the Communists parties have learnt this by heart. Somehow, even the significant section of non-Gandhi leadership of Congress at state level seem to have learnt this the hard way, but somehow, something is missing at the top. The ecosystem wants the Congress top leadership to remain 'glued to core values of secularism' which ironically gets translated as being 'anti-Hindu' in public perception. The public reacts, and the ecosystem reacts further in the same direction. The public reacts further in disapproval. And this is becoming a chain reaction of sorts, one feeding to the other and entire non-Congress political ecosystem, including the BJP as well as most of the current and erstwhile UPA allies, is happy reaping the benefits of this self-destruction by the Congress eco-system.

Modi and Technology

But truth is always stranger than fiction, and myths become accepted as reality when it comes to controversial personalities. One such myth about Narendra Modi is that he became controversial and persona non grata for 'secular' Indians after the horrific riots of 2002. That's simply not true. The fact is Narendra Modi became a controversial and polarising figure even before took oath as chief minister of Gujarat. The fact is, the entire opposition led by the Congress boycotted his oath-taking ceremony in October, 2001. In October 2001, journalist Sheela Bhatt who still writes on Modi wrote for the portal *Rediff.com*: "The Congress will boycott the swearing-in ceremony of Gujarat's new chief, Narendra Modi, today, October 7. Gujarat State Congress Committee president Amarsinh Chaudhary told rediff.com, "The BJP [Bharatiya Janata Party] government is spending Rs. 3-4 crore on the function, which is just not acceptable to us when the state's coffers are empty and the government has not even paid wages to the labourers who toiled during the drought.... The media-savvy Modi has left nothing to chance. He has even issued a press release about three websites, narendramodi.com, gujaratindia.com and cmgujarat.com that will webcast the show live."[4] Notice two things: the uncompromising dislike (to use a mild word) of the Congress of Modi even before he assumed power and propensity of Modi even in that era to use technology and the Internet. In 2001, forget politicians, even many journalists were not familiar or comfortable with the Internet and ideas like 'webcasting' except as an exotic new thing that you could play around with. One of the authors had personally witnessed in 1997 the way Modi used computer databases to keep records of election trends and political profiles of each and every assembly segment in Gujarat. It was extremely impressive considering majority of the media persons in Delhi newsrooms were still struggling to survive in paperless office environment back then. And yes, he was always a generation ahead on keeping the latest technology phone, a fact any journalist meeting him in late 90s would confirm.

Even otherwise sober and objective analysts and commentators succumb to single out Hindutva as the dominant, if not only, reason for the rise and rise of Modi. Data and evidence from economic performance as well as elections seem to suggest otherwise. No doubt, Modi has never hesitated to flaunt his Hindu credentials. One of the first major acts of his after becoming Prime Minister in 2014 was to take the then visiting Prime Minister of Japan Shinzo Abe to Varanasi and witness the Ganga Aaarti in all pomp and glory. Another defining image is of Modi meditating in a 'cave' near the holy Kedarnath temple soon after campaigning for the 2019 Lok Sabha elections got over. And of course, during election campaigns, he often plays the Hindu card. The last member of the Gandhi family to unabashedly display their Hindu identity before, during and after elections was Indira Gandhi.

But when you analyse the astonishing pro-incumbency track record of Narendra Modi, Hindutva is just one element. In this book, we have identified and analysed three primary reasons that have driven the pro incumbency phenomenon in this century. Modi has successfully capitalised on all three. For one, he has carefully cultivated a personality cult and made elections presidential. Second, he has, thanks to swelling tax revenues, unleashed welfare schemes that no political leader before him could do. And third, he has ruthlessly exploited the weaknesses of his opposition rivals when it comes to convincing voters that he is a better bet. We also identified economics as a possible fourth reason though we did not categorise it as one because welfare triumphed economic performance during electoral choices. But even when it comes to economic performance, his stint as Gujarat chief minister was remarkable for sustained economic growth. Forget just industrialisation and foreign investments. In the chapter on "Economics versus Identity", we have quoted well known columnist and frequent Modi critic Swaminathan Anklesaria Aiyar who said the average annual agriculture growth rate in Gujarat in one decade under Modi was the highest ever perhaps in the history of the world. In subsequent pages, we will elaborate on these factors in more detail. But first, let's see if Modi is destiny's child as many think he is.

A lifelong RSS worker, Modi was assigned to the BJP by the Sangh Parivar to play a political role. He first acquired some fame as the man who organised the launch and first phase of the Ram Janambhoomi Rath Yatra led by L.K. Advani in September, 1990. His second brush with publicity and fame came in 1992 when he helped the then BJP president Murli Manohar Joshi hoist the Indian tricolour at Lal Chowk in Srinagar when Jammu & Kashmir was being torn apart by Islamist terrorism. But the BJP Gujarat had many taller and more popular leaders when the party first won power on its own in 1995. In the subsequent internal party feuds and shenanigans that followed, Modi became collateral damage and was virtually exiled from his home state in the late 1990s. He continued his grassroots work in Punjab, Haryana and Himachal even as he gradually emerged as a BJP spokesperson when private news channels started proliferating. He seemed destined to play a secondary role as numerous RSS and BJP folks have done before him. But destiny had other things in store for the bearded 'pracharak'.

First came the monstrous earthquake of January 26, 2001 that devastated Gujarat. Then came the seeming inability of the state government led by chief minister Keshubhai Patel to handle the rehabilitation efforts in a competent manner. And then came electoral shocks for the BJP in the state. Even as it became evident that Keshubhai Patel was becoming more and more unpopular in the aftermath of the earthquake, local election results started confirming the anecdotal evidence. The Congress defeated the BJP in a string of panchayat elections. That was followed by a shock defeat for the BJP in the Ahmedabad municipal elections that even the Congress had not anticipated. The top leadership of the BJP in

Delhi was deeply worried. After all, Gujarat was a hard fought and won crown jewel for the party and a loss in assembly elections due in 2002 would be a massive setback. Even as the party brass was mulling options, the result of a Lok Sabha bye-election in the state became a final wake up call. Nisha Gautam was the second wife of Amarsinh Chaudhary, the first tribal chief minister of Gujarat is an important Congress leader. She won two back-to-back elections from Sabarkantha constituency in 1998 and 1999. Unfortunately, she passed away in 2001 leading to bye-elections that were held in September, 2001. Congress candidate Madhusudan Mistry (who later became a close aide of Rahul Gandhi) scored a thumping victory. That triggered frenzied confabulations in Delhi and Narendra Modi, who had been 'exiled' from his home state, was sent back as chief minister. The rest, as the much-abused cliché goes, is history.

Modi has never looked back since then. It would be instructive to examine the factors that have resulted in enduring pro-incumbency verdicts enjoyed by Modi, both as chief minister and prime minister. Not just for those love and follow Indian politics, but also for future leaders who dream of winning elections and keep winning them. The first factor we have identified and analysed in this book while explaining pro-incumbency is the personality cult. Narendra Modi was a virtual nonentity for Indians prior to 2001 and became a national—even a global figure—only after the 2002 Gujarat riots. Diligently following the Chinese proverb since then, he has somehow managed to transform every challenge and crisis into an opportunity. In the process, he has acquired a larger-than-life image to the extent that could possibly surprise even him.

The Gujarat Model

BJP-nominated Rajya Sabha member and former journalist Swapan Dasgupta analysed Modi the personality in a piece for the journal *Seminar* soon after the 2007 assembly elections in Gujarat: "In Gujarat, a beleaguered Congress quite rightly gauged that its only hope of ousting Modi and the BJP was to convert the assembly into a fragmented election. With Modi's personal popularity at dizzying heights and no focused anti-incumbency, the Congress sought to conduct a low-key campaign based on an aggregate of local grievances. At one level, it hoped to bolster its traditional support among Kshatriyas, Dalits, Adivasis and Muslims—the KHAM combination forged by Madhavsinh Solanki in the 1980s—with accretion of votes from the Leuva Patels and Kolis. It sought to prey on the caste-based dissidence in the BJP led by former Chief Minister Keshubhai Patel...Sonia Gandhi's 'maut ke saudagar' speech on December 1 at Navsari upset the state Congress' calculations. The BJP, which was looking for opportunities to raise the level of the campaign, naturally seized upon this remark. Modi expediently interpreted the remark as an insult to Gujarat's pride and dignity. "Do I, a son of Gujarat, look like a maut ka saudagar?" he asked at his meetings, evoking the inevitable cries of No, no. 'You must pay Soniaben back for this insult to Gujarat'...It speaks volumes for Modi's innate self-confidence (his detractors call it megalomania) that he was unmoved by the intensity of the assaults and the carefully aimed snubs directed at him. He deliberately chose to make himself the centre of the election campaign. A more cautious politician would have taken shelter behind the party or retreated into a shell. Not Modi. He revelled in controversy and wanted more. He put himself directly in the line of fire. The results were there for everyone, except the wilfully blind, to see."[5]

That comes from someone who supports Modi. What about his detractors of whom there are legion? Right at the beginning of the chapter, we have quoted Ashish Nandy and Aakar Patel. Let's add one written for *Time* magazine by Aatish Taseer with a headline "India's Divider In Chief": "Modi's victory was an expression of that distrust. He attacked once unassailable founding fathers, such as Nehru, then sacred state ideologies, such as Nehruvian secularism and socialism; he spoke of a 'Congress-free' India; he demonstrated no desire to foster brotherly feeling between Hindus and Muslims. Most of all, his ascension showed that beneath the surface of what the elite had believed was a liberal syncretic culture, India was indeed a cauldron of religious nationalism, anti-Muslim sentiment and deep-seated caste bigotry. The country had a long history of politically instigated sectarian riots, most notably the killing of at least 2,733 Sikhs in the streets of Delhi after the 1984 assassination of Indira Gandhi by her Sikh bodyguards. The Congress leadership, though hardly blameless, was able, even through the selective profession of secular ideals, to separate itself from the actions of the mob. Modi, by his deafening silences after more recent atrocities, such as the killing of more than 1,000 people, mostly Muslims, in his home state of Gujarat in 2002, proved himself a friend of the mob. He made one yearn for the hypocrisies of the past, for, as Aldous Huxley writes, at least "the political hypocrite admits the existence of values higher than those of immediate national, party or economic interest." Modi, without offering an alternative moral compass, rubbished the standards India had, and made all moral judgment seem subject to conditions of class and culture warfare."[6]

That brings us back to the issue we highlighted right at the beginning of this chapter: the allegation that Modi is anti-Muslim and that he is on a quest to forge a 'Hindu Rashtra' by demolishing the Nehruvian secular democracy that was crafted after 1947. While both the authors pay attention to 'perception' and rhetoric, they 'respect' and have more faith in data and numbers. Let's look at the numbers. If Modi was indeed an ogre who deliberately discriminated against Muslims, their role in government as well as governance should have declined considerably, if not drastically after he became Prime Minister. From a purely political perspective, Modi critics are right when they say that the BJP doesn't have a single Muslim as a Lok Sabha member and barely any as an MLA. But what about other wings of the government. This is what Sanya Dhingra wrote for the *print.in* in 2020: "According to the CSE results released by the UPSC Tuesday, a total of 829 candidates have cleared the latest exam. Muslim candidates comprise 5 per cent of this, as has been the trend over the last few years. Muslims are believed to constitute nearly 15 per cent of India's population. The number of Muslim candidates picked last year was 28, or 4 per cent of the 759 candidates recruited.

For the 2016 batch, for the first time in history, 50 Muslims were selected through the UPSC, with 10 making it to the top 100. In the 2017 batch, too, 50 Muslims were selected through the exam...Since 2016, the per centage of Muslim candidates has remained around 5 per cent, which is a big feat, considering that, since Independence, this number was around 2.5 per cent," said Zafar Mahmood of the Zakat Foundation, which grooms Muslim candidates for the UPSC."[6b]

Ironically, supposedly pro-Modi media platforms are either bemused or unhappy with his government for 'appeasing' Muslims by encouraging more and more of them to join the civil services. There was an avalanche of outrage by Hindutva handles on social media in April, 2022 when the Minister for Minority Affairs Mukhtar Abbas Naqvi officially launched yet another 'free coaching centre for Muslims' to prepare for civil services examinations in Navi Mumbai. In fact, most hardcore Hindutva supporters of Modi on Twitter now call him 'Maulana' Modi! The magazine *Swarajya* (originally launched by C. Rajagopalachari, the friend-turned-fierce critic of Nehru for his socialist policies, in 1958 and relaunched in 2014) is openly pro-Modi. Yet, even it looked askance at his government's decision to encourage more Muslims to join the civil services. In a column for the magazine in 2020, Arihant Pawariya wrote: "I have observed the debate around allegations of pro-Muslim bias in selection of officers by the Union Public Service Commission for the prestigious posts of IAS, IPS, IFS etc., with amusement. As soon as Sudarshan News TV anchor Suresh Chavhanke announced doing a special segment on the possible institutionalised bias in favour of Muslim candidates in UPSC entrance exams, many former and current civil services officers came forward to vehemently deny such charges. They wrote to the Prime Minister and even went to the extent of calling the anchor a bigot... Nonetheless, the reason why one terms the raging debate over pro-Muslim bias as amusing is because the Rajinder Sachar Committee Report in 2006 had recommended exactly the same—to increase diversity of Muslims in employment, housing societies and education. More importantly, the government of India had accepted the suggestion and made it its official policy to improve diversity more than a decade ago. So those who believe that there is no affirmative action in favour of Muslims are on shaky ground when the government itself is implementing such a policy openly."[6c] The authors wonder if a media platform favourably disposed towards the Congress, like *NDTV* for instance, would write critical stuff against the Gandhi family or the party they control.

In fact, the data available with the authors clearly suggests that an increasing number of Muslims are voting for the BJP. When the most 'moderate' and supposedly 'pro-Muslim' Atal Bihari Vajpayee led the BJP, pre and post-election surveys by C-Voter, CSDS and many other credible bodies would report ow barely 2 per cent to 3 per cent Muslims voted for the BJP. Under the 'anti-Muslim' Modi, that per centage has jumped to almost 10 per cent nationally. One of the authors distinctly remembers a TV show after Modi had won the Gujarat assembly elections in 2012. The psephologist turned politician Yogendra Yadav too was in the same show. When the author pointed out that about 23 per cent, or almost 1 in every 4 Muslims had actually voted for Modi, Yogendra Yadav, who was principal architect of Lokniti program of Election Studies at the prestigious CSDS, also insisted that there is hardly anything new in that finding as their post poll surveys showed similar trends. The author was simply trying to make a point the 'communal' Modi got more Muslim votes in Gujarat than a 'secular' Nitish Kumar could ever manage in Bihar, even after being championed by majority of Left-Liberal media for turning down 'BJP of Modi'. Of course, Yogendra Yadav appeared visibly shocked that so any Muslims had voted for a 'mass murderer' and 'Maut Ka Saudagar' like Modi but tried to explain the phenomenon as something like forced voting under fear and persecution.

Fast forward to 2022 elections of Uttar Pradesh, which was arguably way more polarised on religious lines due to the narrative of 'Bulldozer Baba' for CM Yogi Adityanath. The data from C-Voter, CSDS and Axis, the three most important election data pointers of contemporary India, pointed that while Muslims overwhelmingly voted for SP. It was their swing towards Akhilesh Yadav that actually left BSP and Congress as completely bankrupt electorally. CM Yogi, arguably belongs to that section of 'New' BJP which offends the Muslim electorate by stating that they don't need their votes for winning elections. Yet, the same data sets of C-Voter, CSDS and Axis also point out that almost 1 in 10 Muslims also voted for BJP. In fact, the C-Voter data set which studies this phenomenon in greater depth, found while only about 7 per cent Sunni Muslims voted for BJP there were staggering 27 per cent Shia Muslims voting for the BJP even when the party had offered the most anti-Muslim face that if could offer as its CM face. We have also studied all the earlier studied in Bihar which showed the Pasmanda Muslims, or the bottom of the pyramid in Muslim demographics did vote for social welfare schemes of Nitish Kumar thus making a dent in MY equation of Lalu Yadav. Add to that the constant news cycles of persecution of Shia and Ahmedia Muslims coming from 'Islamic' Pakistan, and equally constant news cycles of India under Modi having real good equations not just with Saudi Arabia, but even more so with high seat of Shia geopolitics: Iran; you can see the wheels between the wheels of different narratives driving the Muslim Politics of Hindi heartland. Yes, the 'new' BJP is unhesitatingly 'anti-Muslim' in its narrative and actions on the ground. Yes, a huge majority of Muslims treat the party and its leaders as their enemy and 'clear and present danger'. Yet, the growing number of Muslims, particularly Shia and Pasmanda Muslims, who are openly supporting Modi is not just an eye-opener but completely out-of-syllabus for the students of public perceptions and public psychology.

One of the authors has been openly advocating for inclusion of Shia and Ahmedia minorities of Pakistan in the list of prosecuted minorities of CAA which includes Buddhists, Christians and Sikhs apart from Hindus, but leaves out Muslims as pointed out by all those opposing the CAA. The author feels that it would be the right thing to do purely based on the facts and current situation of minorities in Pakistan. Clearly the 'new' BJP wanted to drive home the point that for them the 'non-Muslim' demographics matter the most. However, the election expert working in the thought process of the same author also wonders what would be the reaction of Shia, Bohra, Ahmedia and 'minorities within the minority' Muslims if the Modi government actually would have done that!

It is up to readers to judge whose judgement is clinically, sociologically and metaphorically sound. Our focus is on the unerring ability of Modi to make himself the topic of discourse.

In 2002, he harangued against 'James Michael Lynghdoh', the Election Commissioner who was not allowing him to contest elections and seek a fresh mandate. And he linked his persona with 50 million people of Gujarat. As Swapan Dasgupta has written, he did something similar in 2007. In the 2012 assembly elections, when things looked more comfortable to him, Modi unfurled his national ambitions by linking his own persona with the 'Gujarat Model' of development. In the 2014 Lok Sabha elections, he constantly boasted of his 56-inch chest while mocking his rivals. When the intemperate and politically foolish Mani Shankar Aiyer of the Congress declared that the man was fit only to sell tea at the Congress headquarters, Modi and his fans promptly organised 'Chai Pe Charcha' sessions all over the country where the poor son of a tea-seller was pitted against the Delhi Dynasty. The narrative was constantly set by Modi: it was he the humble backward caste Indian who represented the aspirations of similar Indians against a rotting feudal order that lorded over India from Delhi like the Mughals and the British did. In 2019, Rahul Gandhi offered him an opportunity on a platter by accusing him of corruption in the Rafale fighter aircraft deal and publicly announcing from rallies: "Chowkidar Chor Hai." Modi promptly changed the words in his Twitter profile to 'Main Bhi Chowkidar', followed by the entire Union Cabinet and tens of millions of his fans. Modi added further spice to this blitzkrieg by comparing himself as the 'Kamdar' versus Rahul the 'Namdar'. Poor Rahul Gandhi had no chance, as the 2019 election results showed.

In fact, he never stood a chance if we closely examine how Modi has used his own unique brand of economic empowerment and welfarism to create a base of voters that cut across caste lines, though he failed to breach the 'Muslim' fortress in his quest for votes and electoral legitimacy. When he was chief minister of Gujarat, Modi not only held dazzling investment summits that attracted global CEOs, but he also walked the talk. The Nano car (now a case study in the failure of hype) was a dream project for the head of the Tata group Ratan Tata. In an unusually bold move for a Marxist, the then chief minister of West Bengal Buddhadev Bhattacharya offered both land and fiscal incentives to Tata

Motors to set up a manufacturing plant at a place called Singur to manufacture the Nano. Much was offered to locals by way of compensation and job promises. But Mamata Banerjee, then in opposition led a strident and violent agitation against the plant to the extent that it became virtually impossible for Ratan Tata and his team to execute their plans. In less than a week, Narendra Modi offered land and other incentives to Tata Motors in a Gujarat town called Sanand with all bells and whistles. A grateful Ratan Tata accepted the offer and Nano moved to Sanand. While the Nano failed, Sanand is now a bona fide automotive hub in India. Singur remains a wasteland of dashed dreams and aspirations. Despite having a reasonably high base, Gujarat remained one of the fastest growing economies of the country when Modi was the chief minister of the state.

As editor of *The Indian Express*, Shekhar Gupta used to travel during elections and write a column called "Writings on the Wall". This is what he wrote on the eve of the 2012 assembly elections in Gujarat: "Are they (companies) here because the moneybags love Narendra Modi? They are here because Gujarat provides them ample power, industrial peace, rail and road infrastructure, law and order and a non-rent-seeking bureaucracy and political class. They have reason to be grateful to Modi. And so do millions of Gujarati beneficiaries of this boom. That's why they keep re-electing Modi. Not because a thousand Muslims were killed under his watch in 2002.... Driving to Limdi from Godhra, we make a short stopover at a lone house on the road in village Ghoomni, near Neemkheda. Kamlaben Mawi, may be in her late forties, lost her husband, Kanubhai, to a heart attack last year. She now takes care of her 70-acre family farm. In her home, the TV is on, showing Rahul Gandhi speaking, live, at a rally. I ask her if I can flick channels to check how India are doing at Nagpur and she says, forget it, they are hopeless, we need a new team. Do you get power, I ask. And the answer is, of course, 24 hours. For her agricultural connection, she says, power comes on alternate weeks, during the day or night. There is no power problem. And water? It used to be, but now she has installed 'teepak padhhati' (drip irrigation system) and there is water in the check-dam close by. Then I ask her, shamelessly, her caste and her daughter-in-law says they are 'Hindu Bhil'. So here is Kamlaben Mawi, a Bhil tribal with zero education. But she can take three crops from a 70-acre farm using drip irrigation. She can also lecture you on what is wrong with Indian cricket. It tells you several things. First, that one unique Gujarati trait is entrepreneurship, and this cuts across caste, ethnicity and religion. Second, that power, or electricity, is the great new equaliser and force-multiplier even in the most distant rural, tribal India. Combined with 24-hour TV, it can even fill the knowledge and literacy gap. And third, that by continuing to harp on Modi's 'false' claims of 24-hour power and rural anger, the Congress has got its basic politics all messed up."[7]

When Modi launched his assault on the throne of Delhi, it was actually economic performance and growth that was the centrepiece of his campaign. In every other public rally, he tom-tommed the Gujarat model and repeated ad nauseam his 'mantra' that the government has no business to be in business. Nationalism and a wee bit of Hindutva was always there, but if you look closely at his almost one year-long campaign (that started with his speech at Shri Ram College of Commerce in Delhi with the half glass full metaphor), it was the promise of improving the economic situation of 'neo middle class aspirational' Indians that became his signature theme. The slogan 'Acche Din' was part of the package along with hologram rallies. When he did become Prime Minister after the BJP astounded the world by winning a majority-282 seats-on its own, Modi seemed determined to pursue what he had done in Gujarat for 13 years: his own brand of empowerment-based welfarism married to economic reforms.

Pausing Economic Reforms

But something did change. On August 15, 2014, Modi delivered his first speech as Prime Minister from the ramparts of the Red Fort. Critics sniggered when he spoke of his number one priority which was to build a toilet in every home so that women in India do not have to face the daily indignity and humiliation of open defecation. His critics sniggered, guffawed and snickered. The so called Lutyens Delhi acolytes tut tutted about how Modi had debased the post of the PM by talking about toilets from the ramparts of the Red Fort, a place from where Jawaharlal Nehru used to speak about the vision of a scientific and forward-looking India as a global leader. Never mind the fact that the toilets are a tool to bring down crime against women in rural India. A majority of the sexual crimes against women happen when they go out in the fields for sanitation purposes, particularly in the dark. They are the most vulnerable as there is no security of male members of the household is around and the overwhelming majority of such crimes go unregistered. It goes without saying that the biggest chunk of such crimes happen against women coming from lower strata of the society.

The sniggers became louder when Modi announced that he would ensure every poor person in India—particularly females—will have a bank account via his Jan Dhan Scheme. The primary aim of the scheme was to enable poor Indians to have a bank account even if they had no money to deposit in that account. It was supposed to empower them and act as an incentive to earn more. For years after the launch of the scheme, critics kept writing 'exposes' in the media about how silly the 'zero balance' was because most of the bank accounts had no money in them. Both the toilets and the zero balance accounts have silenced the critics; silenced metaphorically because every time a scheme pushed by Modi shows visible signs of success, his critics become even more strident and often hysterical.

Parameshwaran Iyer had resigned from the IAS in 2009 and was a global consultant-cum-advisor who worked principally with the World Bank and had more or less settled in the United States. Soon after Modi became Prime Minister, Iyer was invited to meet the Prime Minister to discuss the issue of open defecation and how to solve the problem. Iyer had prior field experience on the issue in countries like Vietnam as a member of the World Bank. Santa Dhingra of the portal the *print.in* interacted with Iyer in January 2021 after he had 'completed' his role in the Swachh Bharat Mission and written a delightful book about it. Here are some excerpts from that feature that showcase how Modi used dedicated professionals to craft a success out of a seemingly impossible task:

"Aap wahin hai na jo IAS chhod ke bhaag gaye the? (Aren't you the person who ran away from the IAS?)" This is how Parameswaran Iyer recalls his first interaction with Prime Minister Narendra Modi. Handpicked by the PM to deliver the Swachh Bharat promise, Iyer would go on to become the name synonymous with the project that made India open defecation free (ODF). The interaction is one of many nuggets from his four-year stint with the Swachh Bharat Mission (SBM) that Iyer has penned down in his new book *Method in the Madness—Insights from My Career as an Insider-Outsider-Insider*...Iyer worked with four ministers during his term—Chaudhary Birendra Singh, Narendra Singh Tomar, Uma Bharti and Gajendra Singh Shekhawat, all of whom he had a good working relationship with. However, he was answerable for the delivery of the SBM to the 'Big Boss himself', PM Modi. Iyer had over time developed an extremely healthy relationship with Modi, whose political capital he immensely leveraged to deliver on SBM, he says. He recalls a top official in the Prime Minister's Office telling him: "No other secretary to the government has utilised the PM's mass appeal for a flagship programme as much as you have." "In the four plus years that I worked on SBM, we ended up doing a record 10 major public events with the PM, something no other national flagship programme has come even close to achieving," Iyer writes."[8]

But Modi did falter and fail while trying to implement the Gujarat model across India. Along with toilets and zero balance Jan Dhan accounts meant to empower the poor, Modi also brought in legislation to change land acquisition laws in a move that was clearly aimed at wooing private sector investors. The previous UPA regime had passed a Land Acquisition Bill that made it extremely difficult, and in some cases virtually impossible, for private companies and entrepreneurs to acquire land to setup manufacturing plants or other business-related purposes. His 'pro-poor' bill was prodded by the Left leaning supra constitutional body the National Advisory Council headed by Sonia Gandhi. To be sure, poor farmers and other landholders had been consistently given a raw deal when the government or private businesses acquired land in the past. But the UPA Bill went to the other extreme, sending an implicit message in as many words to private investors that they were not really welcome. Modi got the Bill amended to make it more business-friendly and actually retained provisions that would ensure land owners got a good price during acquisition. Thanks to a majority in the Lok Sabha, the amended Bill cleared the lower house. But the NDA did not have a majority in the Rajya Sabha and the Bill got stuck. There was ferocious criticism of the Bill; the signature tune being that the newly arrived Modi regime was throwing hapless farmers and land owners to the 'capitalist' wolves. For many months, Modi personally led the campaign to defend the new Bill and describe how it was actually pro farmer. (The same story was repeated in 2021 with the Farm Laws). But then the humiliated 'leader' of opposition Rahul Gandhi came up with the 'Suit Boot Ki Sarkar' jibe and for once, even the ever articulate Modi appeared at a loss for words.

On both occasions the public sentiment swelled against the farm- and farmer-related bills. The C-Voter Annual Report Card in 2015 found almost 70 per cent Indians saying the Land Acquisition Bill was anti-farmer and anti-poor. It was one the rare occasions when Modi lost a perception war. The bill was duly rolled back. The entire episode got repeated in 2021 when an overwhelming majority said Modi government should not do anything that makes farmers unhappy. The farm laws were rolled back as well. On both occasions Modi was taken aback by the unexpected groundswell against the bills. But on both occasions, he simply accepted the mistake, not that the bills were wrong or bad, but that he could not 'properly' convey the benefits of the Bills to common Indians. On both occasions, immediately after the roll-back his personal rating, which by the way remained high even when public was critical of the Bills, went even further up. Can't really blame the opposition for being completely clueless that when on both occasions they won the match on perception war hands down; then how come the same public is giving the trophy to Modi?

But public perception and investor's perceptions are two different animals. Modi abandoned the Bill and the message that went out to investors was definitely not encouraging. The man had failed to do what he had done so well in Gujarat as chief minister.

After all, it had taken him less than two weeks to 'acquire' land in Sanand and offer that not just to the Tata group to manufacture the Nano car, but also to other companies, domestic as well as global. The decision to abandon the Land Bill definitely cost the Indian economy. After that, till the end of his first term, Modi virtually gave up on pro-investor policies and concentrated on being the big daddy of welfare schemes. Populism scored over economics. Sure, the first tenure was marked by landmark economic policy changes like the GST and the Insolvency & Bankruptcy Code. But these moves would pay dividends only in the long term, as they are doing now five years after they came into force. The other major economic policy move, demonetisation was hugely disruptive. That and the hangover of the bad loans crisis created by the previous UPA regime meant investors became wary and cautious. This is reflected in hard numbers. By the time Lok Sabha elections were due in 2019, the GDP growth rate on a quarterly basis had dropped from more than 8 per cent to less than 4 per cent. It is primarily welfare schemes and to an extent an upsurge in 'nationalism' post Pulwama and Balakot that delivered a bigger mandate to Modi in 2019. If voters had cast their ballot based on GDP growth rate figures, his government would have been thrown out.

Analyst Mohammed Zeeshan wrote for *The Diplomat* in December, 2020, clearly explaining why Modi's efforts at reforms have kept stumbling and faltering since he first became Prime Minister in 2014: "For the past six years, Indian Prime Minister Narendra Modi's passionate supporters have built and nurtured an impressive personality cult, casting the prime minister as a strongman leader who gets things done." The campaign has landed two historic electoral victories so far. To many middle-class Indians, Modi's strongman image is attractive, because they believe that only a strongman leader can deliver the important but politically difficult reforms necessary to liberalize the Indian economy Yet, whenever he has attempted to be an economic reformer, all these things—the personality cult, the strongman tendencies, and the passionate support base—have turned out to be Modi's bane, not his boon...If Modi wishes to reform the Indian economy, he will have to publicly rebuke such rhetoric.

For reforms to succeed in a vast and diverse democracy like India, aggression does not work. There has to be a broad consensus, to bring multiple players—including the intended beneficiaries—on board, so that all stakeholders are able to plan and act as needed for the reforms to succeed. All this needs widespread debate and discussion, including multiple rounds of questioning and clarification with the government, before the reforms are finally rolled out.

Yet, none of this has ever happened. When these farm reforms were passed, they were brought out by circumventing the parliament—in the form of an ordinance. The government also removed the Question Hour during the truncated monsoon session of Parliament this year, sparking fears that Parliament was now no more than a mere notice board for policies and laws that have already been concluded beforehand. And the prime minister himself has not held a single press conference in six years.

This strongman-style 'shock and awe' approach, including aggressive propaganda against critics, has hindered the Modi government's ability to implement any reform meaningfully."[9]

As we all know, Modi was compelled to announce the repeal the repeal of the three farm laws in November 2021. Zeeshan is right to some extent when he talks about the need to engage more meaningfully with stakeholders while pursuing on implementing reforms. One big success was the manner in which the late Arun Jaitley as Finance Minister engaged, talked, cajoled and bargained with all state governments many of them not ruled by the BJP or the NDA) before the GST Bill became law in 2017. There was simply no way GST could have happened unless every state government came on board. To that extent, yes, analysts like Zeeshan are right. But they also tend to overemphasise the 'authoritarian' bit. If Modi was truly authoritarian in the classical sense, he would have simply ignored protests and criticism and ensured the both Land Acquisition and Farm Bills remained law in the statute books. The fact that even a '56-inch strongman' like him succumbed to perceived pressure means he listens and adapts. The problem, according to many analysts and insiders within the BJP is that apart from Modi, the regime has a terrible shortage of effective communicators to spread the essence of reform measures and how they actually help the average Indian. There is no dearth of articulate, well read, confident and persuasive leaders in the BJP who can communicate in English, Hindi and even other local languages. It remains a mystery why they are not fielded to propagate reforms while either inarticulate or overly aggressive spokespersons do the job.

Modi learns from mistakes, his own or even others, very quickly. But the authors are completely clueless how any why he has allowed the worst set of party leaders to continue as communicators and spokespersons. The fact is that BJP when in opposition has always made headlines by keeping their best of the best articulators as official spokespersons. But when in power, that set gets transferred to ministerial responsibilities and they are replaced by worst of the worst possible lot. Today if you look at the intellect and mannerisms of huge majority of BJP spokespersons, they reek of such ill-mannered arrogance that every time they open their mouth their party must be turning away a new set of voters. In short; in worst of the times, in their as opposition, the BJP puts their best of suave, sophisticated, well learned faces forward. And when in power, their worst of the ignorant arrogant lot are made their representative. This was true even in times of NDA-1 under Atal-Advani duo. And the same is continuing in NDA-2 and NDA-3 under Modi-Shah combine.

So, there is hardly any secret that in times of crisis, the party infrastructure collapses in communication front, only for Modi to hold the fort all alone and repair the damage on his own, most of the times cutting a sorry figure in public. The fact is that the public knows this situation better than the experts and most of the time cutting a sorry figure or even saying sorry on national television ends up in immediate recovery of the Prime Minister's popularity ratings. The foul-mouthed set of arrogant party spokespersons could probably suit the agenda and personality cult of Amit Shah or Yogi as Prime Minister, but not Narendra Modi as Prime Minister. In all the years after 2014 victory, whenever any crisis has hit the Modi Government, more than the actual crisis, it's the crisis communication that has been the real bad news.

Reforms are Back

But there is good news too that has been buried because of two years of pandemic. The second term of the Modi term has been decidedly reformist and forward-looking. First, the seemingly small but unmistakable message to private investors that this government now really means business. Despite strong protests even from within sections of the Sangh Parivar, apart from the Luddite intellectuals who write apocalyptic columns for media outlets, Air India was privatised and sold to the Tata group. One could say Air India was given back to the Tatas because it was the legendary J.R.D. Tata who had launched Air India before India became a free country; only to see Jawaharlal Nehru nationalise the airline in 1953. The government did not earn any money from the sale; in fact, it lost money as a substantial part of the massive debts of Air India had to be virtually written off. But the message to investors was clear, and important.

However, public perception is all always supportive of disinvestment news, as these steps are seen as something which will end up wiping out government jobs. And the issue of unemployment remains on top of the public agenda along with the inflation. The C-Voter polls for Start News in 2003-2004 also found that people were not very supporting of the these moves in NDA-1. The generic feeling is, you can't create new jobs, at least don't take away the existing jobs that government has been taking care of. Somehow, again in a communication disaster, the Government has been unable to poster up the jobs that are created by profit making companies when the Government gets away from the loss-making ones. To our surprise, the snap poll done for ABP recently, the C-Voter researchers found that a big number was still not appreciate of giving away Air India, that too to Tatas, who all along are considered the best and most responsible employers in Indian public perception. In the Globe C=Scan C-Voter CSR studies, the Tata Group always came on top in terms of the most regarded and respected Indian companies which do good for the society. The much-awaited turnaround of Air India might change that perception about disinvestment.

A much bigger message was sent by Finance Minister Nirmala Sitharaman when she announced new corporate tax rates that are probably most competitive and attractive in the world, including investor favourites like Singapore. Now that the existential threat of the Covid pandemic is receding, the economy will see the impact of these corporate tax cuts. Then there is the Production Linked Incentive scheme launched across a slew of sectors that has begun to pay dividends. Merchandise exports from India crossed $ 400 billion for the first time in 2021-22; with the growth led by engineering goods and consumer electronics and components including mobile phone handsets. Total exports too broke all records, clocking ore than $ 670 billion. LIC has been listed on the stock exchanges. India has signed a free trade agreement with UAE and Australia and till the time this was written, was committed to signing another one with United Kingdom by October, 2022. Clearly, the reformist Modi who had withdrawn into a shell post the 'suit Boot' jibe is back with a vengeance. Critics keep saying he has sold India to the Ambanis and Adanis. But this time, he seems to be taking the rhetoric in his stride.

And the data regarding public perception certainly backs up this claim to optimism. Indians are eternal optimists, but the Covid pandemic even tested the nerves of that optimism. In the C-Voter Daily Tracker, people always mentioned that their day today life is tough. But in the very next question on how do they expect the next six months or a year is going to be, they always answered in majority: "it will be better". For the first time post-covid, that Optimism took a hit in mid-2021 when the number of people who were 'undecided' or who said 'worse' were bigger than number of people who said they were optimistic about a better future. This was the same time when the West Bengal election rallies continued even when Covid was rampaging across the country. Not that Modi was the only politician who continued the rallies, every ranging from Mamata Banerjee to Rahul Gandhi did the same. But the Indian public reacted in a way the elders in a family react to some young guy's wrong doing saying: "We expected others to be this careless and reckless, but how could YOU do the same? We expected you to do better...". And all of a sudden, we watched the approval rating of Narendra Modi plummet in second week of April 2021 onwards. The moment C-Voter Tracker numbers came out in media, there was a radio silence and next thing we know Modi went incommunicado working only on the vaccine part, as if going all out fire fighting for the damage control. From the highs of almost 70 per cent approval rating, at one point of time in May 2021 his rating crashed to as low as 36 per cent, the worst he ever had to face. But as the vaccination program rolled out, slow and steady his ratings started to repair. By July the worst was over for him and by December he was back in 50 per cent plus positive rating. It took the crushing victories in Uttar Pradesh and other states in early 2022 for him to breathe easy with his rating touching 60 per cent plus numbers, which are Modi's personal benchmarks for popularity.

Analyst and commentator Sandeep Ghosh who has worked extensively in the private sector explains the new reformist avatar of the Modi government in a piece for *moneycontrol.com* in February, 2022: "Two years into his second term, Modi's nuanced economic policy is becoming more obvious to discerning observers. In a narrow sense Atmanirbhar Bharat can be interpreted as a renewed call for Swadeshi. It dovetailed into Modi's previous campaign of 'vocal for local'. But, in reality, far from being protectionist it is an invitation for making Indian industry globally competitive. Apart from technology and indigenous capability, two imperatives for being part of international supply-chains are cost and scale. A large part of China's success has been its ability to leverage the vast domestic market and developing skilled manpower. Atmanirbhar Bharat is a step in that direction. As Modi pointed out on a lighter vein, industrialists have always been linked to politicians. This is not a new phenomenon. Even Jawaharlal Nehru and Indira Gandhi were accused of being partial towards big business houses such as the Tatas and Birlas. However, contrary to popular belief, these relationships are not based only on quid-pro-quo. If Nehru and Indira Gandhi leaned on some industrialists it was because, when in a fledgling economy not everyone had the capacity to undertake large investments. Similarly, in the global arena, countries such as Japan and South Korea were able to break the hegemony of

Western conglomerates by leveraging the might of home-grown corporations such as Toyota, Honda, and Samsung.

India too will need some big boys to find a toehold in the world economic ecosystem. To berate Indian enterprise, comparing them with variants of COVID-19, would be doing the nation a disservice."[10]

Try and fix the complex, complicated and strange bits of this jigsaw puzzle and you will start getting an idea of why Narendra Modi is the pro incumbency symbol of the 21st century. In a genuine democracy, the authors feel that Franklin Delano Roosevelt of the United States, Jawaharlal Nehru of India and Margaret Thatcher of the United Kingdom were the symbols of political leaders not only of pro-incumbency, but also of truly transformative epochs that changed political and economic discourse and narratives. As we have discussed in detail in an earlier chapter, FDR not only won four consecutive presidential elections, but also convinced Americans that welfare of the poor was good for the overall economy. Jawaharlal Nehru not only won three consecutive Lok Sabha elections, but also convinced Indians that even a flawed democracy with all its warts was better than other alternatives. Perhaps the toughest challenges were faced by Margaret Thatcher; and not just because she was a woman leader. Britain was facing a crisis on all fronts-economic, social, political and geopolitical when the Iron Lady became prime minister in 1979. But then she won three consecutive elections and changed the country fundamentally, for better or for worse depending on your ideological inclinations. So pervasive has been her impact, despite bitter and often abusive opposition from her critics, that even the rival party the Labour had to talk her language before it got another prime minister in the form of Tony Blair. The authors think Modi's rise, his missteps and his sustained popularity resembles that of Thatcher. Perhaps where the 'fascist', 'autocratic', 'intolerant' Modi differs from her is that he 'surrendered' in the case of Land Acquisition and Farm Laws while Thatcher never ever surrendered and went all guns blazing even after she was ousted in a coup by her own party colleagues. Modi and Thatcher have one more thing in common though: while FDR and Nehru came from privileged families, the other two were born in very ordinary, working-class families. Their struggles and their rise, in that sense, is even more remarkable.

The big question that engages not just the sycophantic admirers and abusive critics of Modi, but also commentators and scholars is: can he match the record set by Nehru of winning three successive parliamentary elections? When it comes to the man himself, Modi seems to have already started campaigning for the 2024 elections. And do remember, he has never lost an election. But anything is possible in politics. Inflation, unemployment and middle-class distress might just lead to a surge of anger against his government to the point voters will say "Let's look for something else". It happened in 1977, in 1989 and in 2004. But do we have an opposition that can capitalise on that possible anger and anti-incumbency against the current Modi regime? The authors think it is possible, but a tall order. And why is that?

We have all read the story about that fabled old man in a village who, on his deathbed, summoned his sons engaged in a dispute. We know how the warring sons realised their folly after failing to break a bunch of sticks and decided to present a 'united front'. Now, there are two serious issues with this fable in contemporary times: the old man would summon his sons and daughters. Second, and more important, is the question of what happens to the squabbling sons and daughters if the old man passed away without imparting this life lesson.

The first question to ask is: are the myriad opposition parties and personalities really interested in actually forging a combined opposition force? Many doubt whether that is so.

Even if the answer is 'yes', the second question is: what will make such a hypothetical 'Mahagathbandhan' (grand alliance) a force that the Indian voter thinks can deliver a better government than the National Democratic Alliance (NDA)?

The authors are not very optimistic of a resounding 'yes' to the first question. Just one piece of hard evidence from the tiny state of Goa that sends two members to the Lok Sabha will explain the reason. In 2017, the BJP literally 'stole' a mandate that was almost certainly against it. It won 13 seats compared to 17 won by the Congress in an assembly of 40. The sitting Chief Minister of the

BJP lost in his own seat. The Congress was short of just three seats. There were 10 'others' who won on an anti-BJP mandate. And yet, it was the BJP that formed the government.

Let's forget morality lectures and come back quickly to 2022. The BJP was unpopular and was staring at 10 years of accumulated anti-incumbency sentiments. Both Arvind Kejriwal of the Aam Aadmi Party (AAP) and Mamata Banerjee of the Trinamool Congress announced that they will fight 'separately' and defeat the BJP without the Congress. The AAP at least has been around in Goa for years. But why Mamata Didi decided to rush headlong into Goa will remain a mystery.

The outcome: the BJP wins 20 out of 40 seats, and the Congress 12. The BJP's vote share was 10 per cent more than the Congress's. The AAP and the Trinamool together polled 12 per cent anti-incumbent votes, which would have almost certainly gone to the Congress in their absence. No rocket science here, just simple maths.

The BJP gets the support of five more MLAs and forms the government for the third successive time. If ambitious chieftains like Mamata and Kejriwal cannot bury their egos for a tiny state like Goa, what makes you think they will do it when the big throne in Delhi is at stake?

Colleagues of Kejriwal think they were working hard for the last five years in Goa, and they feel that their tally could have been way better if the Trinamool would not have made a last-minute entry.

Post-Punjab, we have to take their assertion seriously. As we write this, the AAP has formally announced their intent to contest elections in West Bengal. Who exactly will they end up hurting? Modi or Mamata? Will Modi and the BJP not ruthlessly exploit, probe, inflate and pamper these egos to ensure that it wins a third successive term in 2024?

Of course, the dominance displayed by the BJP in the 2022 assembly elections might be a wake-up call for them with a ringing alarm that chimes: "we will swim or sink together come 2024".

Since anything is possible in politics—and a week is a long time in politics—let us assume that all opposition parties would listen to the sage counsel offered by the 'unofficial' opposition patriarch, Sharad Pawar, who has been plaintively repeating ad nauseam that a combined opposition with the Congress inside that tent is a minimum necessary condition for defeating the BJP-led NDA in 2024. Every time a Mamata Didi or a KCR comes calling, he mumbles this mantra.

Let's face it. The veteran grandmaster of political moves, who was once an ambitious Prime Minister aspirant chieftain in 1991 when the Congress settled for a 'safe' P.V. Narashima Rao, has a very valid point. No matter the scale of parties' sweeping victories in assembly elections in a state or two, fighting the BJP at a national level without the Congress and hoping to dent the Modi juggernaut is delusional, wishful thinking that will take these chieftains nowhere in 2024.

Remember, a similar clutch of chieftains formed a 'united front' sans the BJP in 2009 to dislodge the Congress-led UPA. The modest and unassuming Manmohan Singh took the Congress from 145 to 206 Lok Sabha seats as a consequence. Even his ardent admirers will admit that Singh was no charismatic electoral magician. Imagine what a still indefatigable and charismatic Modi is capable of doing.

In any case, it is all about primary school-level arithmetic. Congress still retains a 'national' core vote base of close to 20 per cent. How can we just arrogantly write it off as dead, buried and gone, and simply refuse to co-opt the party in a defining battle in 2024?

The Congress is still in direct, bipolar competition with the BJP in 195 Lok Sabha seats. Add 20 of Kerala where it has direct equity in the contest, and the tally goes to 215 Lok Sabha seats where the Congress is in the game for winner or runner-up contest.

Now, add the 101 seats in the United Progressive Alliance (UPA)-ruled states of Jharkhand, Maharashtra and Tamil Nadu, where the Congress is still seen as a valuable junior partner. We have not added Bihar in this as Tejashwi Yadav has already dumped Congress.

So, for all practical matters, the Congress and the current UPA allies are in a direct, bipolar contest in 316 Lok Sabha seats. Do the regional chieftains with Prime Ministerial ambitions expect to win a majority by successfully wiping the BJP out in the remaining 227 seats? Last we heard in arithmetic, 227 was supposed to be 45 seats short of the magic figure of 272 in the Lok Sabha. Or do they expect the Congress to come crawling to them in 2024 in the event the BJP falls well short of 272?

And why exactly should Congress do that when the upper limit for Mamata Banerjee remains 42 seats (considering she will win all the seats in West Bengal) and Arvind Kejriwal it remains just 20 seats (considering he will win all seats in Delhi and Punjab)? Let's just leave K. Chandrashekar Rao with a saturation of 17 seats in Telengana alone.

Besides, why blame the Gandhis alone for the dynastic approach when almost all the parties in the opposition camp are doing the same thing? From the Samajwadi Party (SP), the Rashtriya Lok Dal (RLD), the Rashtriya Janata Dal (RJD), the Jharkhand Mukti Morcha (JMM), the Indian National Lok Dal (INLD), the Biju Janata Dal (BJD), the Dravida Munnetra Kazhagam (DMK), the Telangana Rashtra Samithi (TRS), the Shiv Sena (SS), the Nationalist Congress Party (NCP), the Shiromani Akali Dal (SAD), the National Conference (NC), the Peoples Democratic Party (PDP), right up to even the Trinamool Congress, everyone is practising dynastic rule within their party structure. The only exceptions—so far—are the Aam Aadmi Party (AAP) and the Left.

Modi knows this, and this is why his election speeches are now more concentrated around the opposition of dynasties. Even Narendra Modi doesn't single out the Congress for being dynastic. So, why should voters single out the Congress on this matter?

The only person within the UPA rank and file with Prime Ministerial ambition is Sharad Pawar, and he clearly knows his maths and these equations rather well. Not without a reason, he keeps underlining that without Congress, any anti-BJP front will remain a non-starter.

If there was a Pulitzer, Nobel or Magsaysay award for being the most vehement and relentless critic of the Modi regime, the portal *Wire* would win it hands down. Analyst Ajay Gudavarthy wrote the following pearls of wisdom for the portal in 2021 "No other political party and government must have designed the number of strategies the current regime has in mustering an electoral majority and in trying to maintain social hegemony. It is a story of wheels-within-wheels. One strategy follows the other to cancel out the ill-effects of the previous one and then the next to cancel out its ill-effects in turn. It is a kind of carpet bombing of multiple, varied and blatantly contradictory strategies that has bamboozled the opposition either into confusion, submission or blanking out and unable to create an alternate narrative. By the time the opposition picks up the loose ends of the strategy of the BJP-RSS combine, they would have already moved on to many other agendas, programmes and propaganda. One strategy pre-empts the next and it is well-thought-out, even if it at times gives the impression of being contingent...The current regime is ending up antagonising a majority of the citizenry, beginning with students, Dalits, Muslims, women, and now the farmers. These electoral and social strategies are also intended to maintain support, even if they are opposed to the agenda and programmes of the current regime. It is not about convincing or building consent but about creating conditions that do not leave one with any other option, like in the case of Owaisi getting Muslim support—which only consolidates the Hindu votebank...What this kind of sustained fragmentation through multiple strategies does is to realise that social consent is on the decline and electoral possibilities can only be won by fragmenting and dis-empowering those forces opposed to the current regime."[11] Look at the irony, apart from the bitterness. The current regime seemingly has antagonised the Dalits, the backward classes and the poor and yet they are fooled into voting for Modi! Till opposition parties give up this "Ashish Nandy School of analysis", they have no chance.

Clearly, the regional chieftains have to climb down a notch or two from their perches towards the ground reality. But the 'entitled' Nehru-Gandhi dynasty has to climb down a lot more from their now-imaginary thrones. Mamata Banerjee, K. Chandrasekhar Rao and Arvind Kejriwal might let Modi win 2024 and remain content for another few years ruling their regional fiefdoms, but they will simply not accept Rahul Gandhi as the putative leader of the opposition.

And why should they? We are not talking about egos here, but their political instincts. It is doubtful if any other major politician of India has such a miserable electoral track record and continues to make decisions for the party, officially as president or actually as non-president.

If there was even an iota of hope left about his ability to conceive smart political strategies, the manner in which Rahul and his sister Priyanka Gandhi destroyed the Congress in Punjab (and sank Uttarakhand along by keeping Harish Rawat occupied in the Punjab mess rather than leaving him to clean up the Uttarakhand mess) in the run-up to 2022 leaves no further doubt except in the minds of family cronies and sycophants.

The Gandhi family has to accept that their glory days are history and they must express willingness to climb down from their high horse and accept a possible non-Congress man or an ex-Congressman like Sharad Pawar as the leader of a credible national alternative. In short, if they are serious, they should remain a part of the UPA omnibus but let an efficient driver drive it.

Besides, even the Congress can very well do better with a non-Gandhi leader in its leadership role. Electorally speaking, the vote share 'won' by this remnant of the Gandhi family in its best performance in 2009 was a little above 28 per cent. That was still less than the Congress vote share of 29 per cent in 1996 under Narasimha Rao; the much-celebrated 'historic win' of Sonia Gandhi in the 2004 election was actually just a repeat of what Congress under Sitaram Kesri got in 1998 elections. Sonia Gandhi managed 145 seats with 27 per cent votes in 2004, while locked-in-the-AICC-toilet fame, Sitaram Kesri won 141 seats with 26 per cent votes in 1998 for Congress.

What next if the 'dynasty' actually displays the humility to accept reality and forge a 'united front' against the BJP for 2024, where they are not the automatic leaders from the front or from behind the scenes?

The chances of that happening don't appear very high, but let's assume that anything is possible in politics. If this 'united front' is serious about defeating Modi, it must first start by forgetting Modi. No matter who the joint opposition leader is, if s/he is pitted against Modi in 2024 as a national alternative, it's a lost cause.

Can a clutch of super-ambitious and ego-driven regional chieftains, and a supremely entitled 'royal' family, do all this and more in less than two years and start campaigning together for 2024? Well, to again issue the cliché, a week is a long time in politics and stranger things have happened, like castles built on sand staying firm even against a strong breeze.

As many discernible and sensible analysts have been saying since before 2019, Modi will keep making himself the main issue during Lok Sabha elections. The only way to blunt that as a weapon is to focus on the poor performance of BJP leaders (and a big number of inefficient BJP chief ministers) in delivering 'economic' and material well-being on bread-and-butter issues. The opposition must keep hammering the message home to voters that they deserve a better future and a better government. In effect, the opposition has hope only if the Indian voter casts her ballot in 2024 as if it were a series of assembly or some other local municipal elections in their state. In other words, they will have to make it a contest of 543 local municipal elections with hyper-local issues rather than a single national election with national leadership as the only issue.

For all practical purposes, India has been voting as a Presidential system rather than a Parliamentary system. For a long time, the Congress benefited from this, but now, the tables have turned. Going back to the basics of a decentralised, local, first-past-the-post system will be the only way they can ask voters to look beyond the current binaries of pro-Modi/anti-Modi mandates.

As long as the Opposition keeps asking people to defeat Modi, the results would ensure a pro-Modi mandate. If they continue their campaign on an anti-Modi narrative, Modi will remain the centre of discussion. The more you campaign against him, the more he wins.

The more you campaign against him, the bigger mandate he manages to get. It's a circular logic, working like an unstoppable centrifugal force, throwing out the opposition to the periphery. And the entire opposition (and the media sympathetic to them) is only spinning this wheel faster after every defeat. As a meme from the 2020 Indian film *Chhalaang* says, 'Technique Hi Galat Hai Tumhari (your very technique is flawed).'

Quite frankly, the Gujarat assembly elections towards the end of 2022 will be a kind of trailer of what could possibly happen in 2024. Going purely by livelihood issues, the ordinary voter has every right to be incensed with the BJP in the state as well as the centre in a classic case of double anti-incumbency. Cooking oil prices are well above Rs. 220 per litre. Vegetable prices simply refused to come down during the previous winter and remain high. One LPG cylinder costs Rs. 1,000. One litre of petrol is well above Rs. 100. So if she decides to vote against the BJP, she would have legitimate reasons for doing so. But whom does she vote for, if against Modi? Does the other offer her a credible solution to her family's economic woes apart from rhetoric against Ambanis and Adanis? She gets even more confused when Congress leaders abuse each other in public. Add the drama injected by the Aam Aadmi Party and the whole thing becomes a circus.

Of course, Modi can still lose as the word invincible was perhaps invented by a mad man in England. But to whom?

References

1. https://www.insafbulletin.net/archives/2235

2(a). https://www.uscirf.gov/countries/india

2(b). https://www.economist.com/leaders/2020/01/23/narendra-modi-stokes-divisions-in-the-worlds-biggest-democracy

2. https://churumuri.blog/2009/05/27/mathew-55-mathew-107-manmohan-2009/

3.

4. https://www.rediff.com/news/2001/oct/07guj.htm

5. https://www.india-seminar.com/2008/581/581_swapan_dasgupta.htm

6. https://time.com/5586415/india-election-narendra-modi-2019/

6(b). https://theprint.in/india/governance/5-muslims-among-new-civil-services-recruits-only-one-in-top-100/474488/

7. https://archive.indianexpress.com/news/modi-and-the-art-of-the-sell/1046856/0

8. https://theprint.in/india/parameswaran-iyer-modis-ias-man-for-

swachh-bharat-reveals-how-the-mission-was-achieved/595169/

9. https://thediplomat.com/2020/12/on-economic-reforms-modis-strength-is-his-weakness/
10. https://www.moneycontrol.com/news/opinion/in-pm-narendra-modis-economic-policies-both-karl-marx-and-adam-smith-are-out-of-date-8057571.html
11. https://thewire.in/politics/bjp-carpet-bombing-strategy-opponents-fragmented

□

8
LOOKING AT 2032

Perhaps the most abused cliché in contemporary times is the profound saying: "Nothing is permanent". When it comes to politics, the proverb is unerringly apt and telling. Through the book, we have seen, discussed and analysed how pro-incumbency became the dominant phenomenon in Indian politics, particularly electoral politics, in the 21st century. The map shown in the introductory chapter sums it up pretty well: the movement of electoral verdicts from anti-incumbency to pro-incumbency. We have also seen how this phenomenon is not associated with the rise of the BJP and the dizzying ascendancy of Narendra Modi. More non-BJP chief ministers have shown their remarkable ability to win, and keep winning elections, than the BJP ones. But all good things must come to an end. And the authors are convinced a time will come when this overwhelming dominance of pro-incumbency verdicts will again be replaced by tales of angry and disillusioned voters throwing out leaders who once looked invincible.

Anything is possible. In 2000, when the Prime Minister that India never had Jyoti Basu stepped down as chief minister of West Bengal after a continuous spell of 23 years and 234 days in office, most pundits thought that this was new record that would never be broken since anti-incumbency verdicts were still the norm in those days. The same year, a seemingly reluctant and unusual politician Naveen Patnaik became chief minister. And barring ill health or some other exigency, he is set to break the record set by Jyoti Basu. It is almost like records set in the arena of sports. Sooner or later, they tend to be broken.

Look at Kerala. For about five decades, power changed hands between the Congress led UDF and the CPI(M) led LDF every five years after assembly elections. The pattern had become as common as the arrival of monsoon every year. And when the results of the 2019 Lok Sabha elections were announced, it looked as if Kerala would stick to its routine of throwing out the incumbent state government when assembly elections would be held in 2021. The Congress was once again humiliated and crushed by the Narendra Modi juggernaut in the 2019 elections. The challenger Rahul Gandhi lost the family bastion Amethi to Smriti Irani. But both he and the party found solace and a sliver of salvation in Kerala. He personally won big time from the Wayanad constituency and the UDF pulverised the LDF by winning 19 out of the 20 Lok Sabha seats in the state. But wonder of wonders, in 2021, against all odds, chief minister Pinarayi Vijayan and CPI(M) strongman not only won a second term but a bigger mandate. Pundits appeared surprised, and some even shocked. But credible polling agencies including C-Voter had forecast that Kerala too would join the pro-incumbency bandwagon in 2021.

The late and legendary actor Sean Connery was resurrected as James Bond in the movie *Never Say Never Again*. In Indian politics, one could invoke the classic *Saheb, Biwi Aur Ghulam*. The movie showcased how a jaded, effete and out of touch and sync aristocracy was gradually replaced by a brave and, to some, frightening world of new possibilities and opportunities. The movie was redolent with pathos and tragedy. And yet, it also heralded the arrival of a new era. Something similar has happened in Indian politics. We are not talking just about electoral verdicts. We are talking about a wholesale shift in social, political and economic power structures. The old ruling class of India, English-speaking and often deracinated when it came to their Indic roots is being ruthlessly elbowed out by mostly desi subalterns who don't give a toss about old certainties and consensus. Lalu Prasad Yadav remains a boisterous example of this new class of rulers. Narendra Modi, in his own way, of course, towers over them all. The old elite is not pleased, and often resorts to cringeworthy snobbery to reflect how bitter it is about losing both power and the narrative.

In May 2022, Prime Minister Narendra Modi went on a whirlwind three-day tour of Germany, Denmark and France to exchange notes with leaders of those countries. While in Denmark, the Queen accorded him an official reception where visuals showed him being escorted by exquisitely uniformed palace courtiers towards a dining table that glittered with silverware and cutlery. A self-declared saviour of the 'Idea of India' and unrelenting Modi critic named Rupa Gulab sneered in a Twitter post: "Does he even know how to use the cutlery?" Predictably, her nasty and condemns ending remark created the usual Twitter firestorm that lasts a few hours or a few days at most. But the authors think, that one tweet displayed the helpless rage and bile of the old ruling elites more than their patronising attitude.

Look at the list of pro-incumbency leaders in contemporary times led by Modi. Barring Naveen Patnaik, virtually none of them comes from the traditional ruling elite that is more comfortable with English than their own language; virtually none of them (to borrow from that pathetic and pitiful lady Rupa Gulab) was born with a silver spoon in the traditional sense. Virtually all of them have come up the hard way. Some, like Mamata Banerjee, have learnt valuable lessons in violence and intimidation from the Marxists and outdone even their ruthless control over local institutions, including the media. Some, like Yogi Adityanath have created a heady concoction of religious divisiveness and development that seems to work wonders at the polling booth. Who said transformational change doesn't have ugly consequences and doesn't claim collateral damage? It has always been so in history. The French Revolution of 1789 was accompanied by an orgy of senseless violence where even the revolutionaries were executed and slaughtered along with the Emperor, the Queen and the palace courtiers. The story was repeated in 1917 in Russia when the Marxists grabbed power. And in 1979, the Marxists got a taste of their own medicine in Iran. They allied with hardline Islamists loyal to Ayatollah Khomeini to oust the Shah of Iran and usher in a new 'egalitarian' state. Within a year, virtually all the Marxists had been slaughtered by the followers of the Ayatollah. In that sense, we should consider ourselves lucky that the old order is giving way to the new in a more orderly manner.

Coming back to the primary theme of this book: will the pro-incumbency phenomenon become a permanent feature of Indian politics? The answer is: both yes and no. As we mentioned in the introductory chapter of the book, the Congress enjoyed a virtual monopoly over political power between 1947 and 1967. Yes, the first elections were held in independent India in 1951-52. But the British had organised elections in 1946 and Jawaharlal Nehru had become Prime Minister of the British colony called India in 1946. That kind of monopoly was absolute. And while the BJP has indeed emerged as the dominant political party of India and runs a relentless and formidable election machine, it will never achieve what the Congress enjoyed for 20 years between 1947 and 1967. The pro-incumbency phenomenon that we have witnessed in the 21st century is far more diffused and genuinely more democratic. It is extremely unlikely for the BJP, for instance, to even dream of coming to power in the next decade or so in states like Kerala and Tamil Nadu. Even if displays superhuman stamina and manages the seemingly impossible in the distant future, it might have lost its traditional stronghold to a new set of challengers by then. So, we can safely say that the age of single party dominance is well and truly over. Remember: politics abhors a vacuum. So, while it looks at the moment that the BJP is invincible when it comes to Lok Sabha elections, it is a matter of time before social, economic and political churn throws up a 'credible' challenger to the party. In the 1980s, the pioneers of psephology and electoral analysis led by the venerable Prannoy Roy coined the term TINA—There Is No Alternative—to suggest that the Congress would continue to remain dominant despite occasional reverses. Within a decade or so of that, the Congress started its march towards history; history in this case being a march towards electoral irrelevance. At the moment, a coalition looks most likely to have a chance of stopping Narendra Modi equalling the record set by Jawaharlal Nehru by winning three consecutive Lok Sabha elections. It looks unlikely, but then anything is possible in politics.

Why do the authors say yes to the question over continuing pro-incumbency verdicts? One reason is the politics of personality cults. Thanks to social media and growing polarisation, personality cults have become a common feature across the world. And they cut across ideologies. Look at India. Pinarayi Vijayan is a diehard Marxist belonging to a party where individuals are supposed to be always subservient to the party. And yet, he has built an unmatched personality cult around himself to the point that that he is now more important than his own party. Many Marxists are unhappy with this. But they have to keep their thoughts to themselves because Vijayan single-handedly ensured that the Left rules at least one state in the country. Compare him with Yogi Adityanath, a diehard Hindutva fellow traveller who makes L.K. Advani of the Ram Janambhoomi Rath Yatra fame a committed 'secular' politician! Unlike Vijayan, Yogi had Modi to help him win Uttar Pradesh again in 2022. But make no mistake; unlike the 2017 UP assembly elections verdict where it was Modi, and Modi alone all the way, the 2022 elections had the personality cult of the 'Bulldozer Baba' looming over it all the time. So, it doesn't matter which party or ideology they belong to. For instance, take Arvind Kejriwal who often overshadows even Narendra Modi in using taxpayer-funded advertisement campaigns to strengthen his personality cult. Even his supporters today have no clue about his ideology. It is just Arvind Kejriwal. Of course, if at all Arvind Kejriwal can be accused of following any ideology, it would be the ideology of freebies.

Freebies brings us to the flip side of the answer to the question about the durability of the pro-incumbency phenomenon. Our answer is no. That might seem surprising, since every political party seems to be in a race to offer freebies to voters. In the chapter on welfare schemes propelling pro-incumbent sentiments, we have analysed how successful leaders have used 'freebies' to keep voters happy. We showed how K.C. Rao of Telengana pre-empted Narendra Modi by offering direct cash transfers to virtually all farmers in the state before dissolving the assembly and calling for early elections.

Predictably, he won a bigger mandate for a second consecutive term. Arvind Kejriwal has perfected the art by offering 200 units of electricity and 20,000 litres of water free to all residents of Delhi. His party has done something similar after winning a huge mandate in Punjab. But as the late Nobel Prize winning economist Milton Friedman famously said: there is no such thing called a free lunch. Discerning commentators not blinded by ideological leanings are already raising alarm bells over the sheer unsustainability of this freebie culture. And voters are not fools, though many so-called pundits in India think they are. It is a matter of time before the chickens come home to roost and voters realise that freebies can actually be bad for them. The summer of 2022 has already seen massive shortages of power. The simple reason beyond all the blame games and rhetoric that surrounded the power crisis is that state electricity boards are virtually bankrupt thanks to 'free electricity' and have no money to pay power producers. Of what use will be 'free' electricity if there is no electricity? To repeat, it's a matter of time before wisdom will dawn on both voters and politicians.

At a more fundamental level, the most remarkable achievement of the Narendra Modi government has been to deliver to ordinary Indians what should have been delivered decades ago: toilets at homes, concrete houses for the poor, free gas connections, free medical insurance, bank accounts and electricity connections to virtually every household. In a few years, virtually every household will also have piped water supply. This is the pinnacle of welfare. By the end of this decade, the Indian voter will not be yearning for these basic necessities. At the same time, even if the centre and the states govern the country very poorly, the economy will grow at 5 per cent a year for more than a decade by which time India will be transiting from a low income to middle income country. After that, these freebies will not play such a dominant role in electoral politics. Like in most mature democracies, economics will slowly replace welfare as the primary issue. To be sure, identity politics will always be there and will often trump economic issues. But then, who said democracy was or will be perfect?

The authors are convinced that when better qualified and more skilled researchers and analysts write a book like this in 2032, the pro- and anti-incumbency debate will still be going on. The personality cult will still be there. Identity politics will still be there. But much more would also have changed; some for better, and some sadly for worse.

□□□